BIBLICAL ANIMALITY
AFTER JACQUES DERRIDA

SEMEIA STUDIES

Steed V. Davidson, General Editor

Number 91

BIBLICAL ANIMALITY
AFTER JACQUES DERRIDA

Hannah M. Strømmen

SBL PRESS

Atlanta

Copyright © 2018 by Hannah M. Strømmen

Library of Congress Cataloging-in-Publication Data

Names: Strømmen, Hannah M., author.
Title: Biblical animality after Jacques Derrida / by Hannah M. Strømmen.
Description: Atlanta : SBL Press, 2018. | Series: Semeia studies ; Number 91 | Includes bibliographical references and index. | Description based on print version record and CIP data provided by publisher; resource not viewed.
Identifiers: LCCN 2018014640 (print) | LCCN 2018018767 (ebook) | ISBN 9780884142980 (ebk.) | ISBN 9781628372120 (pbk. : alk. paper) | ISBN 9780884142973 (hbk. : alk. paper)
Subjects: LCSH: Animals in the Bible. | Theological anthropology—Biblical teaching. | Creationism—Biblical teaching. | Derrida, Jacques.
Classification: LCC BS663 (ebook) | LCC BS663 .S77 2018 (print) | DDC 220.8/59—dc23
LC record available at https://lccn.loc.gov/2018014640

Printed on acid-free paper.

Contents

Acknowledgements

Thanks to an intriguing remark by Nicholas Royle as to "animals and Derrida," an idea lodged that gradually took on life, crept inside the covers of the Bible, and made a home there. This idea would perhaps have remained only an idea if it had not been for Yvonne Sherwood. Her intellectual flare remains an inspiration. Particular thanks are also due to Denise K. Buell, for her patience with earlier versions of this book and for invaluable advice along the way. I thank the Semeia Studies editorial team and SBL Press, particularly Steed V. Davidson, Nicole Tilford, and Kathie Klein.

I am grateful for the College of Arts scholarship I received from the University of Glasgow that enabled much of the research that led to this book. Many in Glasgow enriched my time there, and I thank particularly AKMA and Margaret Adam, Johnathan Birch, James Currall, Kevin Francis, Rebecca Henderson, David Jasper, Lee Johnston, Samuel Tongue, and Alana Vincent.

In the process of writing this book there were many who have played important roles, wittingly and unwittingly. Fatima Tofighi has been an inestimable intellectual companion and friend: may our conversations always be ringing with laughter! Stephen D. Moore gave constructive feedback for which I am hugely grateful. Colleagues at the University of Chichester, particularly Tommy and Hannah Lynch, Ruth Mantin, Graeme Smith, Stephen Roberts, Mark Mason, Ben Noys, and Fiona Price, have offered unstinting support and encouragement. I thank Fatima Tofighi and Rachel Moriarty for double-checking the Hebrew and Greek. Most particularly I thank Ulrich Schmiedel, for too much to be named or known: what would I do without you?

Finally, I would like to thank my parents and siblings: Einar, Mary, Kristian, Sigrid, and our old dog Ben. To this most marvelous family I dedicate this book.

Hannah M. Strømmen, Chichester, January 2018

Abbreviations

Acts Thom.	Acts of Thomas
AHR	*The American Historical Review*
Ann.	Tacitus, *Annals*
AS	*Aramaic Studies*
BArch	*The Biblical Archaeologist*
BBCom	Blackwell Bible Commentaries
BBHRS	Blackwell Brief Histories of Religion Series
BCT	*The Bible and Critical Theory*
BLS	Bible and Literature Series
BMW	The Bible in the Modern World
BSIH	Brill's Studies in Intellectual History
CBOTS	Coniectanea Biblica, Old Testament Series
CBR	*Currents in Biblical Research*
CMP	Cultural Memory in the Present
Con	Concilium
CPSSup	Cambridge Philological Society Supplementary Volumes
CR	*CR: The New Centennial Review*
CriticalSt	Critical Studies
CSCP	Continuum Studies in Continental Philosophy
CTAIHS	Collection des travaux de l'Académie internationale d'histoire des sciences
Divinations	Divinations: Rereading Late Ancient Religion
EA	Encounters with Asia
EAC	Essays in Art and Culture
EC	Epworth Commentaries
EP	European Perspectives
Epis. Fam.	Cicero, *Epistulae ad Familiares*
EPS	Environmental Philosophies Series
ETP	Ecocritical Theory and Practice

FCNTECW	Feminist Companion to the New Testament and Early Christian Writings
FIOTL	Formation and Interpretation of Old Testament Literature
FT	The Frontiers of Theory
GBP	Great Books in Philosophy
Gen. Rab.	Genesis Rabbah
HACL	History, Archaeology, and Culture of the Levant
HDR	Harvard Dissertations in Religion
Herm	Hermeneia
Hist. eccl.	Eusebius, *Historia ecclesiastica*
Hist. nat.	Pliny, *Historia naturalis*
Hist. Rom.	Livy, *The History of Rome*
HM	Heythrop Monographs
HRP	*The Harvard Review of Philosophy*
HRS	How to Read Series
HSM	Harvard Semitic Monographs
Hypatia	*Hypatia: A Journal of Feminist Philosophy*
ICC	International Critical Commentary
ISPR	Indiana Series in the Philosophy of Religion
JBL	*Journal of Biblical Literature*
JECS	*Journal of Early Christian Studies*
JRS	*Journal of Roman Studies*
JRT	*Journal of Religion and Theatre*
JSNT	*Journal for the Study of the New Testament*
JSNTSup	Journal for the Study of the New Testament Supplement Series
JSOT	*Journal for the Study of the Old Testament*
JSOTSup	Journal for the Study of the Old Testament Supplement Series
LHB	Library of Hebrew Bible
LNTS	Library of New Testament Studies
MC	Medieval Cultures
Meridian	Meridian: Crossing Aesthetics
MJPR	Modern Jewish Philosophy and Religion
MSRHC	Medicine, Science, and Religion in Historical Context
NCBC	The New Cambridge Bible Commentary
NIGTC	New International Greek Testament Commentary
NRSV	New Revised Standard Version
NTT	New Testament Theology

OBO	Orbis Biblicus et Orientalis
OH	Oxford Handbooks
OLR	*The Oxford Literary Review*
OTG	Old Testament Guides
OTM	Old Testament Message
OTR	Old Testament Readings
OTT	Old Testament Theology
OWC	Oxford World's Classics
PC	Penguin Classics
PCPhil	Perspectives in Continental Philosophy
PhilPR	*Philosophy and Phenomenological Research*
Post	Posthumanities
PT	Playing the Texts
RA	Religion in America
RC	Routledge Classics
RCC	Religion/Culture/Critique
Readings	Readings: A New Biblical Commentary
RP	Religion and Postmodernism
RT	Radical Thinkers
SAQ	*South Atlantic Quarterly*
SBT	Studies in Biblical Theology
SCT	Studies in Continental Thought
Sci	*Science*
SemeiaSt	Semeia Studies
Signs	*Signs: Journal of Women in Culture and Society*
SNTSMS	Society for New Testament Studies Monograph Series
SNTW	Studies of the New Testament and Its World
SPOT	Studies on Personalities of the Old Testament
ST	Signposts in Theology
StASRH	St. Andrews Studies in Reformation History
T&TCT	T&T Clark Theology
TA	Thinking in Action
TES	Tampere English Studies
TP	*Textual Practice*
VC	Verso Classics
VTSup	Supplements to Vetus Testamentum
WA	*World Archaeology*
WBC	Word Biblical Commentary
WUNT	Wissenschaftliche Untersuchungen zum Neuen Testament

Introduction: The Question of the Animal

What is termed the "question of the animal" is one of the foremost challenges in the humanities. Briefly put, the question of the animal pertains to the issue of human/animal difference: To what extent, and in what ways, are humans and animals different, or indeed similar? Generally speaking, animal studies seeks to move away from anthropocentric attitudes and to reject an absolute distinction between humans and animals. In these debates, the Bible is frequently blamed as a weighty anthropocentric inheritance. I aim to move these debates further through close engagement with the biblical archive. What might a biblical inheritance constitute for thinking about animality? Can anything definite be said in the slippery name of the biblical? By examining four significant texts in the biblical archive for the topic of animals, I demonstrate the importance of probing the question of the animal further with regard to the Bible, both in light of the nuances, tensions, and ambiguities of biblical literature, and for exploring the possibilities of inheriting this complex and composite corpus otherwise—beyond biblical blame.

The biblical texts I explore fall into two main groups. First, texts that especially address questions of eating: namely, Gen 9 and the aftermath of the flood where humans are given animals to eat; and the question of clean/unclean animals in Acts 10. Second, texts that address questions of power and politics: the book of Daniel with its lions, animal-king, and hybrid animal visions; and the battle between the Lamb and the Beast of Rev 17. These different and disparate texts provide the material and momentum to show important instances of *how* "the Bible" conceptualizes humans, animals, and gods as well as how it characterizes the relationships between them. I propose that often in the same spaces in which these characterizations might be fixed as detrimental to animal life lie also the possibilities of seeing animals radically otherwise.

Specifically, I engage the biblical archive by examining and building on Jacques Derrida's work on the question of the animal. What does it mean to read the Bible after Derrida? In his work on animality, which I discuss in more detail below, Derrida provides an important starting point by taking up the topic of human/animal difference and in problematizing assumptions about this difference in philosophical texts and traditions. Before attempting such a response with this study, I address three questions in this introduction. First, why the question of the animal? Secondly, why the Bible? And finally, why Jacques Derrida as an interlocutor? I devote a rather long explication of Derrida's contribution to animal studies in this introduction because it provides the theoretical underpinnings to the chapters that follow. It is worth noting the larger picture in this part before drawing on aspects of Derrida's thinking as they help to unpack the biblical texts I analyze.

Humanity's Identity Crisis

The surge of interest in the topic of animals in the humanities has accelerated in the last few decades, with research steadily receiving more and more critical attention, reaching a pitch in the last ten years. Earlier scholars such as Peter Singer, Richard Ryder, Andrew Linzey, Tom Regan, and Mary Midgley fought for academic attention for animals in the 1970s and 1980s—focusing on animal rights and animal liberation—by building on the pioneers of utilitarianism Jeremy Bentham and John Stuart Mill for an appeal to decrease the suffering of animals. In the 1990s, the debate continued to explore the differences between humans and animals and what this might mean both philosophically and politically (Sheehan and Sosna 1991; Garner 1997; DeGrazia 1996). This is coupled with feminist issues of exclusion and marginalization in Carol J. Adam's work (1990, 2004, 2018; Adams and Donovan 1995, 2007; Adams and Fortune 1995). The turn of the century has seen an increase in interest, with a range of thought-provoking scholarship on animals, from Stephen R. L. Clark's *The Political Animal: Biology, Ethics, and Politics* (1999), Matthew Calarco and Peter Atterton's *Animal Philosophy: Essential Readings in Continental Thought* (2004a), and Cary Wolfe's *Zoontologies: The Question of the Animal* (2003) to Marc R. Fellenz's *The Moral Menagerie: Philosophy and Animal Rights* (2007), Paola Cavalieri's *The Death of the Animal: A Dialogue* (2009), and Calarco's *Zoographies: The Question of the Animal from Heidegger to Derrida* (2008), to mention only a few significant examples.[1] This scholarship engages histori-

---

1. The increase in scholarship on this topic is only continuing, with a number of

cally, ethically, and philosophically with animal issues, from questions of the human/animal distinction and whether it can be retained to extensive discussions of consciousness, rights, tradition, rationalism, and Darwinism (e.g., Fellenz 2007); psychoanalysis, microorganisms, and DNA (e.g., Roof 2003, 101–20; Hird 2009); as well as concepts of technology and pets, such as Donna J. Haraway's well-known discussion of "cyborgs and companion species" (2003, 4).[2]

Clearly, the debate over animal welfare, rights, and status is attracting much attention in current scholarship, engaging with contemporary popular attitudes to animals, such as the fashion and food industry, as much as with philosophical theories and cultural legacies. An important factor for the rise of animal studies comes from the natural sciences and critical engagements with scientific research. Zoological, ethological, and ecological research has provided the empirical grounds and impetus for reassessing dominant assumptions about the differences between human and animal life. Merely one example is tool use, commonly thought to be a uniquely human characteristic. Research done in behavioral ecology shows, for example, that New Caledonian crows can be observed not only to use tools frequently but also to manufacture tools, create new designs to suit their needs, and select sophisticated tools according to a particu-

---

prominent animal-focused publications. To name a few, Cavell et al. 2010; Beauchamp and Frey 2011; Donaldson and Kymlicka 2011; Rudy 2011; Norwood and Lusk 2011; DeMello 2012; Cohen 2012; and Tyler 2012.

2. For scholarship that engages historically, ethically, and philosophically with animal issues, see particularly Calarco 2008 for the continental philosophy tradition and Clark 1999 for a thorough discussion of philosophical traditions on animals, particularly Aristotle and Plato, that also touches on slavery, children, women, kings, and apes in relation to rethinking the concept of the animal. For questions of the human/animal distinction, see, for instance, Calarco's (2008) thesis that human/animal distinctions should no longer be maintained and that we must move away altogether from anthropological modes of thought. Calarco concludes with a critique of Derrida for maintaining the terms human and animal despite his criticism of the absurd distinction on which they are founded, calling this a rarely dogmatic moment in Derrida's writing (3, 10, 143–48). In my view, it is rather that Derrida (e.g., 2004, 66) insists on a number of limits and distinctions. Further, it is not a matter of simply erasing the word animal (or human) and thus acting as if the problematic issues surrounding these words go away. For "cyborgs and companion species," see also Haraway 1990 and 2007. Haraway (2003, 16) focuses on dogs and what she calls the "implosion of nature and culture in the relentlessly historically specific, joint lives of dogs and people, who are bonded in significant otherness."

lar task.[3] The destabilization of concepts and characteristics thought to be exclusive to humans has set in motion something of an identity crisis. As Wolfe (2003, xi) points out, such knowledge has "called into question our ability to use the old saws of anthropocentrism (language, tool use, the inheritance of cultural behaviors, and so on) to separate ourselves once and for all from animals." He argues that the humanities are "now struggling to catch up with a radical revaluation of the status of nonhuman animals" (xi). Troubling the absolute distinctions between humans and animals has opened up most pertinently, perhaps, questions of ethics in reflecting on the status of animals in relation to humans and a concomitant attempt to rethink the exclusivity of *human* rights and strictly *human* ethical considerations.[4]

Wolfe (2003, xi) also draws attention to new theoretical paradigms over the past few decades: cybernetics, systems theory, and chaos theory, paradigms that "have had little use and little need for the figure of the human as either foundation or explanatory principle." Technology has played a key part in this rethinking of the human. In her now famous "A Cyborg Manifesto" in *Simians, Cyborgs, and Women: The Reinvention of Nature* from 1991, Haraway discusses the boundary breakdown between human and animal, as well as between animal-human (organism) and machine. We are, she writes, "creatures simultaneously animal and machine, who populate worlds ambiguously natural and crafted" (149). We are "cyborgs, hybrids, mosaics, chimeras" (177). Rather than continue what she calls the "border war" of human/animal and human-animal/machine, she calls for pleasure in the confusion of boundaries as well as responsibility in their construction. Emphasizing new technologies, she suggests that a cyborg world might be "about lived social and bodily relations in which people are not afraid of their joint kinship with animals and machines" (154).

Concern and compassion for animals is nothing new. From Pythagoras to Theophrastus, Seneca to Porphyry, Percy and Mary Shelly to Arthur Schopenhauer, Bentham, John Locke, and Mill to Jacques Derrida, the

---

3. There are numerous studies now that testify to characteristics thought to belong only to humans observed in various animal species, such as the research done by Jane Goodall, Arthur Schaller, and Dian Fossey, developed from the founders of modern ethology, Niko Tinbergen and Konrad Lorenz. More about the New Caledonian crows can be found on the website of the Oxford University research group on Behavioral Ecology: http://users.ox.ac.uk/~kgroup/tools/introduction.shtml.

4. See for instance Regan 2004 and Waldau 2011.

debate around attitudes to, and appropriation of, animals has existed. But from an increased interest in animals burgeoning in the 1970s, the last three decades have seen this interest gain momentum toward rethinking more radically and systematically about animal life as a subject in the humanities. The "question of violence and compassion toward animals has, in a certain sense, become one of the leading questions of our age" (Calarco 2008, 113). It is not a question that has simply appeared on the academic scene as if from nowhere. As Stephen D. Moore (2014a, 2) points out, the challenge to the human/animal hierarchy could be placed "in a continuous line with the interrogations of the male/female, masculine/feminine, heterosexual/homosexual, white/nonwhite, and colonizer/colonized hierarchies entailed in feminist studies, gender studies, queer studies, racial/ethnic studies, and postcolonial studies." Certain dualisms have been dominant that work to mirror the self not only where the self is human but where the human is a *man*, and such dualisms, as Haraway (1991, 177) writes, have been "systemic to the logics and practices of domination of women, people of color, nature, workers, animals." The animal question bears important connections with the question of the slave, the native, the Jew, and the woman, as will become clear in the chapters to follow.

The question of the animal does have its own concerns and its own challenges, however, in the fact that those who are at the heart of animal studies do not speak or write in human languages, and so the question of their status as *objects* of study is a perennial one. It may not be a matter of urging animals to seize "the tools to mark the world that marked them as other," as Haraway (1990, 175) puts it, even if we think many animal species are capable of using tools of various kinds. Haraway's insistence on displacing "hierarchical dualisms of naturalized identities" and "retelling origin stories" (175), however, is in many respects what animal studies is about. It is also instructive for my turn to the Bible as a source of origin stories. While the history or prehistory of the animal question is multifaceted, then, there are at least two crises that are important to note. The first, concerning the idea of the human subject, is crucial for continental philosophy and the specifically Derridean focus in this study. The second, the idea of environmental crisis, pertains to a broader context for animal studies and accounts for the urgency and advocacy with which animal studies has been marked.

As for the first crisis, there has been what might be termed a crisis of the subject and the desired "exiting" of an "epoch of the metaphysics of subjectivity" (Jean-Luc Nancy in Derrida 1995b, 257) promulgated most prominently by thinkers such as Martin Heidegger, Emmanuel Levinas, Michel Foucault, Louis Althusser, Jacques Lacan, and Derrida. This crisis has taken shape under the shadow of the Enlightenment era as a critique of conceptualizations of the human subject, particularly around concepts of autonomy, consciousness, freedom, and reason. This Enlightenment subject has come under critique as "absolute origin, pure will, identity to self, or presence to self of consciousness" (Derrida 1995b, 265).[5] Notions of the subject in relation to definitions of humans can be traced as far back as Aristotle's writings, but the idea of the subject as it is understood today comes most clearly to the fore with René Descartes's (1989) famous *je pense donc je suis*, or the *cogito ergo sum*, and what is often called the beginning of modernity.[6] It has become commonplace, as Nick Mansfield (2000, 13) points out, to characterize the modern era as an era of the subject. The intellectual trends sparked by critiques of the subject proffer interrogations of the debt of Enlightenment thinkers, such as Descartes, Immanuel Kant, and Jean-Jacques Rousseau, and the ways in which their thinking undergirds modern conceptions of selfhood as well as sociopolitical structures and institutions.[7]

An important work in this regard is Theodor W. Adorno and Max Horkheimer's *Dialectic of Enlightenment* (1997), originally published in 1944, which put forward a powerful critique of an Enlightenment tradition and rationalist thinking that appeared to go hand in hand with the bloodshed of the twentieth century. They asked why humanity has not entered

---

5. Derrida is being somewhat facetious here in that he is questioning Heidegger's characterization of an "epoch of subjectivity" by giving the example of Spinoza as someone who does not present a metaphysics of absolute subjectivity.

6. As Nick Mansfield (2000, 15) points out, in Descartes "we find together two principles that Enlightenment thought has both emphasized and adored: firstly, the image of the self as the ground of all knowledge and experience of the world (*before I am anything, I am I*) and secondly, the self as defined by the rational faculties it can use to order the world (*I make sense*)."

7. Mansfield (2000) discusses the importance of Heidegger's critiques of the subject as something determined by certain attributes such as consciousness or reason; what Heidegger proposes we ought to consider, rather, is a more fundamental ground for the subject, namely, existence itself, *Dasein*. Foucault's name has stood for a thinking of subjectivity that is not a naturally occurring "thing" that anyone has but rather a construct of dominant socioeconomic, political, and cultural structures and institutions.

into a new kind of living but rather sunk "into a new kind of barbarism" (xi). In 1947, Heidegger (1993, 219) asked in his "Letter on Humanism" how meaning can be restored to the term *humanism*, criticizing ways in which humanism has been understood in relation to man, his essence, and existence.[8] The story for Adorno and Horkheimer ([1944] 1997, xi) was one in which humanity had not met its own expectations and had trusted too much in the triumphs of modern consciousness. The Enlightenment "*must examine itself*, if men are not to be wholly betrayed" (xv, emphasis original). Liberating people from superstition and myths seems, for them, to have resulted in a sovereignty of man (or the autonomy, power, will, and force of the *subject*) that manifested itself in domination and mastery of nature, power, and technology as well as other people on the grounds of calculation and utility (4). As a result of such examinations and critiques, Calarco (2008, 12) suggests the subject has become disassociated from "the autonomous, domineering, atomistic subject of modernity" and now recognizes his or her coming into being by and from events, powers, structures, cultures, and institutions. "The subject, when understood as one who bears and is responsible to an event and alterity that exceeds it," is, then, not a "fully self-present and self-identical subject" (12). This latter idea would be the subject "whose existence and death have been proclaimed in the discussions over humanism and the metaphysics of subjectivity" (12). Discussions of the subject and critiques of the Enlightenment are of course diverse, complex, and multifaceted and by no means form a straightforward consensus. Similarly, the Enlightenment tradition is itself an amorphous and composite web of thinkers far more diverse and multifarious than implied here. But, broadly speaking, particular conceptions associated with Enlightenment thought concerning the subject and its relation to autonomy, reason, freedom, the individual, and consciousness have come under close and critical scrutiny in the last century, a scrutiny that appears

---

8. Heidegger (1993, 226, emphasis original) proposes that the first humanism, "Roman humanism, and every kind that has emerged from that time to the present, has presupposed the most universal 'essence' of man to be obvious. Man is considered to be an *animal rationale*." This is not only a literal translation of the Greek but a metaphysical one as well, he argues. Metaphysics, Heidegger says, thinks of the human being on "the basis of animalitas and not in the direction of his humanitas" (227). The human body and existence is something *essentially* different to animals, according to him, and so humanism and the human must be rethought on this basis. Derrida (1989, 169–73; 2008, 142–60; 2009–2011) critiques Heidegger for this supposition on several occasions.

to have generally taken the form of a crisis as to what the human subject is or might be. These discussions—and the critiques and alternatives that have emerged from them—have been crucial for postcolonial, feminist, race critical, and queer theoretical questions of subjectivity and humanity. It is a matter of challenging what Haraway (1991, 156) calls the "Western" sense of self as "the one who is not animal, barbarian, or woman."

The second crisis is the ecological concern for the natural world, the seemingly detrimental impact of human life and civilization on the world, and the critical attempts to alter attitudes to the world's natural resources, the environment, and the habitat in which humans and animals live.[9] Ecological thought could be characterized as a "humiliating descent" for humans (Morton 2008, 265). Tracing such a descent much further back than the twentieth-century critique of the Enlightenment subject, Timothy Morton (2008, 265) argues that from "Copernicus through Marx, Darwin and Freud, we learn we are decentered beings, inhabiting a Universe of processes that happen whether we are aware of them or not, whether we name those processes 'astrophysics,' 'economic relations,' 'the unconscious' or 'evolution.'" While explaining that the term *anthropocene* has been applied to the period reaching back to the industrial revolution as well as even further back in time, Timothy Clark (2015, 1) suggests that its force as a term is connected to the time after the Second World War, when "human impacts on the entire biosphere have achieved an unprecedented and arguably dangerous intensity." This term has become popular in the humanities as shorthand for climate change, deforestation, overpopulation, and the general erosion of ecosystems (2).

Connecting ecological issues to animals, Val Plumwood (2002, 2) comments that our "failure to situate dominant forms of human society ecologically is matched by our failure to situate non-humans ethically, as the plight of non-human species continues to worsen." She argues that we need to think self-critically about the irrational decisions that are made for "our collective cause" and scrutinize the dominant illusions that inform such decisions (2). Rather than move entirely away from an approach of human-centeredness, however, Plumwood argues that the global crisis we find ourselves in should not result in the idea that it is necessary to choose between human concerns and nonhuman concerns. Rather, it is a matter

---

9. For further discussions of ecology, see, for instance, Morton 2007 and 2010. For a critical discussion of ecology, animality, and humanism, see Ferry 1995.

of recognizing, for instance, how "our own danger is connected to our domination of earth others" and how the human species is not set apart or isolated from other species and ecosystems (124).

A major element of the current ecological crisis is species extinction; animals and their disappearance thus serve as a wake-up call and horror mirror-image to humans. Midgley (2004, 171) calls the relations between humans and the world a "war" against nature and proposes that it is only recently that:

> modern people might actually in some monstrous sense win their bizarre war, that they might 'defeat nature,' thus cutting off the branch that they have been sitting on, and thus upsetting, not only the poets, but the profit-margin as well. To grasp this change calls for an unparalleled upheaval in our moral consciousness.

A double anxiety is embedded in animal species extinction: first, a sense of responsibility and guilt at animals disappearing at what appears an alarming and unprecedented rate; second, a recognition of humans as vulnerable (human) animals who may suffer the same fate if a balance is not regained of sustainability in the ecosphere. The ecological crisis and concern for the environment have functioned as a profound challenge to what is now condemned as human sovereignty. Critical questions as to human superiority and a self-serving human culture are rife in debates over the state of the world today, and much of this debate figures as a powerful indictment of humanity, calling for radical change. Such change is not merely about practical alterations to some human lifestyles, industry, and culture—existing at the cost of the natural world and its resources—but about *attitudes* to the concept of humanity and its place in the world.

Rethinking human superiority could potentially set in motion a wide-ranging critical examination of practices that are central to human life, such as the appropriation and exploitation of natural resources and the commodification and commercialization of animals in the food, sport, and fashion industry. Part of such a rethinking inevitably involves questioning notions of progress, particularly in facing up to the dismal forecasts of climate research and in formulating potential solutions. The question of the animal, Calarco (2008, 1) exhorts, "should be seen as one of the central issues in contemporary critical discourse," rather than tucked away somewhere distant as a niche in applied ethics. Moral philosopher Christine Korsgaard (2009, 3) writes that animals are:

conscious beings, who experience pleasure and pain, fear and hunger, joy and grief, attachments to particular others, curiosity, fun and play, satisfaction and frustration, and the enjoyment of life. And these are all things that, when we experience them, we take to ground moral claims on the consideration of others.

Why, then, are animals ipso facto excluded from such consideration? Fellenz (2007, 5) calls this exclusion an "inattention" on the part of moral philosophers and suggests it is "the challenge philosophy must face in the coming century" (6).

The question of the animal might be summed up, then, as: (1) an appeal to face and challenge the industrialization, commercialization, exploitation, and objectification of animals and the suffering this entails in the contemporary world; (2) a concern and care for the impact of anthropocentrism for wider ecological, environmental, political, and ethical issues; and (3) a critical engagement with conceptions of the subject in light of current philosophical and scientific discourse, along with a commitment to reevaluate concepts of the "human" and "animal" in scientific, political, literary, religious, and philosophical traditions, past and present.

Biblical Blame

What does the Bible have to do with any of this? The Bible is a crucial archive to explore in the context of animal studies because much contemporary philosophy on the animal refers to the Bible (either explicitly or implicitly) as an anthropocentric cultural weight to blame for humanity's superiority complex. In much the same way as feminist scholars have argued for the importance of critical engagement with the patriarchal structures of the Bible, it is necessary to engage critically with the ways in which this scriptural archive has seemingly also trod animals underfoot. A main aim of my study is to probe more closely the assumptions about the Bible put forth in this regard—particularly, as I go on to discuss, the way that the Bible becomes a corpus assumed to contain anthropocentric attitudes based on a handful of citations, if that. To apportion blame to a complex canon of texts from vastly varying times, places, styles, contents, and contexts as if dealing with a singularly coherent work is at any rate a dubious practice. I engage with the Bible precisely because of its importance in cultural memory as a powerfully persistent archive with a complex diversity of characters—animal, human, divine. The Bible demands more sustained attention in order to grapple with its texts in light of the concerns and criticisms of animal studies.

Scanning the field of contemporary philosophy on the question of the animal, it is interesting to note that in measuring blame for the concept of the human as a superior being, the Bible is frequently brought up in the beginning, in introductions to rigorous discussions over the status of animal life. Seemingly, this is done to name and shame the Bible as blamable without putting it under much, if any, critical investigation. Engaging with the status of animals in the world, the Bible is held accountable for our rigid, exclusive, and inflated notion of the human. Anchoring popular and philosophical conceptions of the animal in the deeply entrenched anthropocentric structures of Western intellectual thought, the tendency is to mount the Bible as an originating stable point of blame, to be put on trial, hurriedly condemned without prosecution, and thereby rushed to the marginal spaces of muted censure. Of course, no scholar says exactly this: I will take the Bible to court and put it on trial for the killing and eating of millions of animals and for intensive farming, hunting, fur-production, pet-keeping, and other similar practices so commonplace in the Western world. Nonetheless, there is an implicit assumption that the Bible is responsible for the current ideological underpinnings that justify animal abuse. While it is not afforded the privilege of closer examination—perhaps deemed somehow unquestionable—the Bible nonetheless persistently stands accused of sacrificing the animal in favor of the human, thereby acting as scaffolding for the metaphysical assumptions that have traditionally held the human in place, central and aloft. The human is privileged by the divine, the prime receiver of the logos: a powerful gift that has long equated humans to sovereign masters over the nonhuman in creation. Turning to significant recent publications in animal studies, already mentioned above, demonstrates this marked tendency.

For instance, Wolfe (2003, x) writes in *Zoontologies* that "the animal as the repressed Other of the subject, identity, logos" reaches "back in Western culture at least to the Old Testament," and yet none of the diverse contributors to this exciting collection of articles follow up on this particular Old Testament heritage. It is briefly brought to the fore only to be dropped again as a muted point. In Singer's (2004, x) preface to *Animal Philosophy*, his second reference to the long history of animals having "no ethical significance," or at least "very minor significance," is Paul (after Aristotle), further mentioning Augustine and Aquinas. It is from this vantage point that Singer opens up into "most Western philosophers" (x). In the introduction to the same book, Calarco and Atterton (2004b, xvii) contend that the transition from Aristotle's man as "rational animal" to simply "rational being" (in which "man" is exclusively and exhaustedly subsumed) was made "all the easier by the biblical story of man being made in the image of god and having dominion over the animals." A biblical story, then, is thought to have smoothed the passage from thinking of the human as a certain *kind* of animal in creation, to the human as something else altogether in light of his ability to reason.

In *Zoographies: The Question of the Animal from Heidegger to Derrida*, Calarco (2008) discusses Levinas and the ethical relation to the other, who for Levinas is necessarily a *human* other. Calarco turns Levinas's position on its head, drawing his own "neoreligious" conclusion where the encounter with the animal is "transcendent," a "miracle," but is quick to avoid this turn to religious language by affirming his resolve for a "complete shift in the terms of the debate" (59), as if he were echoing Levinas's (2004, 47) own words: "enough of this theology!" He goes on to warn that we must adopt a hypercritical stance toward the "ontotheological tradition" we have inherited, "for it is this tradition that blocks the possibility of thinking about animals in a non- or other-than-anthropocentric manner" (Calarco 2008, 112). A theologically oriented tradition is not merely to blame, then, but is also a stumbling block for contemporary attempts to think about the animal. In the introduction to *The Political Animal: Biology, Ethics and Politics*, Clark (1999, 5) references a number of specific biblical passages[10] to demonstrate "these commands, these tacit bargains" as implicit in owning animals and yet not treating them as mere things. His is a more positive account of the biblical legacy but remains in this case nonetheless elusive, never expanded upon in the main body of the argument.[11]

In Cavalieri's (2009, 2) *The Death of the Animal: A Dialogue*, one of her "speakers" (the first essay of the book is a dialogue-shaped discussion) suggests we need to instate "distance from the revered legacy of our history, what I am referring to in particular is the idea that some points, or perspectives, of the past should be rejected as archaic." The same speaker warns that although narrative form is something humans have always "craved" and "cherished" as modes of understanding self and world, we

---

10. Namely, Lev 19; 22; 23; 25; 26; Deut 22, 25; Ezek 34; Prov.

11. Clark (2013) has dealt more explicitly with religion and animals elsewhere.

must ensure that "such narratives are not translated into normatively hierarchical frameworks," as "they determine roles and questions of status" (5). This becomes more explicitly directed to the biblical tradition when she writes that according to "the most widespread" of these culturally and conceptually determining narratives, "human beings were made by God in his own image, while nonhuman beings are mere creations. The latter are only a preparatory work, while the former are the apex of creation, directly molded by God" (5–6). This reference is put forward with confidence, without recourse to a specific biblical text, context, or sustained analysis. The assumption is that we already know what she is talking about—the point speaks for itself. Cavalieri uses this point as a synecdoche for the history that has justified the systematic subjugation and suffering of animals: "such a story supports the normative implication that humans are superior beings, entitled to use nonhumans as they see fit" (6). What Cavalieri seemingly calls for is violence toward the so-called sacred, a fundamental purge or erasure of the biblical trace. Without further ado, she suggests, this particular conceptual corpse needs burying. A relic of the past, it still clutters our thinking of the animal and thus demands immediate iconoclastic action. Invoking the ethical dimension inscribed in the question of the animal—issues of "right and wrong," as she puts it—this is a point of some urgency, lest we allow the biblical to run wild and cause all sorts of further havoc (2).

Fellenz (2007, 31) picks up on the same point and sums up the blame in the following statement: "the traditional ethical models found in Western philosophy and theology have been premised on human uniqueness: the belief that as rational (perhaps ensouled) beings, humans have a putative value and destiny that surpass that of any other animal." He writes about "the religious concept of animals as part of the *human dominion*" (2, emphasis original) and points out the necessary "proximity" between human and animal within religious sacrifice, which is also the prerequisite for scientific experiments on animals for human gain; it is a case of life and living in a way that corresponds (13). Whether this is a point that accords greater significance to animals in biblical accounts of sacrifice or not, the relation Fellenz sets up implicitly foregrounds biblical sacrifice of animal bodies as the origin of scientific experimentation on animals. This is an interesting point but one that surely needs validating through specific reference to biblical sacrifice narratives, rather than ploughing forth under the assumption that we all know what exactly takes place in such sacrificial structures. Fellenz also refers to biblical and classical Greek stories to convey the way in which the transformation of humans into animals is a frequent trope used to signify punishment (16). One of the foundations for assuming the ontological inferiority of animals is, according to Fellenz, "theological in nature," embodied in the religious myth that "we humans are ensouled beings, created in the image of a God who made the world, including the animals, for our use" (34). He does present some of the ways in which Christian theologians have worked against this trend but stays clear of specific textual references to the Bible, and ultimately, the theological arguments are swept under the carpet. Saying "we need not rely on them, nor become entangled in other theological complexities" (36) is a sweeping motion reminiscent of Cavalieri's (2009, 4) proposed disentanglement from the biblical.

Of course, these are all *philosophical* texts on the moral and ontological status of animals. Why should they engage with biblical texts? Further, this is not to say they are necessarily wrong. The point is rather that in order to respond to the question of the animal as it relates to our cultural and religious inheritance, it is problematic to plot an uncritical notion of the Bible as the origin point, especially without revisiting these textual sites. To hold up the cultural inheritance of the Bible and its theologies without thinking more precisely about what is meant by the "theological," "God," "human," and "animal" in these contexts is to propagate a myopic acceptance of this legacy as well as its wholesale rejection on terms that are all too opaque.

Even if these contemporary philosophical references are merely the result of religion's "prolonged stammerings" (Bataille 1989, 96) in the world today, the Bible nonetheless plays a significant part in both fundamental beginning and ensnaring tangle. It represents a dangerous, labyrinthine structure that serious philosophers would be better off avoiding, as if that messy business is a job for biblical scholars alone. If it were not for the fact that the above-mentioned philosophers are producing valuable and timely publications on the animal and that all point to the Bible as culpable, this troublesome biblical body of literature *could* feasibly be left for biblical scholars to dissect in the dark or for theologians to peruse in peace. Instead of attempting to erase the biblical trace violently, we would be better off turning toward that textual body, responding to it, going through its pockets anew, and reviewing the strange and fantastical, domestic and divine characters that inhabit its spaces. As Laura Hobgood-Oster (2014, 216) points out, to view such a tradition—she is specifically addressing the Christian tradition—as wholly negative is "mistaken or at least incomplete."[12] It is perhaps a matter of adopting what Yvonne Sherwood (2004b, 14) has called "slow motion biblical interpretation": an interpretive practice with the biblical archive that is "caught up in a complex relationship of exultation-mourning, gratitude-disappointment, fidelity-betrayal," "a mode of interpretation that, instead of dividing the world into those who accept or reject a given religious inheritance (in a large act of choice that seemingly exonerates us from the intricacies of inheritance thereafter), implicates us all in little acts of micro-choosing and micro-decision" (14).

Important work has been done to challenge the trend of equating religion, particularly Judaism and Christianity, with anthropocentrism. Paul Waldau (2013) calls for inquiries about religion and animals that do not resort to generalization, noting Lynn White Jr.'s (1967, 1205) infamous thesis that "especially in its Western form, Christianity is the most anthropocentric religion the world has ever seen." Elijah Judah Schochet's (1984) *Animal Life in Jewish Tradition: Attitudes and Relationships* and Robert M. Grant's (1999) *Early Christians and Animals* are two significant resources for Judaism and Christianity and their relationships to animals. Ingvild Sælid Gilhus's (2006) valuable *Animals, Gods and Humans: Changing Attitudes to Animals in Greek, Roman and Early Christian Ideas* is a welcome contribution to the contextualization of the Judeo-Christian attitude to animals in the Greco-Roman world. Hobgood-Oster (2008) provides a wide-ranging reading of animals in the Christian tradition that have largely gone unnoticed in her *Holy Dogs and Asses: Animals in the Christian Tradition.*

The earliest example of a Christian theological response within animal studies has been Linzey's work, such as *Animals on the Agenda: Questions about Animals for Theology and Ethics*, which investigates both Christian scripture and tradition to question whether this tradition is irredeemably speciesist (Linzey and Yamamoto 1998).[13] In another publication, in collaboration with Rabbi Dan Cohn-Sherbok, Linzey and Cohn-Sherbok (1997, 1) aim to give an account of "the positive resources available within

---

12. In this article, Hobgood-Oster provides accounts of speaking animals in the Christian tradition as a response to the question of the supposedly *Word*-obsessed Christianity and its exclusive connection to humans and human language.

13. The introduction is named: "Is Christianity Irredeemably Speciesist?" *Speciesist* signifies when one species is deemed superior to another. See also Linzey 1976, 1987, and 1994.

the Jewish and Christian traditions for a celebration of our relations with animals." While not uncritical, Linzey's project has been oriented around a positive revaluation and redemption of the Bible and the Judeo-Christian. David L. Clough's (2012) systematic theology on animals and his work with Celia Deane-Drummond (2009) and with Deane-Drummond and Rebecca Artinian-Kaiser (2013) have been particularly important for establishing the role of animals in the theology and religious studies fields. These works rigorously chart and challenge theological traditions with regard to the concerns of animal studies, take note of animal symbols and rites in religious practice, and grapple with ethical theories and practices. Charting a broader religious field, Lisa Kemmerer's (2011) comprehensive *Animals and World Religions* engages with animal activists in different religious traditions. Waldau and Kimberly Patton's (2009) *A Communion of Subjects: Animals in Religion, Science, and Ethics* is a further sign of more wide-ranging engagement with religion in relation to the concerns of animal studies.

While there is more work done on animal studies in theology and religious studies so far, there is also notable scholarship arising more particularly with regard to the Bible. Studies such as Kenneth C. Way's (2011) *Donkeys in the Biblical World: Ceremony and Symbol*, Tova L. Forti's (2008) *Animal Imagery in the Book of Proverbs*, and Deborah O'Daniel Cantrell's (2011) *The Horsemen of Israel: Horses and Chariotry in Monarchic Israel (Ninth–Eighth Centuries B.C.E.)* are helpful resources within the field of animals in the Bible, but as Ken Stone (2014, 290) points out, these are strictly historical-critical resources that, although useful, do not provide a critical engagement with, or connection to, the questions raised by animal studies today. Moore's (2014a) *Divinanimality: Animal Theory, Creaturely Theology* and Jennifer L. Koosed's (2014a) *The Bible and Posthumanism* are important contributions that model close biblical engagement with a critical theoretical bent. Both volumes provide rich engagements with the theoretical stakes of animal studies and the ambiguities of religion and its scriptures. In the introduction to *Divinanimality*, Moore (2014a, 11) states that "if the animal-human distinction is being rethought and retheorized, then the animal-human-divine distinctions must be rethought, retheorized, and retheologized alongside it." A significant tenet of *Divinanimality* is that there are considerable resources, in that most religious scriptures and much of theology predates "the Cartesian realignment of human-animal relations in terms absolutely oppositional and hierarchical" (11). As Koosed (2014b, 3) argues, the Bible "contains multiple moments of disruption, boundary crossing, and category confusion: animals speak, God becomes man, spirits haunt the living, and monsters confound at the end." All the essays in *The Bible and Posthumanism*, as Koosed (2014b, 4) points out, demonstrate the complexity of biblical texts and traditions. It is imperative to build on this burgeoning scholarship, multiplying perspectives and critical attention to foster broader as well as more detailed discussions. What I add with my own study is a more sustained attention to themes of animality by charting a specific trajectory across the biblical corpus with regard to the killability (and edibility) of animals and notions of proper and improper sovereignty.

The themes of killability and sovereignty are bound up with one another through the issue of human versus divine powers to give and take life. Are humans given a sovereign power to reign over animals, as seems to be the case in Gen 1:26, where humankind is given "dominion over the fish of the sea, and over the birds of the air, and over the cattle, and over all the wild animals of the earth, and over every creeping thing that creeps upon the earth"?[14] This dominion is by no means settled by this verse when it comes to the biblical texts that follow Genesis, or even within Genesis itself. Human sovereignty is frequently deemed improper, a misplaced hubris that forgets the vulnerability and mortality of humans. The challenge to such sovereignty causes splinters in the idea of animals as killable objects, subject to human sovereignty. When human sovereignty is destabilized, humans and animals are in many ways on a par under the only proper sovereign: God. The human/animal boundary thus frequently experiences slippages, as every living creature exists in the hands of the divine sovereign; all the living are vulnerable and mortal, human or nonhuman.

The Biblical Archive and Cultural Memory

The Bible is referred to in the name of a particular textual, cultural-religious inheritance as memory and authority, and it is necessary to turn anew to this referent with the question of the animal in mind. It would be better to speak (as I already have) of "the biblical archive" in referring to the Bible, thus drawing in notions of multiplicity, preservation, power, and legacy more explicitly. Thinking critically about issues of multiplic-

---

14. All biblical references are taken from the NRSV, unless stated otherwise.

ity in the biblical inheritance, it is important to unmask the seemingly organic point of origin for which terms such as the *Bible* or the *Judeo-Christian* stand, as if the Bible was homogenous, congruent, and a monolithic corpus or that noticeable theological differentiations exist between Judaism and Christianity. I argue that the Bible is neither a pure origin for anthropocentrism nor a straightforward source for anthropocentric thinking. Indeed, the case can be made that individual texts in the biblical archive can be interpreted as fostering current understandings of human dominance, centrality, and superiority. At the same time, however, these same texts frequently radically problematize such an anthropocentric understanding in the relationality that conditions life with and as animals.

Undoubtedly, the Bible has been influential in countless ways. Whether it is frequently read in detail is another question. In his influential *Religion and Cultural Memory*, Jan Assmann (2006) theorizes the ways in which individual memory is never wholly distinct from social memory. He explores how societal norms and practices emerge from such collective memory. In "the act of remembering we do not just descend into the depths of our own most intimate inner life, but we introduce an order and a structure into that internal life that are socially conditioned and that link us to the social world" (1–2). Individual memory—and its formation, structure, and order—is mediated through a particular context, culture, and society and is thus caught up in what he calls "collective memory." Assman suggests that "the task of this memory, above all, is to transmit a collective identity. Society inscribes itself in this memory with all its norms and values and creates in the individual the authority that Freud called the superego and that has traditionally been called 'conscience'" (6–7). This kind of memory is, he writes, "particularly susceptible to politicized forms of remembering" (7). We might see the above references to the Bible as a symptom of a collective memory of the Bible *as* anthropocentric. Particular pieces of its archive are remembered and reinforced socially through repetition of its supposed meaning. One such example would be the much referred to *imago Dei* in Genesis—that is, humans being made in God's image—and the concurrent "memory" that this straightforwardly signifies human superiority. Such reinforced memory and its consequences might explain the anxiety felt in regard to the Bible as a cultural canon whose content is still remembered in today's world, in more or less oblique ways. The fuzziness that accompanies any attempt to calculate *how* such memory functions or *what* it denotes merely exacerbates the anxiety, making such "memories" all the more elusive and uncontrollable, thus harder to erase or even to admit their presence as a dominant norm.

Importantly, Assmann suggests that norms are to some extent naturalized by appearing to represent the individual beliefs of a person, as separate from particular cultural archives. Such beliefs are thus thought to be natural as either singular or universal ("common sense") rather than culturally constructed and part of a larger fabric of influences and influxes. Cultural archives are of great importance, whether consciously acknowledged or not, as Assmann (2006, 7–8) points out: "both the collective and the individual turn to the archive of cultural traditions, the arsenal of symbolic forms, the 'imaginary' of myths and images, of the 'great stories,' sagas and legends, scenes and constellations that live or can be reactivated in the treasure stores of a people." Cultural archives, then, are crucial for understanding both individual and collective forms of memory and how they continue to influence norms, values, and practices in the present and for the future. Assmann holds that there "is no understanding without memory, no existence without tradition" (27). Noting Heidegger's and Derrida's writings on archives, Assmann argues that the discussion emerges "as a form of memory that constitutes the present and makes the future possible through the medium of symbols … permeated by the political structures of power and domination" (27). This attention to the way political structures of power and domination affect the present and the futures that are possible concurrently is of vital importance for the question of the animal. Political structures and authoritative archives condition thinking and acting in the world today with regard to power (or the lack of it), but crucially, as Assmann implies, they also shape the future. In other words, if perceptions of animals today as killable *things* are shown to be linked to particular myths or cultural legacies, these perceptions might appear rather less natural or common sense. If, on the other hand, such understandings are reinforced by recourse to discursive strategies of myths and narratives as to the "natural" or "original" order of particular hierarchies, then the right to reign over animals might appear fully justified, and the idea that animals could be treated or thought of otherwise would remain unthinkable.

In light of the blame apportioned to the Bible, it is imperative that this hybrid body of texts is examined with critical attention to the complexities and tensions that mark its varied topography. Exactly *how* this canon has influenced past and present views of animals is perhaps impossible to map out. But to trawl over some of its terrain today considering the questions posed in animal studies and attempt to identify in what ways the biblical archive could be seen to reinforce ideas of human superiority—and in what ways it might resist such ideas—is a task that this study attempts.

Following Jacques Derrida

Derrida was arguably one of the most influential if not infamous thinkers of his time. The names *Derrida* and *deconstruction* have, as Sherwood's (2004b, 5) assessment demonstrates, been frequently divided between religious mystification and secular demystification, both "encroaching totalitarianism and encroaching relativism."[15] Alternately critiqued for "impotent bookishness" and "totalizing power," he "serves as a cipher for perilous regression (into childhood 'play,' or the occult world of Jewish mysticism), and also for dangerous acceleration beyond the borders of the humanities and the human and humane" (Sherwood 2004b, 5–6). From his early work in the 1960s and 1970s—with the seminal *Writing and Difference* ([1967b] 2001) and *Of Grammatology* ([1967a] 1998), through *Glas* ([1974] 1986), *Dissemination* ([1972] 1983), *The Truth in Painting* ([1978] 1987), *Of Spirit* ([1987] 1991), *Specters of Marx* ([1993] 2006), and *Rogues* (2005b), to mention only a few—to the two posthumously published volumes *The Beast and the Sovereign* (2009–2011), he has done nothing if not spark debate amongst critics and followers. Prolific and diverse in his interests, Derrida wrote on phenomenology, Marx, Plato, Freud, drugs, 9/11, the poetry of Paul Celan, the death penalty, Franz Kafka, democracy, the South African truth and reconciliation commission, Abraham and animals, as well as on the terms and neologisms he is so well known for, such as "*écriture*," "*différance*," the "khora," and "deconstruction" (and this is not an exhaustive list).

Perhaps what characterizes Derrida's style of thinking the most is a sustained attention to texts—their details, marginalia, and tensions—marked by a deep respect for the legacies and traditions with which he engaged as well as a ceaseless capacity for imaginative, radical, and surprising interpretations. Peter Sedgwick (2001, 192) calls Derrida "amongst the most controversial of post-war European thinkers," because "he is a thinker who has sought to challenge a number of what he argues to be deeply rooted presuppositions that dominate the practice of philosophi-

---

15. See also Sherwood and Hart 2004, for a discussion of the relationship between Derrida's work and religion.

cal enquiry" (193). As Derrida-scholar Nicholas Royle (2009, ix) puts it: "He questions everything. He refuses to simplify what is not simple. He works at unsettling all dogma." It is perhaps no wonder, then, that he has "consistently provoked anxiety, anger and frustration, as well as pleasure, exhilaration and awe" (xi). In his *In Memory of Jacques Derrida*, Royle (2009, xi) writes that Derrida "was the most original and inspiring writer and philosopher of our time. He made—and his writing still makes and will continue to make—earthquakes in thinking." Earthquakes in thinking *what*? Or *who*?

One answer to this is in thinking about the human and animal. Derrida analyzes issues at the heart of the two crises I referred to earlier, namely, the question of the subject and the question of the human as a sovereign figure in the world. His later work forms a significant contribution to the question of the animal. In the philosophical tradition associated with the crisis of the subject, Derrida is a significant figure, both indebted to, and critical of, thinkers such as Heidegger, Adorno, Levinas, and Foucault. Derrida (1995b, 268) argues that despite all the challenges to the understanding of the "subject," the discourse on the subject "continues to link subjectivity with man." Already in 1968, Derrida (1969, 35) addresses the question of "man" and suggests that the history of the concept of man has not been sufficiently interrogated, as if "man" were a sign without historical, cultural, and linguistic limits. A large part of Derrida's later work engages with concepts of the human and man in the Western philosophical tradition, the question of the animal, and what a different subjectivity might look like—one that takes account of animal life, and not merely as inferior to human life. This can be most powerfully and succinctly found in the 1997 Cérisy lectures, posthumously published as *The Animal That Therefore I Am* (2008).

Related to this work on the human subject and animals, he also dedicated many seminars toward the end of his life to concepts of sovereignty—the sovereignty of the human—and figures of beasts in philosophical, political, cultural, and religious canonical works. These are gathered in the two posthumously published volumes of *The Beast and the Sovereign*, transcribed from his final 2001 to 2003 seminars. In these seminars, Derrida (2009, 26) explored the often-paradoxical representations of the political human as superior to animality and political humanity as animality. He sets out to pose "the great questions of animal life (that of man, said by Aristotle to be a 'political animal,' and that of the 'beasts') and of the treatment, the subjection, of the 'beast' by 'man'" (2009, editorial note). Michael B. Naas (2008, 63) points to this central concern of sovereignty in the last two decades of Derrida's work as "the root of many of the philosophical concepts Derrida wished to reread and many of the contemporary ethical and political issues he wished to rethink." The most prominent issues would have been religion, hospitality, democracy, and justice.[16] These themes are all present in Derrida's thinking of animality.

In "Violence against Animals," Derrida (2004, 62) proclaims that the "question of animality" is not merely one question among others. He explains how he has long considered it "decisive":

> While it is difficult and enigmatic in itself, it also represents the limit upon which all the great questions are formed and determined, as well as the concepts that attempt to delimit what is "proper to man," the essence and future of humanity, ethics, politics, law, "human rights," "crimes against humanity," "genocide," etc. (62–63)

Derrida (63n3) explicitly draws attention to the persistent interest he has taken in the question of the animal and the many references to it in his work. Situating himself like a Robinson Crusoe on an island unto himself, Derrida (2008, 62) claims he has always been exempt from what philosophy has called, with such imprecision, "the animal":

> I am saying "they," "what they call an animal," in order to mark clearly the fact that I have always secretly exempted myself from that word, and to indicate that my whole history, the whole genealogy of my questions, in truth everything I am, follow, think, write, trace, erase even, seems to me to be born from that exceptionalism.

What Derrida contributes to animal studies, then, is a wide-ranging critique of a dominant line of thinkers in Western philosophy, particularly the continental philosophy tradition. He provides suggestions for how we might begin to follow such traditions differently. From "Aristotle to Lacan, and including Descartes, Kant, Heidegger, and Levinas" (2008, 12, 27, 32, 54, 59, 89) these thinkers are "paradigmatic, dominant, and normative" (54) in regard to the philosophical understanding of the "human." Derrida's repeated references to this "Western philosophical tradition" intentionally situates him as following this tradition, participating in its

---

16. See, for instance, *Rogues* (2005b), *The Gift of Death* (1995c), *Of Hospitality* (2000), and *On Cosmopolitanism and Forgiveness* (2001).

legacies, but determinedly inscribing his own philosophical signature on this tradition in a powerful indictment of its philosophical treatment of animals. Derrida (2008, 54) further justifies their prominence in his work by arguing that they:

> constitute a general topology and even, in a somewhat new sense for this term, a worldwide anthropology, a way for today's man to position himself in the face of what he calls "the animal" within what he calls "the world"—so many motifs (man, animal, and especially world) that I would like, as it were, to reproblematize.

It is not that this tradition is homogenous but rather that it has been "hegemonic" when it comes to human/animal distinctions, so that it is in fact a discourse "*of* hegemony, of mastery itself" (2004, 63, emphasis original). In *The Animal That Therefore I Am*, Derrida (2008) undertakes this reproblematization, focusing on the above-mentioned canonical figures. For *The Beast and the Sovereign* seminars, he expands his canon with a wide range of writers in volume 1: Jean de La Fontaine, Thomas Hobbes, Rousseau, Niccolò Machiavelli, Giorgio Agamben, Gustave Flaubert, Gilles Deleuze, Edmund Husserl, Celan, and D. H. Lawrence, as well as goes over Aristotle, Paul Valéry, Levinas, Lacan, and Heidegger again. Volume 2 focuses on interpreting Daniel Defoe's *Robinson Crusoe* and Heidegger's *The Fundamental Concepts of Metaphysics: World, Finitude, Solitude.* The figures Derrida examines are not put forward as an exhaustive archive of Western philosophy for rethinking the conceptualization of the human/man but do form an impressively expansive exploration and multifaceted critique of some of the key texts and thinkers for the Western world.

Derrida's (2008, 40) thesis is bold, with enormous implications for grappling with the most dominant thinkers in the history of Western philosophy:

> I'll venture to say that never, on the part of any great philosopher from Plato to Heidegger, or anyone at all who takes on, as a philosophical question in and of itself, the question called that of the animal and of the limit between the animal and the human, have I noticed a protestation based on principle, and especially not a protestation that amounts to anything, against the general singular that is the animal.

He traces an agreement between philosophical sense and common sense "that allows one to speak blithely of the Animal in the general singular" and suggests that this "is perhaps one of the greatest and most symptomatic *asinanities* of those who call themselves humans" (41, emphasis original).

Derrida stands seemingly solitary in the continental philosophy tradition in paying attention to animal issues despite, as Calarco (2007, 6) reminds us, this tradition priding itself on its engagement with concrete ethicopolitical subjects of thought. Singer echoes this in his affirmation that a philosophical impetus is necessary to bring about practical change in relation to animals but that continental philosophy has failed to provide one. What philosophical incentive to challenge the way nonhuman animals are treated, Singer (2004, xii) asks, has come from philosophers in the continental tradition, thinkers such as "Heidegger, Foucault, Levinas, and Deleuze, or those who take the work of these thinkers as setting a framework for their own thought?" His answer is "as far as I can judge, none," revealing perplexity as to "why such an extensive body of thought should have failed to grapple with the issue of how we treat animals" (xii). Singer asks what this failure signifies in the alleged attempts to question and critique prevailing assumptions and dominant institutions. At the same time, as I implied earlier, of course these thinkers *have* formed an important part of rethinking animality in terms of bringing questions of the subject, freedom, ethics, and the other to the fore. It would arguably be impossible to imagine animal studies today without this continental tradition. Derrida, however, is one such thinker who explicitly drew attention to such practical and philosophical issues and whom Singer fails to mention.

Despite Derrida's own insistence on the topic of animality, to which he dedicated his whole life, little sign of this can be found in the scholarship that poured out in the aftermath of his death. In their book *Encountering Derrida: Legacies and Futures of Deconstruction*, editors Allison Weiner and Simon Morgan Wortham (2007, 1) write that he leaves us behind with "a wealth of writings that touched upon nearly every aspect of the philosophical enterprise, publishing an enormous body of texts that crossed—and reinvented—a host of disciplinary fields." But, perhaps because it predates the posthumous publication of *The Animal That Therefore I Am*, none of the contributors to this volume mention the question of the animal. Perhaps for similar reasons, Ian Balfour's (2007) edited collection, *Late Derrida*, does not bring the animal issue to the fore. The same is the case for Madeleine Fagan, Ludovic Glorieux, Indira Hašimbegović, and Marie Suetsugu's (2007) *Derrida: Negotiating the Legacy*. Royle's (2009, 157–58) *In Memory of Jacques Derrida* touches briefly on Derrida's *The Animal That Therefore I Am* but does not leave the impression that this was a particularly central topic for Derrida. Calarco (2007, 1) bemoans the "dearth of writing on this theme by his followers and critics" and asserts that from "the very earliest to the latest texts, Derrida is keenly aware of and intent on problematizing the anthropocentric underpinnings and orientation of philosophy and associated discourses" (2).[17]

Naas's (2003, xix, emphasis original) *Taking on the Tradition: Jacques Derrida and the Legacies of Deconstruction* looks at how Derrida's work has prompted a rethinking of tradition, legacy, and inheritance in philosophy, writing of "the incredible power of the tradition, its way of recuperating the most heterogeneous and marginal elements, *and* its great fragility, its vulnerability to the very gestures of reception that make it—along with our history and our origins—possible in the first place." While Naas touches on concerns that are close to the animal as the forgotten, foreclosed topic Derrida emphasizes in the Western philosophical tradition, he does not mention animality specifically. Naas continues to argue that one "begins by listening to the canon because the canon always gives us more than we imagine, more than we could have expected, because the canon always gives us, in its folds, something noncanonical, something that can never be simply included in the curriculum" (xxix). This *more* arguably could refer to the foreclosed animal subjects that Derrida follows and to which he responds, what he argues has been what philosophy forgets, namely, "the animal can look at me" (Derrida 2008, 11). In other words, the animal is not merely an object of study, of comparative interest or symbolic significance. It "has its point of view regarding me. The point of view of the

---

17. Attention to this aspect of Derrida's work is growing, albeit in rather niche corners. A notable example is Leonard Lawlor's (2007) *This Is Not Sufficient: An Essay on Animality and Human Nature in Derrida*. In 2007, the *Oxford Literary Review* published a special issue on Derrida and animals, entitled *Derridanimals* and edited by Neil Badmington. See also Berger and Segarra 2011, Krell 2013, and Turner 2013. With the exception of Lawlor, these are situated at the fringes of animal studies with a somewhat idiosyncratic approach, focusing more on particular and sometimes eccentric human-animal encounters or specific concerns in Derrida's work. Krell (2013), for instance, offers a summary and close reading of *The Animal That Therefore I Am* and *The Beast and the Sovereign* seminars, involving also a critical response with particular focus on Derrida's reading of Heidegger's 1929 to 1930 lecture on world, finitude, and solitude. Turner (2013) draws on Hélène Cixous extensively and takes a somewhat idiosyncratic approach, with essays on insects, moles, worms, and sponges as well as lions, elephants, and wolves. It is less strictly tied to Derrida's corpus per se, taking its point of departure from Derrida into other avenues.

absolute other" (11). As Derrida says, "nothing will have given me more food for thinking" than the alterity of the animal (11).

Greater attention to this aspect of Derrida's thought is emerging, however, as can be seen from, for example, Aaron S. Gross's (2014) *The Question of the Animal and Religion*, Judith Still's (2015) *Derrida and Other Animals*, and Sarah Bezan and James Tink's (2017) *Seeing Animals after Derrida*. Bezan and Tink (2017, x) posit that the environmental and ecological criticism that coincided in many ways with Derrida's turn to the animal has been supported and developed by debates around the "anthropocene" as well as by the nonhuman turn in thought of new materialism, speculative realism, and object-oriented philosophy. Although much of this goes in different directions than Derrida, they reflect that "Derrida's work has become part of a wider series of theoretical approaches to the animal and the environment since its inception" (Bezan and Tink 2017, x). As Gross (2014, 121) contends, Derrida "helps us to attend to animals differently but also to the knot in which the animal is bound to other core concepts," without relegating animals as a stepping stone to more supposedly worthy subjects. "Derrida shows how we need to reconsider our own subjectivity to responsibly consider animals and how we must confront out own being-confronted-by animals—by individual animals in our lived-in world—to reconsider our own subjectivity" (121).

What Derrida ultimately calls for in his work on animality is threefold: (1) greater vigilance in philosophical thought over the supposedly distinct differences between humans and animals; (2) compassion and an awakening to the animal other as a condition for ethics—an awakening that is linked to Derrida's dream for an unconditional hospitality; and (3) responsibility in the face of a horizon of justice that will always be to some extent excessive, incalculable, and impossible but that nonetheless demands our interminable response with respect to the other as *any* other.

While the term *deconstruction* is indiscreetly bandied about in all manner of contexts, usually in alliance with a vague sense of the postmodern project divorced from Derrida's work, on the one hand, or used synonymously with his signature as a thinker, on the other, I am somewhat uneasy about its use, especially in light of the frequent misuse and misunderstandings that weigh it down.[18] As a ghost that cannot be wholly

---

18. Perhaps what haunts deconstruction most visibly today is the banality associated with its vague alliance with a popculture postmodernism.

purged, however, I would like to grapple with the idea of deconstruction specifically in relation to the so-called distinction(s) between what we call humans and what we call animals. This can be described by the figure of the threshold[19]:

> The threshold not only supposes this indivisible limit that every decon-struction begins by deconstructing (to deconstruct is to hold that no indivisibility, no atomicity, is secure), the classical figure of the threshold (to be deconstructed) not only supposes this indivisibility that is not to be found anywhere; it also supposes the solidity of a ground or a founda-tion, they too being deconstructible. (Derrida 2009, 309–10)

The word threshold (*seuil*), Derrida (2009, 310) explains, comes from the Latin *solum*, which means soil "or more precisely the foundation on which an architectural sill or the sole of one's feet rest." What this means, "and this is the gesture of deconstructive thinking," is "that we don't even con-sider the existence (whether natural or artificial) of any threshold to be secure, if by 'threshold' is meant *either* an indivisible frontier line *or* the solidity of a foundational ground" (310).

However, to stop here would be to succumb to the abstraction into which so many explications of deconstruction fall. Deconstruction is not merely about acknowledging the instability of any threshold or limit between one concept/thing and another, or merely about breaking down such boundaries by pointing to their fragility, thus equating "deconstruc-tion" (as it so often is) with its near-homonym "destruction." This would be to open up what Derrida calls the abyss and remain content to cease thinking in the face of such a void. As Chrulew (2006, 18.3) notes, there is a perhaps uncharacteristic earnestness in Derrida's thinking about animals that needs to be taken into account. For Derrida (2009, 333–34), what is called for is both "a greater vigilance as to our irrepressible desire for the threshold, a threshold that *is* a threshold, a single and solid threshold," an openness to the fact that there may in fact be no threshold, and a recogni-tion that "the abyss is not the bottom nor the bottomless depth" of a hidden base. "The abyss, if there is an abyss, is that there is *more than one* ground [*sol*], more than one solid, and more than one single threshold [*plus d'un*

---

19. This is perhaps a play on Levinas (1969, 173): "the possibility for the home to open to the Other is as essential to the essence of the home as closed doors and windows."

seul seuil]" (334, emphasis original). What the deconstructive task would consist of, then, is examining critically *what* threshold is upheld as natural, single, and seemingly indivisible, and what other thresholds might be unmasked or unmaskable in the critique of such a supposed central threshold. Where does a threshold lie? But further, what does it hold *inside*, and what (or who) *outside*? How is it constructed as a threshold? Who are the masters and inhabitants of the house, and who are strangers, foreigners, or even enemies lurking outside? Concepts of house, home, threshold, and its insiders/outsiders become hugely important to Derrida's discourse on animality. It is, for him, part and parcel of a thinking of a hospitality that is unconditional and an ethics that is spatial and temporal: *in* a place, a specific context, at a threshold that is both shared and divisive, and *with* a singular other who is both potentially threatening and loving, never determined (or determinable) in advance as one or the other.

Humans, Derrida (2008, 32) suggests, have given themselves this word *animal*, "as if they had received it as an inheritance" to construct a threshold; they have "given themselves the word in order to corral a large number of living beings within a single concept," the animal. Animals thus remain outside, on the other side of this threshold, as killable, edible, huntable, trappable, containable: as nonothers and nonneighbors, accepted in proximity as exceptions in the case of pets or as machines for human use. Of course, this is putting the point starkly, and Derrida does participate in a certain polemical trend that marks animal studies.[20] Such polemics, however, are perhaps justified in light of the urgency of challenging the threshold that allows for intensified animal farming industries, genetic crossbreeding and manipulation, hormone treatment, experimentation, cloning, and artificial insemination all for the "putative well-being of man" (Derrida 2008, 25). Derrida calls the question of the animal an *event* and condemns the dissimulation that allows for a diversion from, or deferral of, confrontation with this event. "However one interprets it, whatever practical, technical, scientific, juridical, ethical, or political consequences one draws from it, no one can today deny this event—that is, the *unprecedented* proportions of this subjection of the animal" (25, emphasis original). This is a repression of sorts, a symptom that demands immediate attention and long-term treatment that no one can seriously

---

20. For a critique of some of the polemical, even extreme strands of animal studies as they relate more specifically to environmentalism, see Ferry 1995.

deny any longer: "men do all they can in order to dissimulate this cruelty or to hide it from themselves; in order to organize on a global scale the forgetting or misunderstanding of this violence, which some would compare to the worst cases of genocide" (26). As Gross points out (2014, 135), there is a structure that links genocide to violence against animals—namely, a sacrificial structure—as well as similarities in "the scale, coordination, the application of technology, the writing bodies, the willing perpetrators, the disavowals." Derrida (2008, 28–29) speaks of a "war." Gross (2014, 131) explains that Derrida's reference to war should not simply be regarded as a polemical metaphor. The reference signals rather the "immense mobilization of resources, social (local, regional, national, global) planning, an intensified use of technologies, destruction of environments, and mass killing" that characterize warfare (131–32). "And just as war has become intensified in modernity—sword to gun, bomb to nuclear bomb—so has the war against animals" (132). The war against pity toward animals has also been waged, he argues, in the academy as much as within religious traditions (136). Critical attention to the complicity and participation in such a war is now an urgent matter (137).

I have called Derrida's response to the question of the animal an awakening to the animal other as a condition for ethics. Why? Peggy Kamuf (2010, 10) argues that "wakefulness, or alertness" are traits Derrida "consistently assigns a positive value." She points out that this key part of his vocabulary is a testament to the legacy of modern philosophy, at least since the Enlightenment and perhaps especially with Kant and his call for vigilance.[21] What she calls Kant's "wake-up call to critical, non-dogmatic philosophy" has continued to resonate ever since, and she argues "nowhere in a more thought-provoking fashion than in Derrida's writings of the last half century" (10). Wakefulness is "the very condition or possibility of critical reception and inheritance" (10). But wakefulness to what or whom? To the other, in an ethical relation that is a response and responsibility to this other, which Derrida proposes must also be the animal other. Before pursuing this further, it is necessary to add a preliminary note on the reference to ethics here. When Derrida refers to ethics in relation to animality, he is seemingly referring to two things. The first is the specific moral practices and laws that govern the interactions between humans and animals;

---

21. Kamuf (2010, 10) recalls Kant's comment that it was reading David Hume that woke him from his "dogmatic slumber."

the second is to the self-other relationship as an always already ethical relation. Simply put, *ethical* in this second sense is bound up, not with specific moral prescriptions, but with a state of responsibility to and for the other, to whom something of me is due. When I mention the awakening to the *condition* for ethics, then, I mean to the conditions under which this encounter takes place in determining this something in regard to whom the other is or can be.

It is important to note that Derrida's notion of an awakening to ethics is partly based on a critique of Heidegger and the authority of wakefulness that Derrida criticizes Heidegger for deeming a human power or property.[22] It is, he writes, on the basis of questions of sleep and waking that Heidegger announces his typology of beings—stone, plant, animal, man (Derrida 2008, 149).[23] Derrida emphatically does not follow Heidegger in this regard on positing a *human* straightforward, exclusive, and authoritative consciousness as wakefulness. The other important reference for Derrida's awakening is its connection to his critique of Levinas and his ethics of the face of the other who is a determinedly *human* other.[24] Derrida (2008, 106) questions Levinas's ethics and suggests it remains a dormant ethics: "it is a matter of putting the animal outside of the ethical circuit." And this, he writes, "from a thinker that is so 'obsessed' (I am purposely using Levinas's word), so preoccupied by an obsession with the other and with his infinite alterity" (Derrida 2008, 107). Derrida retorts:

> If I am responsible for the other, and before the other, and in the place of the other, on behalf of the other, isn't the animal more other still, more radically other, if I might put it that way, than the other in whom I recognize my brother, than the other in whom I identify my fellow or my neighbor? If I have a duty [*devoir*]—something owed before any debt, before any right—toward the other, wouldn't it then also be toward the animal, which is still more other than the other human, my brother or

---

22. Derrida is mainly engaging with Heidegger's (2001) 1929 to 1930 lectures, published as *The Fundamental Concepts of Metaphysics: World, Finitude, Solitude*.

23. Heidegger in turn draws on Aristotle for his discussion of wakefulness and sleeping.

24. Derrida retells Levinas's story of the dog named Bobby in a concentration camp, whom he calls "the last Kantian dog in Nazi Germany." Derrida (2008, 113–17) deals with this passage extensively and cites John Llewelyn's question to Levinas at the 1986 Cérisy conference as to whether animals have a face.

my neighbor? In fact, no. It seems precisely that for Levinas the *animot* is not an other. (107, emphasis original)[25]

Derrida is attempting, in Calarco's (2007, 4) words, to think "a thought of the same/other relation where the same is not simply a human self and where the other is not simply a human other." In the notion of awakening, Derrida is thus indicting the philosophical tradition he criticizes with a myopic, docile, negligent attitude when it comes to the question of ethics in the face of animals. "So long as there is recognizability and fellow, ethics is dormant. It is sleeping a dogmatic slumber. So long as it remains human, among men, ethics remains dogmatic, narcissistic, not yet thinking. Not even thinking the human that it talks so much about" (Derrida 2009, 108). The unrecognizable is the awakening (108). Sedgwick (2001, 217) explains how:

> Philosophy, for Derrida, takes place in the world first and foremost as an ethical mode of thought: it concerns the relationship between thinkers (philosophers) and the limits of what they can think. Their duty is to pay attention to these limits. Paying attention to these limits, refusing to think in terms of an already secure future for philosophical thought, is the duty of philosophy itself and of those who practice it.

Having critiqued ideas of response and responsibility as properties thought to be exclusively human, Derrida is both calling for a more radical response and responsibility on the part of human animals in his call for an awakening to the animal other as a condition for ethics, but he is also at the same time questioning the autonomy and authority assumed to be inherent to such powers of wakeful response and responsibility. As he puts it, we

---

25. *Animot* is a term Derrida coins in French to signify (in sound) *animaux*, animals in plural, rather than the animal in general singular, to mark the absurdity of what such a general singular animal could possibly mean. But it also refers to *mot* ("word") and his emphasis on this *word* animal, the attention paid to what a word means, and what powers words can have for cramming such a vast multiplicity of living beings into this verbal enclosure as an opposition to humans. In *Rogues*, Derrida (2005b, 60, emphasis original) writes similarly: "pure ethics, if there is any, begins with the respectable dignity of the other as the absolute *unlike*, recognized as non-recognizable, indeed as unrecognizable, beyond all knowledge, all cognition and all recognition: far from being the beginning of pure ethics, the neighbor as like or as resembling, as looking like, spells the end or the ruin of such an ethics, if there is any."

must cast "doubt on all responsibility, all ethics, every decision" (Derrida 2008, 126). Such doubt, he says, "on responsibility, on decision, on one's own being-ethical, seems to me to be—and is perhaps what should forever remain—the unrescindable essence of ethics, decision, and responsibility" (126). His awakening to ethics, then, is a relation that is always in question and always undecidable. Wakefulness can never be assured as a fully present consciousness; an authoritative, open-eyed seeing; or a wholly controlled knowing, immune from dreams, blindness, the unconscious, finitude, and limitations as well as forgetfulness of what or who also *sees me*. In fact, to be responsible or responsibly wakeful might be to recognize oneself still to be dreaming, to be still asleep. The self-consciousness of the wakeful human, Derrida emphasizes, is a relationship to the other whom I follow, who sees me, and to whom I respond. This provisional wakefulness is what, I argue, characterizes Derrida's idea of the other as an animal other who goes before me—to whom I say, "after you"—and the other as a witness who sees me and who signifies a justice in abeyance, who founds my accountability as the essential possibility for ethics. As I go on to discuss, this otherness for Derrida is imagined in the *nonhuman* other of animal and divine.

In order to be ethics at all, for Derrida, the relationship to the other must be grounded in two principles. One is what he calls the:

> immense question of pathos and the pathological, precisely, that is, of suffering, pity, and compassion; and the place that has to be accorded to the interpretation of this compassion, to the sharing of this suffering among the living, to the law, ethics, and politics that must be brought to bear upon this experience of compassion. (Derrida 2008, 26)

Derrida develops this question of pathos from an invocation of Bentham's question of whether animals can suffer. The form of this question, which is about passivity rather than what laudable traits animals do or do not possess, "changes everything" (27). Compassion ought, as he says, to "*awaken* us to our responsibilities and our obligations vis-à-vis the living in general" (27, emphasis added). This is not an awakening to Heidegger's "authority of wakefulness" (Derrida 2011, 185) but rather to the responsibility demanded toward the vulnerability of life, the always deconstructible limits of humans and animals alike, and a shared finitude in the face of mortality (Derrida 2008, 26). Wakefulness is attention as care and curiosity toward animal others rather than a consciousness deemed exclusively human.

The second principle is developed in Derrida's (2009, 241) interpretation of D. H. Lawrence's poem "Snake" with the "scene of hospitality." Here, the sovereignty presented in the poem is on the side of the snake, not the human who is petty with a learned propensity to violence and who thus attempts to kill the snake that shows up at the watering hole. Analyzing this poetic narrative, Derrida (2009, 243, emphasis added) writes that "Lawrence *awakens to ethics*, to the thought 'Thou shalt not kill,' in a scene of hospitality" in a scene with a potentially murderous, threatening animal. Here lies Derrida's critique of Levinas and Heidegger, in the recognition of the other who goes before me—the snake that is already there at the watering hole—who demands an "after you" from me, the proper ethical response to the other as any other. This is an animal who shares my world, who evokes humility at the heteronomy of this other and the possibility of hospitality.

The question is, Derrida (2009, 244) suggests: "Does an ethics or a moral prescription obligate us only to those who are like us … or else does it obligate us with respect to anyone at all, any living being at all, and therefore with respect to the animal?" Derrida's awakening to ethics is precisely the recognition of the animal as a neighbor, or fellow, not by claiming its sameness to humans but its otherness, and thus is a prime example of the challenge of the other of ethics, who demands my compassion, even in the face of danger or incalculability as to *who* the other is and what it might do. It is a matter of recognizing the other as first, coming before me, and thus admitting a certain powerlessness and divisibility in the "I" who always stands in relation, *seen* by the other, *seeing* the other (239). We are thus talking not about ethical principles themselves in regard to Derrida's awakening to the animal other as a condition for ethics, but to what Calarco (2008, 108) describes as Derrida's protoethics. It is not that this is without practice but rather that such a practice emerges out of the principles described in or by particular, concrete contexts. This is essentially "a matter of acting and making decisions in concrete circumstances, using as much knowledge as possible, and in view of a 'maximum respect' for animals" (115).

One of the most incisive critiques of Derrida's work on animality is Haraway's (2007) *When Species Meet*. She suggests that when Derrida reflects on his cat in *The Animal That Therefore I Am*, the cat is quickly forgotten in favor of "his textual canon of Western philosophy and literature" (Haraway 2007, 20). He does not become curious about what the cat might be doing, feeling, or thinking, despite the fact that he insists that "this is a 'real cat,' not the figure of a cat, or of all cats" (Derrida 2008, 6). Haraway

(2007, 21–22) argues that the question of animal suffering is not the decisive question, albeit an important one. How much more promise, she asks,

> is in the questions, Can animals play? Or work? And even, can I learn to play with *this* cat? Can I, the philosopher, respond to an invitation or recognize one when it is offered? What if work and play, and not just pity, open up when the possibility of mutual response, without names, is taken seriously as an everyday practice available to philosophy and to science? (22, emphasis original).

As my study, inspired by Derrida, is indeed about a textual canon, it might well be the case that real animals are sidelined in favor of the more textually textured wild animals, living things, four-footed creatures, reptiles, and birds of this ancient archive. Furthermore, at least in their textual incarnations, these creatures are not much given to play or work but rather to appearing in covenants, visions, pits, and battles. Derrida's focus on notions of human sovereignty and on suffering and pity, then, might be well placed to grapple with the ancient beasts of Genesis, Daniel, Acts, and Revelation. Haraway's critique is, however, an important one, and I return to it particularly in the conclusion of this book as a reflection on the significance of these biblical texts and their potential legacies.

Animality in the Bible

My study concentrates on the following four texts: Gen 9, Acts 10, the book of Daniel, and Rev 17. I am not presenting them as representative of the Bible or as exhaustive of the theme Bible and animality. They are not the only or necessarily the most natural texts to choose with this question in mind.[26] I chart a particular biblical trajectory by presenting a study that moves from Genesis to the Acts of the Apostles and from the book of Daniel to the book of Revelation. While I am not suggesting lines of connection, continuity, and rupture in any simplified manner with regard to the Christian biblical canon, I tease out the particular themes of kill-

---

26. There are two topics that are perhaps conspicuously absent in my discussion: the Genesis creation stories and the issue of sacrifice. Where attention is given to the Bible in relation to animality, it has mostly been given to these issues, whereas so many other aspects of the Bible have been overlooked. For the Genesis creation stories (Gen 1–2), see particularly Linzey and Cohn-Sherbok 1997, Habel and Wurst 2000, and Cunningham 2009. For the topic of sacrifice, see, e.g., Klawans 2009 and Sherwood 2014.

ability and sovereignty as they relate to animality that I identify as central
to Gen 9, Acts 10, Daniel, and Rev 17. Through close readings of each of
these texts, I propose that it is possible to identify their particular details
with regard to animality while simultaneously positing recurring themes
as they are negotiated in the biblical corpus.

I begin, then, with the scenes of Gen 9 and Acts 10, exploring how they
grapple with the killability and edibility of animals and how they relate to
the idea of the brother or fellow. In Genesis, this is particularly about who
is and who is not killable and who is and who is not included in the covenant with God. For Acts 10, the idea of universal fellowship is entangled
with which animals are and which animals are not allowed to be killed and
eaten. Although the term *animal* might not be deployed in the original
languages of Hebrew and Greek, the category of animality can arguably be
seen as a key space where notions of self and other are worked out.

From these discussions, I turn to notions of sovereignty in Daniel and
Revelation. In these texts, the idea of human versus divine sovereignty is
paramount, and for both texts, the political is depicted as animal. In these
two chapters, then, I examine the way political and politicized depictions
of animals sustain adverse conceptions of animality as well as shore up
sympathy for, and solidarity with, animals as a shared state of finitude
under the divine sovereign. Perceptions of who or what is killable and
who or what is sovereign are key to the biblical terrain I map out. These
two themes—killability and sovereignty—are ways of designating proper
zones of power and proper zones of otherness; the one who is sovereign
can kill (and eat) the one who is other. But what I show in these texts is that
zones of sovereignty and otherness are problematized and problematic.

None of the biblical texts I analyze uphold a conception of the human
as stable and sovereign or of the animal as straightforwardly and simply
killable. But the texts do simultaneously play out moments in which
boundaries between human and animal, and between divine and animal,
become sporadically set and strategically employed. Many biblical stories,
as Koosed (2014b, 3) points out, "explore the boundaries of the human
in ways that destabilize the very category of the human." But engaging
with texts in the Bible is not merely about the blurring of boundaries.
Rather, such an engagement is about exploring particular manifestations
of animal, human, and divine in their relationships, imagined boundaries and identities, interdependence, affection and animosity, and affinity
and alienation. Calarco (2008, 240) states that Derrida's work has "only
scratched the surface of this project of deconstructing the history of the

limitrophe[27] discourse of the human-animal distinction." His hope, then, is that scholarship will continue building on Derrida's thought across different institutions, contexts, texts, and discourses (Calarco 2008, 240). One such geography to be explored further is precisely the Bible, read after Derrida. Biblical texts are texts to "think with, to think about how we think and categorize, divide and decide" (Sherwood 2014, 251). I return, then, to the slow-motion reading I noted earlier, hoping to offer close readings of the biblical texts that take account of their tensions and disruptions, strangeness and symbolism, as well as their more literal and seemingly straightforward meanings.

Perhaps in tension with the pace of such a reading, such a project cannot but hope to respond to the urgency and contemporaneity of Derrida's question of the animal in regard to this ancient archive called Bible. Picking up on what Sherwood says of Derrida's Bible, this straddling of the ancient and the urgent—the past and the present—involves responding to a further invitation set in motion by Derrida: namely, turning to an edition of the Bible that is not locked into the past as a wholly contextual study seeking out origins, intentions, and ancient meanings. Rather, as I demonstrate in this book, such an interpretive practice would entail picking up Derrida's Bible as "an edition of uncertain date: in one sense ultra-contemporary, constantly thinking the biblical *cum tempus*, with time—that is with change, flux, interpretation, revision—and with the time(s)" (Sherwood 2004b, 4). After all, "every reading is not only anachronistic, but consists in bringing out anachrony, non-self-contemporaneity, dislocation in the taking-place of the text" (Derrida 2011, 87). Turning to the four biblical texts that inhabit different spaces of the biblical archive, then, I address their characters with curiosity as to how they might be read today, always already haunted by how they may or may not look back and let the ancient "speak" to the (post)modern as much as the (post)modern to the ancient.

---

27. The *limitrophe* refers to the particular limits drawn between humans and animals that are necessarily endless, in order to keep multiplying the powers of the human—*throphe* or *throphy* alluding both to growth, topic, and nourishment. As Moore (2014a, 5) explains, *limitrophy* is a strategy Derrida himself uses, not to efface the limit between humans and animals but to complicate and fold it, to thicken and divide it, multiplying it further in ways that demonstrate the strategies used against animals and those that reveal the impossibility of many such starkly drawn limits.

1

The First Carnivorous Man

Genesis is one of the most popular parts of the Bible to turn to, either implicitly or explicitly, for discussions of the biblical archive in regard to animals.[1] If the Noah stories count amongst the most famous biblical texts (Moberly 2009, 102) and the story of Noah in Gen 6:9–9:29 is "one of the best-known stories in world literature" (Arnold 2008, 96), then they are certainly worth examining for the question of biblical legacy and animality.[2] Although the earlier creation myths in Genesis are more often cited in animal studies and Noah's ark is a more familiar image of human-animal interaction, Gen 9 plays out a decisive moment in the biblical archive over the relations between animal, human, and divine. Genesis 9 is one of the texts in the biblical archive that could be held up as blamable for its attitude to animals. It is the text that follows the story of the flood, in which God exterminates all creatures except those God has warned: Noah, his household, seven pairs of clean animals, a pair of unclean animals, and seven pairs of birds, "to keep their kind alive on the face of all the earth" (7:1–3). After the two creation myths of Gen 1 and 2, Gen 9 presents a third creation, almost a recreation. After Adam as the first man, Noah becomes a "new Adam, the first of a new human race" (Westermann 1994, 479). Here we find an origin story of the first carnivorous man, as Noah, the new head or man of humanity after the flood, is given permission

---

1. See, for instance, Habel and Wurst 2000 and Barton and Wilkinson 2009.

2. Norman Cohn (1996, xi–xii) further lists a number of roles Genesis has played, from "royal and priestly propaganda" to "a message of consolation and hope" for Jews, and for Christians "a prefiguring of salvation." From "an excuse for extravagant flights of fancy and strenuous exercises in pedantry," it has been "deeply involved in the development of scientific geology" from the seventeenth to the nineteenth century, and from the late eighteenth century to contemporary times it has played a major part in discussions between traditional religious beliefs and scientific perspectives (xi–xii).

to eat animals.[3] Genesis 9 thus sets up the relationship between animal, human, and divine after the flood, presenting the conditions of this new world. With its line about humans being made in the image of God (cf. Gen 1:27), Gen 9 seemingly clinches the point, destining humans to be godlike carnivores.

The claim that humans are made in God's image (Gen 9:6) is one of the infamous lines cited as evidence of a biblical anthropocentrism—an anthropocentrism so entrenched that it is still dominant today.[4] To add to the rather smug cozying up of divine and human, the same passage designates the killing of humans wrongful but the killing and eating of animals permissible. As Linzey (1998, 3) pointedly puts it: "While Genesis 1.29 commands vegetarianism,[5] Genesis 9 allows carnivorousness." Seen in this light, Gen 9 is indeed a blameworthy text for a perspective that seeks to think otherwise about human/animal distinctions than merely consumer and consumed. Accordingly, Linzey divides the Bible into "two worlds," one in which "violence and disorder are inevitable, even divinely sanctioned," and the other with the hope and dream of "Isaiah in which

---

3. While Noah, arguably, takes on the role of "man" as a new first sovereign authority, a patriarch, it is perhaps interesting to note, as Lloyd R. Bailey (1989) points out, that there is in fact another, less well-known Noah in the Bible. The "other" Noah is a woman, one of the five daughters of Zelophehad (Num 26:33; 27:1; 36:11; Josh 17:3). As Bailey (1989, 145) shows, the narrative in which she appears is significant for women's right to inherit real estate.

4. This line is also found in the first creation myth of Gen 1:26: "Then God said, 'Let us make humankind in our image, according to our likeness.'" Clough (2009, 145–62) suggests that most readers are still reading Genesis with an Aristotelian worldview rather than Darwinian theories of the natural world. Looking back historically, he notes Philo of Alexandria's reading of Genesis as influential, a reading that affirms human superiority and a qualitative difference between humans and animals. Clough suggests that Aristotelian natural philosophy and Philo's reading have been significant for Christian understandings of Genesis "and the qualitative division between human beings and other creatures on the basis of reason has set the parameters for Christian thought ever since" (145–48). Clough traces other influential thinkers such as Augustine, Thomas Aquinas, Martin Luther, and John Calvin who seem to have agreed to a great extent with Philo. As for humans made in the image of God, Clough writes that discussions in modern interpretation have developed, but its function in providing a divisive demarcation between humans and other creatures remains largely the same.

5. This is a reference to Gen 1:29: "God said, 'See, I have given you every plant yielding seed that is upon the face of all the earth, and every tree with seed in its fruit; you shall have them for food.'"

the lion does not eat the lamb but lies down next to it" (4). How can these two worlds be understood, if there are indeed two?[6] Considering the vast and various texts that make up different biblical canons, it seems unlikely that there should be (only) two such stark worlds, or even two in regard to the biblical world and the world thereafter, in which there is such a thing as animal rights. There is, I suggest, more nuance to Gen 9 than has often been acknowledged.

Genesis 9 tends to be divided into two separate parts: 1–17 and 18–29. I treat these two parts in turn but read their themes in conjunction as a narrative, in view of the relationship between animals, humans, and God in the first part and the emphasis on the way notions of animality play out amongst Noah's human family in the second. In this chapter, I argue that the scenes of Gen 9 are more complex than a mere permissibility of carnivorous power. I propose that the proximity between God's permission for humans to eat animals and his covenant with *all* life evokes a tension in the text over edibility, killability, and accountability. God's promise to account for *all* life marks the power given into human hands to consume animals and, simultaneously, the response and responsibility that will be demanded of them. Building on Derrida's discussion of nakedness and shame in his own reading of Genesis, I propose further that Noah's nakedness in the second part of the chapter points to what is at stake in the covering up of vulnerability shared amongst living animals—human and nonhuman—namely, the changeability of status regarding brotherhood and the human, where a brother and a son or grandson can become relegated to a lower status as a nonhuman. It is not accidental that a crucial legacy of the Curse of Ham story is the dehumanization of African Americans, pivoting precisely on questions of who counts as human and who, or what, as nonhuman, as animal.

As is well known, Genesis is a complex text, or rather a complex set of texts. The "canonizing process" thought to be involved with regard to Genesis has a long history, and it is impossible to speak of *a* coherent composition (Brueggemann 2003, 31). Yet while Genesis may well be "an accretion of sundry traditions, shot through with disjunctions and contradictions, and accumulated in an uneven editorial process over several centuries" (Alter 1997, xi), it is pieced together in this particular way; it persists as a text. This is how I treat it. It is crucial to grapple with the textual tradition

---

6. See Robert Murray (1992, 34) for a similar division into two worlds.

as well as the textual tensions as a multifaceted inheritance. By cross-referencing other parts of Genesis, or in treating chapter nine as a narrative unit, I am not attempting to locate sense or coherence as a result of original composition or authorial intention. Rather, I am reading Gen 9 and its place in Genesis as a part and product of a biblical canon, the legacy of which remains powerful and persistent in cultural memory but frequently obscured as to its interpretive possibilities.

An Animal Covenant?

One way of reading the human-divine dynamic of Gen 9 is to see in this mythology a God who becomes a less sovereign figure of power and presence after the flood while humans become more sovereign in their relationship toward the living, as if God renounces his power as a fearful lord and gives it over to humans. I propose that, nonetheless, the proximity between God's permission for humans to eat animals and his covenant with all life evoke a tension in the text over edibility, killability, and accountability.

Genesis 9 begins with a blessing on Noah and his sons, telling them to be fruitful, thus replenishing the earth with their offspring (9:1). God tells them that the dread of them will be on "every animal of the earth, and on every bird of the air, on everything that creeps on the ground, and on all the fish of the sea": all are delivered into their hands (9:2). The following verse gives permission for everything to be edible (9:3), implying that humans had been vegetarian before but now can eat freely a carnivorous diet. There is a clause, however, according to which flesh with its life-blood cannot be consumed (9:4).[7] Further, killing a human is forbidden (9:6). So far, it appears that God favors the human subjects of this re-creation such that there is a clear hierarchy between the lives of humans, which must be protected, and the lives of animals, which are now edible, which is to say killable. As I go on to discuss in relation to Derrida's (2008, 16, emphasis original) reading of the God of Genesis, this does indeed look like the God who "destines the animals to an experience of the power of man, *in order to see* the power of man in action, in order to see the power of man at work, in order to see man take power over all the other living beings." It is indeed as if "the subject as we know it arrives together with human

---

7. Arnold (2008, 109) explains how the prohibition against consuming blood arises from the priestly conviction, stated frequently in the Bible: blood is life, and life is sacred (Lev 3:17; 7:26–27; 17:11, 14; 19:26; Deut 12:15–16, 23).

vulnerability and a demand not to violate the human, and this inviolability arrives together with the 'sacrificiability' of the animal" (Gross 2014, 141).

Claus Westermann (1994, 17) understands the emphasis on being fruitful in Gen 9 as a form of divinely given human power: a "god-given dynamism," "God's power at work" in humans. The gift of animals—"as I gave you the green plants, I give you everything" (Gen 9:3)—is similarly a gift of power to humans, giving over the "fear and dread" they might feel toward a God who has once blotted out his creation to the animals in their relationship with humans. Fear could also imply elements of reverence, as if it is indeed a matter of proper reverence toward one's master, humans to the divine, and now animals to humans. In this sense, humans do indeed become godlike, in God's image (9:6), with "every animal of the earth," "every bird of the air," "everything that creeps on the ground," and "all the fish of the sea" in their hands (9:2). The difference between killing a human and killing a nonhuman animal for food is thus inserted as part of the conditions for this re-created world. Westermann (1994, 462) concludes, "human existence is now confronted with the necessity of killing."

Genesis 9 might be read as a repentance on God's part for the flood; or, if not outright repentance, then the acknowledgement that it should not be done again (Gen 9:11).[8] In God's promise not to *exercise* such sovereignty, again a repentance is hinted at, and thus God's sovereignty appears diminished. These intimations of nonsovereignty in God are played out particularly with regard to the transfer of the power over animals into the human hand (9:2 [יָד]). As a sign of his promise, he has set his "bow in the clouds" (9:13). Indeed, such an acknowledgement would perhaps hint at an admission of repentance. W. Lee Humphreys (2001, 70) calls this God's recognition of his "overreaction." Deeming the rainbow an "unexpected turn," Bill T. Arnold (2008, 111) reflects on a God who needs to be reminded not to destroy the world again, rather than humans needing the reminder. Walter Brueggemann (2003, 33) argues that Gen 1–11 shows how "the will and purpose of the Creator God is sovereign, but that sovereignty is deeply and categorically under assault from the outset." Another

---

8. This is an implicit promise in chapter 8 (reaching full expression in chapter 9), where Noah builds an altar to the Lord and presents animal burnt offerings. "And when the Lord smelt the pleasing odor, the Lord said in his heart, 'I will never again curse the ground because of humankind, for the inclination of the human heart is evil from youth; nor will I ever again destroy every living creature as I have done'" (Gen 8:20–22).

suggestion, offered by R. W. L. Moberly (2009, 116), is that this is a story about the inevitability of human violence and God's correlative decision to change, if humans will not. Westermann (1994, 473) criticizes the explanation for God's bow as connected "with the image of God as a warrior carrying a bow." Rather, he argues, the Hebrew word for bow comes from an Arabic verb meaning "to bow" or "to bend" (473). The word for blessing with which Gen 9 begins (ברך) can also mean to kneel. In light of God's later promise never again to blot out his creation, it is as if God repents of his violence, blessing his remaining living creatures, as if kneeling before them in repentance and bowing or bending to the remaining life on earth. The offering of animals to humans, then, could be seen as a withdrawal from the sovereign God to the sovereignty of humans.[9] God is casting off the violence marking his destruction in the flood. Humans take God's place in regard to the living. This would tally with Robert Murray's (1992, 34) suggestion that in Gen 9:2, "God reaffirms the grant of sovereignty over animals" set out in the earlier creation narrative. He sees this as the relationship between humans and animals laid bare "*as they are*, not as they were idealized in Genesis 1 and 2, or in any other vision of universal peace" (34, emphasis original).

However, there is a twofold tension in this text between such a reading of human sovereign power and what follows in regard to God's relationship to his creation and his covenant. First, the covenant (Gen 9:9) consists of the promise "that never again shall all flesh be cut off by the waters of a flood, and never again shall there be a flood to destroy the earth" (9:11).[10] This covenant is established with Noah, his sons, the sons of his sons (9:9), "and with every living creature that is with you, the birds, the domestic animals, and every animal of the earth with you, as many as came out of the ark" (9:10). Arnold (2008, 110) remarks on the centrality of this covenant "to the post-diluvian order." But what is involved in this covenant? Is it the hierarchical form Murray (1992, 35) intimates as a veritable

---

9. Mark G. Brett (2000, 34) argues that "the final editors of Genesis were covertly anti-monarchic," discussing particularly the two creation narratives of Gen 1 and 2. But his claim could also be made in regard to the "less" sovereign God in Gen 9 as a postlapsarian condition leaning toward a negative view of human's sovereignty: in the life after the fall, "male rule is a sign of distance from God, not likeness to God" (34).

10. As Jack P. Lewis (1968, 8) points out, a reference to the "waters of Noah" is used in the book of Isaiah to introduce the idea of an unchangeable covenant (Isa 54:9–10).

demythologization? Is it a more supposedly "natural," nonidealized order in which the "partners" may well be "God, humankind and all animals" but where the latter are straightforwardly subordinated to humankind in fear and trembling (Murray 1992, 34)? The covenant arguably adds ambiguity rather than a clear-cut order. The stipulation as to *who* this covenant includes ("between me and you and every living creature of all flesh") is repeated in 9:12, 9:15, and 9:16. Again in 9:17, the inclusivity of this promise is emphasized: "This is the sign of the covenant that I have established between me and all flesh that is on the earth." The references to all-the-living in 9:12 and all-flesh in 9:15 (in Hebrew suffixed as one term joined together) emphasize the unity of this "all" (כל) and the shared condition of *all* life as flesh (בשר) and soul (נפש).[11] David S. Cunningham (2009, 101) highlights how the emphasis on flesh helps "blur the boundaries between human beings and other animals." He proposes this focus on flesh as a resistance to the superiority of humans made in God's image, viewing life forms within this "larger context of all flesh" (114).[12]

---

11. While Noah is associated with being the first carnivorous man, he does have another legacy related to animals. Linzey and Cohn-Sherbok (1997, 27–30) recount a rabbinic story from Gen. Rab. 31.14 where Noah is praised for his care and consideration for animals. In the ark, each day he is said to feed every species its appropriate food at the correct time. They link this to the rabbinic concept *tsar baalei hayyim* ("pain of living creatures"). Although this concept does not come from the Bible, it is based on interpretations of biblical literature concerning the need for care of God's creatures. Peter France (1986, 102–3) tells of another Hebrew legend with a slightly different twist in which a lion suffered a fever while being in the ark and did not like the dry food that was provided for him. When Noah, one day, forgot to feed this lion, the beast struck him so violently that Noah became lame. Because of this deformity, he was not allowed to exercise the office of priest.

12. Cunningham (2009, 114–17) shows how there is an abundance of references to flesh, suggesting that a "nuanced relationship between human beings and animals" can be found in the Bible if the biblical concept of flesh is more closely examined. "Many of the references are to the physical stuff that makes up the body of an animal; notably, whether the flesh is that of a human being or another animal, the same word is used" (Cunningham 2009, 114). Further, the phrase "all flesh" is fairly common, and its meaning appears stable: all living creatures. As well as God's relationship to all flesh in Genesis (Gen 6:13, 17, 19; 7:15, 16, 21; 8:17; 9), he also draws attention to Job 34:14–15; Ps 136:25; and Ps 145:21. As for the New Testament, he mentions the incarnation and Christ as flesh (John 1:14; also, Eph 2:14; 1 Tim 3:16; 1 John 4:2). This is a valuable discussion, but there are tensions. In 1 Cor 15:39, Paul provides an example where flesh is distinctly distinguished into different *kinds*: "All flesh is not the same flesh: but there is one flesh of men, and another flesh of beasts, and another flesh

What happens, then, with the permission to eat animals? In scholarship, this is predominantly perceived as a further fall in Genesis. Robert Alter (1997, 38) comments that this speech "affirms man's solidarity with the rest of the animal kingdom," which is then qualified with "vegetarian man" being given permission to eat animals. Linzey and Cohn-Sherbok (1997, 8) write that in this new creation, "God has now set up the world as a 'kitchen' for human beings." Walter Houston (1998, 12) too suggests that whereas the relationship between humans and animals in Gen 1 could be interpreted to imply a "caring role in regard to animals," Gen 9 undoes such care by introducing "an element of hostility." Houston (12) understands this as showing the way in which the world before the flood was how God originally desired creation to be, but the re-creation afterwards is the compromised version. While the command to procreate in Gen 1:22 is also directed toward animals, and thus "humankind has to share the divine vocation of co-creation with the earth and with other creatures" (Brett 2000, 27), Mark G. Brett also argues that this "radically inclusive" (27) order is compromised in Gen 9 where the "human dominance over animals" is heightened (44). Laurence A. Turner (2009, 45) states: "the relations between humans and animals are brutalized." Julia Kristeva (1982, 96, emphasis original) too comments on this turn as if there were a "*bent toward murder* essential to human beings and the authorization for a meat diet was the recognition of that ineradicable 'death drive,' seen here under its most primordial or archaic aspect— devouring."

But this narrative presents a more nuanced effect than merely the loss of another Eden. Gross (2014, 141) calls it a "complex blend of inclusion and exclusion of animals within the fold of the covenant." This is not merely a collapse into a grim realism on the part of a God whose high hopes have been shattered in the face of human propensities to violence, or what Moberly (2009, 113) calls "the evil-thought clause" from Gen 8:21: "for the inclination of the human heart is evil from youth," as if God had drawn up something like a prenuptial insurance against the future violence humans will commit. Rather, I propose that the proximity between God's permission for humans to eat animals and his covenant with all life evokes a radical tension in the text.

---

of birds, and another of fishes." In any case, Paul's use of flesh has distinct contextual nuances. See Robinson 1957 for a detailed discussion of Paul's use of σάρξ and σωμα in relation to the Hebrew understanding of flesh and the body.

Tension appears in relation to God's words on the edibility of animals, the nonkillability of humans, and God's stipulation that God requires a reckoning of, or for, every life (Gen 9:5). This all-inclusive covenant, Linzey and Cohn-Sherbok (1997, 22) point out, is clear but "is rarely given its due and proper weight." As already mentioned, the power given into human hands to consume animals arises alongside a promise to account for all life. This is connected to God's less sovereign status, allowing humans to live sovereignly. Westermann (1994) comes close to this reading when he concedes that the restrictions concerning life-blood appear to imply caution with regard to the consequences of carnivorousness. If to kill animals is permissible, such killability "carries with it the danger of blood-lust," he writes, or "of killing for the sake of killing, of blood-thirstiness." "One's conduct towards other people is not to be separated from one's conduct towards animals" (Westermann 1994, 465). While the worry about blood-lust is a rather typical reason given for not harming animals—more for its *human* impact than concern for animals—Westermann has hit on the issue with his comment on the differentiation in conduct in interhuman relationships and human-animal relationships that asserts itself in this narrative but remains questionable. Flesh (בשר), with its life (נפש) or blood (דם), is something humans and animals share (9:4). What God says is that God requires the blood of their lives, at the hand of every living creature (the root of the word is חי meaning "alive" or "living") and the hand of humans, emphasizing the common responsibility between animal and human. At the same time, humankind is referred to by the distinct designation "humankind" (אדם), as well as "man" (איש) and "man's brother" (אח). A reckoning will be required from every animal and from human beings (9:5).

Additionally, the reference to requiring a reckoning for *human* life in Gen 9:5 could be read to qualify the words referring to "each one for the blood of another," implying this refers only to human blood. This would fit with the prohibition against shedding the blood of a human that follows in 9:6. But following directly after the reference to the flesh, life, hands, and blood shared by humans and animals alike, and in the reckoning of animal *and* human life, the line "I will require a reckoning for human life" (9:5) and the life of every human being is perhaps no longer wholly assured and immunized against the nonhuman. John Olley (2000, 134) too points out that it "cannot be fortuitous that there is a close linking of permission to eat flesh and strong statements about human killing." Like Cunningham, he notes the striking reference to flesh, signifying humans and animals alike.

Flesh can be eaten in Gen 9:4, but flesh is to be kept alive in Gen 9:8–15 (Olley 2000). This might be an attempt at grounding a stark differentiation between different kinds of flesh and which kind is killable and edible and which kind is not, but these lines are perhaps not as easily drawn as is sometimes made out, even in this origin myth for the first carnivorous man. As Humphreys (2001, 71) points out, "the logic of God in this double couplet (9:6) is problematic when pressed: One who sheds the blood of one who sheds the blood becomes a blood shedder.... The chain could go on forever on an endless feud." The "brother" figure in 9:5 for whom one is held accountable is potentially more open as regards fellowship than is commonly understood. At the least, there is the assertion that animals too will require a reckoning and so appear to be *similarly* accountable to, and accounted for, as humans.[13] Westermann's (1994, 462, emphasis added) point about the "*necessity* of killing," then, is perhaps rather the *possibility* and thus the freedom to kill in relation to animals, a freedom that is haunted by the accountability to God.

In Alter's (1997, xiv) translation of Genesis, where he aims to uphold the "profound and haunting enigmas" he believes Genesis itself cultivates, he laments the loss of the bodily emphasis in translation. He draws particular attention to the repeated reference to the hand, which is so important for Gen 9 in regard to animals: "into your hand they are delivered" (9:2). As James G. Murphy (1863, 227) puts it, animals "are placed entirely at the disposal of man." The hand here might be read as a symbol of capacity for care as well as power, for the potential of compassion and/or violence. To be given something in this sense can mean that it is placed into one's hands as possession or property, but it can also mean to have something *entrusted* to one's care. It could even imply "at hand," that is, available or nearby, as a neighbor. In "*Geschlecht* II: Heidegger's Hand," Derrida (1989, 169–73) examines the way in which Heidegger conceives of the hand as a defining essence of the human but not of animals. This is partly rooted in a distinction Derrida critiques as "seriously dogmatic" in its lack of empirical evidence that distinguishes between the human hand's capacity for giving and the animal claw as taking (173). Here, in Gen 9, it is God who gives into the human hand; the human is the creature who receives or takes.

---

13. Turner (2009, 46) states that the fact that animals are also made accountable ought not to be surprising given the curses placed on the serpent in Gen 3:14–15 (see also Exod 21:28). This speaks against the interpretation of a compromised re-creation which simply accepts human violence.

Further, as already mentioned, when God requires a reckoning, it is at/from the *hand* of every beast or living being as much as at/from the human hand (9:5), as if the properties symbolized by the hand are associated with accountability and God as justice to come for *all* the living. Accordingly, the hand is a site for "good and evil" (Gen 3:5), for responsibility and the space of decision in regard to the life or lives of others. What could be said to take place, then, is that the God of the flood eschews sovereignty to what could be called a justice to come—in which humans and animals are accounted for alike—but in a world where humans abide in a decidability regarding their response as to who is a neighbor and who is not and how to *handle* their fellow creatures as brothers or as bodies to be killed and eaten.

A Justice to Come

I suggest that by supplementing Derrida's (2008) reading of the Genesis creation myths in *The Animal That Therefore I Am* with Gen 9, Derrida's God can be located in a covenant between God and all living beings that shows the "power of man at work" (16), a power given by God in terms of the subjection of animals under humans. However, the covenant simultaneously plays out Derrida's demand for accountability to—and responsibility for—the lives of others, the shame evoked by the crime of excluding the animal from the ethical circuit, and the unveiling of the naked human as animal. Genesis 9 both stages the power of sovereign man in the figure of Noah, whose nakedness must be covered and whose position and propriety must be erected and upheld, but simultaneously complicates this sovereignty in the haunting promise of God to account for *all* life. Permission to kill animals in Gen 9, then, sits uneasily beside the injunction not to kill a fellow human being. In the uneasy proximity to animal life and the deconstructable distinctions that separate a human brother from an animal brother, Gen 9 sets in motion a call for a responsibility that is always already broken, at fault, but at the same time excessive, haunting, and powerful. Building on Derrida's discussion of nakedness, animality, and relationality, Gen 9 provides a textual locus for the figure of God as a horizon of justice to come, albeit an ambiguous one.

With the "reckoning" God will demand "from every animal" "and from human beings" (9:5), it is as if *every* living being will be held accountable in a justice to come. Alter (1997, 39) characterizes the system implemented in 9:5 ("each one for the blood of another") as that of a "retributive justice," since the taking of human life will result in the killer's life to be taken

(9:6). Murphy (1863, 228) calls it the "law of retaliation" or the "axiom of moral equity." While Olley (2000, 139) suggests the covenant spells out an "unequivocal equality" rarely taken account of, he ultimately concedes that Gen 9 falls back upon the "reality of self-centered human violence" which requires divine sanctions. But there is more to this justice than a system of interhuman symmetrical retribution through divinely given sanctions. The emphasis on God's promise to *all* life is a testament to the relationship between God and *all the living*. The proviso appears to be that the God who has blotted out his creation must decrease sovereign power and allow the freedom, decidability, and responsibility to rest between humans and animals. God will, as Derrida (2008, 17) puts it, wait "in order to see." J. G. McConville (2006, 38) places this in a binary: "human interrelationship has the capacity to be benign or internecine." He suggests that this duality and decidability is particularly shown in another pair of brothers over questions of fraternity, competition, and killability, namely Jacob and Esau (Gen 27:41), echoing Cain and Abel (McConville 2006, 38). McConville (169) calls this the "embedding of justice-righteousness in the created order." But arguably, it is more complex than a duality in which one could simply opt for "justice-righteousness" as if it appeared on a drop-down menu for ethical decisions. It is this complexity and ambiguity that Gen 9 plays out.

In Derrida's (2008, 18) discussion of "cat or God," the animal other is the figure whom one is called to live *with* and respond *to*. Derrida is fascinated by the God of Genesis who gives over the naming of animals to the human. This, he says, marks the "finitude of a God who doesn't know what he wants with respect to the animal" (Derrida 2008, 17). Derrida speaks of a "vertigo before the abyss" (18) in the face of "an all-powerful God *and* the finitude of a God who doesn't know what is going to happen to him with language" (17). Interestingly, he admits, this same vertigo strikes him when he is naked facing his cat (18). From this connection, Derrida writes: "I hear the cat or God ask itself, ask *me*: Is he going to call me, is he going to address me?" (18). God retains "the infinite right of inspection of an all-powerful God" (17) and so is seen as a figure in whose sight I am, the figure of a justice to come. But the animal, the finite other, is inextricably caught up in this God and in this question of an address. In a sense, the dizzying fact for Derrida is that both the cat and God in this encounter *see* him, and with his cat he sees the cat see him. Gross (2014, 127) suggests that in some ways "the entire point of Derrida's elaborate discussion of being seen by an animal is not to convey something new but to prompt us to confession, to an acknowledgement of animal gazes as something we have already encountered." Simultaneously, it is as if Derrida is confessing to God potentially seeing and addressing him.

The human, "between the beast and God" (Derrida 2009, 54) is both sovereignly free and *seen* by these figures of otherness who demand response and responsibility. Just as justice "can never be reduced to law, to calculative reason, to lawful distribution, to the norms and rules that condition law" (Derrida 2005b, 149), the relationship to the animal other cannot be wholly inscribed in laws to kill or not to kill. Hence, there is no straightforward command either way, to kill or not kill. This absence of a clear command comes close to Derrida's critique of rights as prescribed by a law, rather than emerging from an ethical relation. For Derrida, rights-based ethics is "locked into a model of justice in which a being does or does not have rights on the basis of its possession (or lack) of morally significant characteristics that can be empirically derived" (Wolfe 2009, 52). Yet the "question of justice" is not reducible to the question of rights—or to the immanence of any juridico-political doctrine (Wolfe 2009, 53). It is always *more*. As Wolfe puts it in regard to Derrida, ethics only as a law-given right in fact reduces "ethics to the *antithesis* of ethics by relying upon a one-size-fits-all formula for conduct that actually *relieves* us of ethical responsibility—an application that, in principle, could be carried out by a machine" (53, emphasis original). In Gen 9, the response to the animal other is left ambiguous, a space of decidability, and thus of radical responsibility; it is a place where compassion can happen but not according to a prescribed law. It is in the relationship between humans and animals, then, that justice can be demanded, precisely because the choice to kill or not to kill *is* a choice. *More* responsibility resides in such human power.

But God is not, for Derrida or for Gen 9, necessarily to be interpreted as a teleological judgment in such a structure of justice. Naas (2008, 9) points out that Derrida resists the theologico-political, rejecting any pure sovereignty—that is, an indivisible, solitary, and exceptional power—such as God. God is both sovereign and nonsovereign in Derrida's interpretations of Genesis. Drawing upon the second creation myth in Gen 2, where Adam names the animals, Derrida (2008, 16, emphasis original) argues that "the public crying of names remains *at one and the same time* free *and* overseen, under surveillance, under the gaze of Jehovah, who does not, for all that, intervene.... He lets him indulge in the naming all by himself. But he is waiting around the corner, watching over this man alone with a mixture of curiosity and authority." Derrida connects the power of the man in naming the animals to the conceptualization of the human as a sovereign set apart from divine or animal creatures, lonely in his sovereignty. But everything happens "as though God still wanted to oversee, keep vigil," marking his own sovereign and—as Derrida puts it—"infinite right of inspection of an all-powerful God *and* the finitude of a God who doesn't know what is going to happen to him with language. And with names" (17, emphasis original).[14]

Derrida's God here is not an indivisible sovereign God but a God who has given over power to humans and will wait to see what happens. While Derrida (2008, 5) stages the human entrance to knowledge in the implicit reference to Genesis with knowledge as "consciousness of good and evil," he does not comment further on how the biblical legacy might either be complicit with the philosophical tradition he critiques or how these references in fact ground his own relational "I" responding to the other as "cat or God" (18). Building on his Genesis reading, Derrida inflects Adam's naming to his own named cat as a particular cat[15] for thinking of the animal other not "as the exemplar of a species called 'cat'" but in "its unsubstitutional singularity" (9). Like the secret, unknown, and unknowable gaze of the animal other, God similarly provokes a "vertigo before the abyss" in the prospect of an address from the other (18). But while Derrida reflects on being seen naked by his animal other, the figure of God is left as something of a haunting remainder.

Just as the God of Gen 9 is less sovereign, eschewing a powerful presence, God as a justice to come might play a similar part to Derrida's democracy to come as the possibility of a prayer for justice as equality without calculation.[16] As Simon Morgan Wortham (2011, 1060) explains

---

14. In his reading of Cain and Abel in Gen 4, Derrida (2008, 42–44) questions whether this too is a case of God reacting to the offering of "sacrificial flesh" and conveys Cain's shame, his hiding and covering of himself, as if naked in the sight of God and in light of the murder of his brother. Derrida suggests that God shows signs of repentance for preferring Abel's animal sacrifice since killing an animal, in a sense, leads to the killing of a brother.

15. On the proper name, Franz Rosenzweig (2005, 201) writes that as soon as a being has its own name, it can no longer be dissolved into its genus; it is its own genus. Derrida alludes to this idea here when he emphasizes the significance of his named cat, perhaps as another oblique comment on Levinas's dog, who also had a name, Bobby, but who does not feature in Levinas's thinking as an ethical subject.

16. See Derrida's (2005a) discussion of a "democracy to come."

it, the democracy to come can never *be* present—just as the God of Genesis will not *be present* to judge. It is rather, a call:

> for unending vigilance, uncomplacent politics, highly singular engagement, and newly creative, newly resourceful decision. Indeed, amid this enduring, vital struggle—one which cannot be resolved by recourse to constructed laws, customs or norms—we find the promise of the future itself, the 'democracy to come' in the here-now. (Wortham 2011, 1060)

After Adam and Eve's fruit-eating in Gen 3, the re-creation that Gen 9 portrays is one in which *more* responsibility is demanded of life and in regard to life, rather than merely a concession to human violence. In fact, such an accountability announced by God from all the living, in the context of his covenant with all life, is arguably a demand for *excessive* responsibility in the face of one's other as every living other. Justice is thus a horizon of expectation that sets in motion the demand for response and responsibility in excessive measure: an impossible responsibility, and the dream, perhaps, of an impossible justice to be done to all-the-living.

Despite the permission to eat animals, their killability is thus not assured but suspended in the unknowability of the justice to come in which *all* will stand to account for their lives and the lives of others. This becomes particularly the case in light of the second half of Gen 9, where the lines drawn as to who is human or brother and who is animal are troubled, and thus who is killable is further problematized.

Exhibiting Noah's Nakedness

As mentioned above, Gen 9 is often divided into two parts, with 9:1–17 and 9:18–29 as separate textual strands. For all that the first half is discussed in relation to animal studies, the second half is not taken into account, nor is the whole chapter read together in this regard. In the second part of Gen 9, Noah is seen uncovered in his tent, drunk and naked, by his son Ham. Ham tells his two brothers of their father's nakedness; they take a garment, walk backwards into their father's tent, and thus cover him up without looking at him. As soon as he realizes what has happened, Noah curses Ham's son Canaan, condemning him to servitude to his brothers.

Turner (2009, 48) points out that, as a "sequel to the Flood story," Gen 9:18–29 is strikingly similar to the sequel to the creation account in Gen 3. Offences are connected to fruit: the fruit of knowledge of good and evil (3:3–6) and grapes from Noah's vineyard (9:20–21). In both narratives, nakedness is a central motif, even though the terms differ (Turner 2009, 48). Both are followed by curses, and both involve covering up one's nakedness: "by God with animal skins in 3:21; by Shem and Japheth with a garment in 9:23" (48). Intimations of sexual crimes preflood are also potentially at play in regard to Noah's nakedness postflood (49). But, as Turner (50) points out, in Gen 3 man and woman come to *know* they are naked, while Noah eats of his fruits without realizing his "true state" (9:21, 24). It is, however, as Turner does not mention, in Noah coming to *know* his own nakedness and his having-been-seen that the narrative pivots. The story of Noah's nakedness plays out the changeability of status regarding brotherhood, where a brother and a son or grandson can become relegated to a lower status as a nonbrother.

Building on Derrida's discussion of nakedness in relation to the human/animal divide, I argue that Noah, the patriarch, is exposed for what he is: naked as a beast, unconscious of his nakedness as if there were no difference between himself and an animal. To compensate for such an exposure of the truth of his naked "animal" state, Noah exercises his power in a performative command that makes Canaan animal-like, of lesser status than himself and his brothers. Famously, as I go on to discuss in more detail, this passage has been used in discourses on race to justify the inferiority of African people. Reading the passage in regard to both race and animality emphasizes the way in which the category of nonhuman or animal can be strategically employed to situate some of the living outside the ethical circuit; such a justifying apparatus must thus be continuously and critically challenged in order to problematize systematic suffering.

Much of biblical scholarship is baffled by the Noah figure of Gen 9:18–29, unable to reconcile him with the righteous Noah under God's protection and viewing the drunkenness, cursing, and apparent injustice of the narrative as inexplicable. This tendency is perhaps the result of the dominant historical-critical method in biblical studies, especially oriented around what Alter (1997, xi) calls the "philologist impulse" "to disambiguate"[17] and the difficulties of disambiguating the Noah of verses 18–29. For example, both Norman Cohn (1996, 14) and John Skinner

---

17. Alter goes on to say that biblical scholars have frequently been "trigger-happy in using the arsenal of text-critical categories, proclaiming contradiction wherever there is the slightest internal tension in the text, seeing every repetition as evidence of a duplication of sources, everywhere tuning in to the static of transmission, not to the complex music of the redacted story" (xlii–xliii).

(1910, 181) solve the issue by arguing that there must be two Noahs, as the drunken Noah simply does not fit the character of the "righteous and blameless patriarch who is the hero of the flood" (Skinner 1910, 181). Westermann (1994, 482) argues for separate authorship or redactions between the Priestly source P and Yahwist source J. David M. Carr's (1996) study of Genesis evades the drunken Noah altogether by ending his interpretation at Gen 9:17. "Bypassing the intriguing story of Noah's sons," Tremper Longmann III (2005, 17–18, 119) moves straight from the rainbow to the Tower of Babel. In Brett's (2000, 46) *Genesis: Procreation and the Politics of Identity*, he writes that whatever "confusion hovers over the culprit of the crime against Noah, the reader is expected to see the curse of slavery as justifiable" and leaves it at that. Humphreys (2001, 66) writes about Noah as "God's select other" but refrains from remarking on the "other" Noah in the postdiluvian world of God's creation. Murphy (1863, 239) notes that we are in no position to know the extent of Noah's guilt in regard to wine drinking, conflating Noah's curse with the mythic explanation of future races. This forms part of a plausible reading also offered, for instance, by Lloyd R. Bailey (1989), which explains that the two narrative sections serve different functions. The purpose of the second half of Gen 9, he argues, is to explain the political and social relations between the groups that Noah's sons represent, shifting from a flood story to an etiology. "This type of literature, attested in ancient societies around the world, intends to explain some presently existing object or custom by means of an 'event' in the past" (Bailey 1989, 159).

The second half of Gen 9 has been deemed an exegetical puzzle since antiquity (Bergsma and Hahn 2005). John Sietze Bergsma and Scott Walker Hahn (25, 27) call this passage a "compressed, elusive narrative" with "awkward features." Noah's curse of Canaan is seen as out of proportion and therefore baffling: "Noah's curse dwarfs Ham's offense" and thus offends our moral sensibilities (Evans 1980, 15). Arnold (2008, 112) argues quite simply that Ham's offense is due to failing to honor his father—a serious offense in ancient northwestern Semitic culture, as is clear from Exod 20:12 and Deut 5:16. One strategy in scholarship has been to *add* to the story, to give it sense, to insist on "more to the story" (Bergsma and Hahn 2005, 25) than is told, speculating as to what this might be.[18] This "more"

---

18. Lewis (1968, 181) argues these verses "perplexed the ancients as much as they do us." Tracing various readings by early Christian writers and in Jewish rabbinic texts,

has mostly taken the shape of a dirty secret, sexual deviancy, something unspeakable. Bergsma and Hahn contend that refusing this "more" to the story is succumbing to a conservatism in regard to anything not made entirely explicit in the text and go on to explain away the awkwardness of the narrative by inserting sexual transgression into the empty space left in the silence of the text itself (36). Alter (1997, 40) relates how the mystery of Ham's transgression toward Noah has remained a conundrum, explaining how some, even as early as the classical midrash, have read into this story a castration narrative between father and son, like the Zeus-Chronos story in which the son castrates the father or, alternately, enters him sexually. A sexual reading is not entirely implausible, as "to see the nakedness of" can refer to sexual activity (Alter 1997, 40).[19] However, as Alter points out, it is also entirely possible that seeing one's father naked was itself a taboo that would warrant a curse (40). Bergsma and Hahn (2005) list paternal incest, voyeurism, and castration as possibilities that have been put forward for what takes place between Noah and Ham.[20] Surveying the sexualized accounts of this scene in scholarship, Brad Embry (2011, 418) explains how paternal incest has been the category most widely accepted in modern interpretations of Gen 9. He argues, however, that voyeurism is the problem because "nakedness is a literary cue that indicates the reality of the Fall" (419). Embry calls the scene of Noah's nakedness a "recognition of the residue of the initial Fall; the naivety lost in the Fall remains in the post-diluvian context as well" (426).

Despite seeing no reason to read maternal incest into the Gen 9 account of Noah and his son Ham, as Bergsma and Hahn (2005, 32) argue, I do agree with their points concerning the theme of humiliation that is seemingly played out in Noah's anger, the possible interpretation of a shift in power dynamics when the father and head of the household is seen naked, and the concurrent anxieties about authority being destabilized. But this can be read in relation to animality and divinity rather than

---

he suggests that the explanations given to the curse of Canaan arise from the particular *Sitz im Leben* of the individual writer.

19. Alter adds that the Hebrews did associate the Canaanites with licentiousness. This view is based, for instance, on the rape of Dinah in Gen 34 and the story of Lot's daughters in Gen 19.

20. Ultimately, they argue that maternal incest is what takes place to explain Noah's curse of Canaan—the illicit offspring of incestuous sexual practice—in order to usurp the place and authority of the father.

purely interhuman hierarchies. In light of God's seeming to repent of the flood, or at least his promise not to exercise such violent authority again, Noah appears to take on a role as sovereign man in his anger at being seen naked. Such a scene could be read as a loss of mastery and thus *being seen as animal*. Noah is, to borrow a phrase from Derrida (2008, 4), "naked as a beast," ashamed at *being seen* in this state by Ham. It is a matter of being seen before knowing one is seen (Derrida 2008, 11). "Nudity is nothing other than that passivity, the involuntary exhibition of the self" (11). With the new order of animals in human hands, Noah desires to uphold such an order of differentiation, with a clear hierarchy of man as master. Here, everything else is subjected, given into human hands (9:2). Brett (2000, 44) holds that in Genesis "overt ideologies of human dominance, male dominance or primogeniture are allowed to stand, but alternative perspectives are juxtaposed in such a way as to undermine the dominant ideology." Noah's dominance as man is precisely undercut and undermined in this scene of naked exposure. If power has been displaced somewhat from God to humans, in whose hands all animals are given, then Noah is arguably asserting a stance of power in regard to his sons in the curse he exclaims. Seeing his father naked is akin to depriving Noah of his power as a man, above his sons and animals.

Here, Derrida's discussion of nakedness in relation to animality might open up a reading of Noah's nakedness that links in with the earlier discussion of animality. From the beginning of *The Animal That Therefore I Am*, Derrida's (2008, 1) concern with nakedness is situated in a reading of Genesis: "Starting from Genesis," confessing to "words that are, to begin with, naked." Derrida's first words echo the first words of Genesis: "In the beginning" (1). He builds on nakedness as a point of departure to posit his condemnation of a "crime" "against animals" (48) and his call for responsibility toward what we "call" the animal (30). Nakedness is one point that divides humans and animals. "Man would be the only one to have invented a garment to cover his sex" (5). This is not only a matter of a piece of cloth or a fig leaf, however; humans are thought to be different to animals because humans can *know themselves* to be naked. Animals, however, are unaware of their nakedness and so are not naked as such (4–5). The issue of nakedness is tied to the assumption that humans are self-conscious creatures, whereas animals do not possess such self-consciousness. Hence, this differentiation on the point of nakedness is less about nakedness per se, but more about the capacity to self-reflect, to be self-aware, self-conscious. Derrida shows how this human self-consciousness becomes connected to the idea of the human as an autobiographical I, capable precisely of saying I, of reflecting on himself or herself and the philosophical dictum "I think therefore I am" that arises from this understanding (34).[21] Without language, animals are thought to lack this I, the thinking that accompanies the I as a defining characteristic, and thus the ability to say "I am" (76). As a result, animals are thought to be incapable of the response and responsibility tied to ideas of language, reason, self-consciousness, and accountability. Derrida suggests that the "I am" functions as an "I can," because in philosophical discourse the human is described according to the powers, properties, and capacities he or she is thought to possess and that animals purportedly lack (93). Derrida's "I can" is an allusion to the French *pouvoir*, meaning both "to can," "to be able," and "power"; he thus proposes that the human "I am" is really an "I can" that is posited as sovereign, powerful, capable, and possessive of properties that set it apart from animals as a superior sovereign figure (27).[22]

Keen to be *more* than a mere beast, Noah's nakedness is something like an upstaging of his authority. He loses face.[23] To repeat Derrida's connection between the idea of manhood and shame:

> Man would be the only one to have invented a garment to cover his sex. He would be a man only to the extent that he was able to be naked, that is to say, to be ashamed, to know himself to be ashamed because he is no longer naked. And knowing himself would mean knowing himself to be ashamed. (2008, 5)

But Derrida's mentioning of shame is not merely to point to the feeling of embarrassment that might accompany being seen naked by another. It is also, as mentioned earlier, to point to accountability. Derrida's critique of a discourse that divides between the properties humans possess and that

---

21. Derrida (2008, 69–87) discusses Descartes and his "I think therefore I am" at some length.

22. *Pouvoir* also of course contains the verb *voir*, which Derrida (2009, 250–51) discusses in regard to an autopsy scene between a sovereign king and an elephant. It is about the power (*pouvoir*) to see (*voir*) the dead animal as a passive object of knowledge that mirrors and magnifies the autonomous, living sovereign figure who does the active seeing.

23. As Derrida (2008, 107–10) discusses in relation to Levinas's ethics, to not have a face, to "lose face" would precisely be to be animal.

animals purportedly lack is inextricably—but only implicitly—caught up in his references to, and readings of, Gen 1–4. He discusses the nakedness of Adam and Eve hiding from God in Gen 3 and extrapolates from there to point to shame, name and naming, accountability, animality, and God. Derrida understands the self-consciousness of the human who knows himself or herself to be naked as shame, alluding to knowledge of naked-ness and the accompanying sensation of shame in Gen 3:10–11. Animals not being naked, therefore not having knowledge of their nudity, is to be without consciousness of good and evil (Derrida 2008, 5). The conscious-ness of "good and evil" is of course a reference to Adam and Eve's fruit-eating, consequent knowledge of good and evil, and banishment from the garden in Gen 3:5. Derrida uses these Genesis references to critique what he sees as the solipsistic sovereignty of the human I in philosophical dis-course. He sees its exclusion of animals as a symptom of the solipsism that makes humans respond and responsible to only a human other, an other who represents the similar and self-same. Derrida implies that the autobiographical capacity of the I is self-regarding, even when it purports to relate to its other, because it is still a human other, reflecting itself in similitude. What is deemed proper to humans—such as reason, language, response, responsibility—has thus become the justification for a sover-eign rule of humanity at the expense of animals. What the justification has refused, however, is a sense of relationality *with* animals; it has resisted a response *to* animals and a *responsibility* for animals.

By orienting the human I around notions of shame in his allusions to Genesis, Derrida inflects autobiographical solitude into a confessional and relational stance. Is there, he asks, "an account of the self free from any sense of confession?" (Derrida 2008, 21). Alluding to Augustine's (2008) *Confessions* and the invention of autobiography, the concept of confession links the human I to notions of fault and guilt, thus pointing back to Adam and Eve after eating the forbidden fruit. Derrida (2008, 48) implies that the confession that accompanies any autobiographical I is the "crime" of depriving animals of everything humans are thought to pos-sess. He demonstrates the artifice of such a construction of difference. This is particularly the case because the nakedness of the body also connotes the vulnerability of exposure to the other, which stresses the impossibil-ity of separating the "I think" from a body. Humans and animals share such embodied states as mortal creatures, however different their bodies may be. Nakedness is the sign of exposed vulnerability. Derrida's theme of nakedness is thus intended to draw attention to the vulnerability of the body as a mortal thing capable of suffering. This "capacity" for suffering counters the "I can" that, Derrida argues, dominates the discourse around the "human" with its properties and powers, in being a negative capacity, a weakness rather than capacity-as-power or *pouvoir*. This is where Derrida's call for compassion in the face of animal life leads: to a compassion that ought to "awaken us to our responsibilities and our obligations vis-à-vis the living in general" (27).

While autobiography marks the solipsism of the sovereign I in a self-rotating self-reflection, Derrida uses the idea of confession to argue that every I is always a response *to*. He calls for relationality, a response and responsibility that is not calculated in advance to exclude any other as too other. Describing himself being naked in his bathroom in the sight of his cat, Derrida is showing the way in which it is not merely a matter of his perspective as a philosophical thinker, a solipsistic, disembodied "I think therefore I am," but rather an acknowledgement of his *being seen*.[24] Thus, Derrida (2008, 9, emphasis original) stages his philosophical discussion of the animal in a *relational* scene where he is being seen by an animal, and not by the idea of an animal, but by a particular cat, an "unsubstitutional singularity," "*this* irreplaceable living being." By calling all animals by the common denominator "animal," philosophical discourse on the animal has refused the multiplicity, irreducibility, and complexity of the living creatures that are subsumed by this designation, which Derrida condemns as a dynamic of power, akin to Adam's naming of the animals in Gen 2:20 but as if he had given them only this one name: *animal*. Derrida's animal other is an irreducible singular other who "can see *me* naked" (59, emphasis original). What philosophy has forgotten is, he suggests—and this is perhaps calculated forgetting itself—that the animal can look at me (11). The animal "has its point of view regarding me. The point of view of the absolute other" (11). The recognition of such a point of view is important because it turns the tables to the animal as a sovereign gaze and the human I as a vulnerable (animal) body. When Derrida writes that as with "every bottomless gaze, as with the eyes of the other, the gaze called 'animal' offers

---

24. There is an implicit reference here to Michel de Montaigne's (1987) *An Apology for Raymond Sebond*, where in section two of the third chapter, Montaigne is commenting on the arrogance of humans presuming themselves to be godlike, calling humans both the most fragile and the proudest of creatures. He mentions his cat and famously asks: when I play with my cat, who can say for certain whether she is playing with me or I playing with her?

to my sight the abyssal limit of the human: the inhuman or the ahuman, the ends of man" (12), he is revealing the unknowability of the other, whose identity will always to some extent remain hidden—unknown and unknowable—just as this gaze reveals the limits of knowledge. He configures this as a secret: "seeing oneself seen naked under a gaze behind which there remains a bottomlessness, at the same time innocent and cruel perhaps, perhaps sensitive and impassive, good and bad, uninterpretable, unreadable, undecidable, abyssal and secret" (12). Thinking of the animal as bare or naturally naked is to strip animals of the potential for secrecy, specificity, and thus otherness. They become reducible objects to the human gaze, transparently inhabiting the properties humans *see* in them, namely, all that is deemed nonhuman.

If only humans are capable of shameful nakedness, and thus also to a certain self-consciousness and self-reflection, then Derrida's turn from the autobiographical to the confessional I is due to a certain idea of guilt. He emphasizes this to distance himself from the autobiography tied to the *human* as an autonomous singular I who freely self-reflects and situates the I as a testimonial figure always already testifying *to* and guilty *of*. For Gen 9, it seems that Noah's anger at *being seen* naked could be read as a symptom of uneasiness as to who or what is animal and the status of all the living, accountable *to* God after the flood in which so much life— animal and human—was obliterated. Noah is described as "a righteous man, blameless in his generation" (6:9).[25] He has lived responsibly, properly, guiltlessly. Feeling himself watched over by God as the only man not blotted out, Noah lives uneasily in the new world, haunted as if his position as the new first man—survivor, carnivore, and a father of fathers—is vulnerable, and if not guilty, he is nonetheless blamable. Eager to uphold his blamelessness and haunted by this desire to remain shameless, Noah thrusts blame outwards at the other who has exposed him lying flat out, unconscious, naked, and drunk in his tent. Noah's shame at being caught

---

25. Lewis (1968, 7) discusses how in postbiblical literature, both Jewish and Christian, Noah is frequently held up as "an outstanding example of righteousness." He notes (177) how the early Christian debates on moral issues by the church fathers were often focused around Gen 9, where Noah's drunkenness "becomes a classic example of the evils of drinking." At the same time, there appears to be a tendency to exonerate Noah. Ambrose, for example, proposes that Noah was not ashamed of his nakedness; Origen and Jerome suggest that Noah may not have known of the effects of wine (177).

in this state must be transferred to another's account. Ham, stepping inside the tent in which Noah lies, trespasses the threshold outside which his father's manhood is erected, properly and clothed before God. Once conscious and covered again, Noah responds with a violent curse, as if he were covering the disgrace of improper nudity with divinelike retribution: "When Noah awoke from his wine and knew what his youngest son had done to him, he said: 'Cursed be Canaan; lowest of slaves shall he be to his brothers'" (9:24–25). As McConville (2006, 36) points out, the covenant with all life earlier in the chapter with its "universalizing picture is disturbed by Noah's curse on Canaan for the enigmatic sin of his father Ham (9:25–27)." But how should such a *disturbance* be understood?

Why Canaan and not Ham? Jack P. Lewis (1968, 178) notes tendencies in later postbiblical literature to make Ham an "archsinner." "The moral interest in Ham's action expressed itself by drawing a warning against the exposure of the body" (178).[26] Ham has been conceived as one who laughed at the vulnerability of his father (178). Westermann (1994, 484) notes the tendency in some scholarship to solve this problem by treating it as an error; thus it is Canaan who sees Noah naked, not Ham. But Westermann fiercely counters this point and says we "must leave the contradiction as it is" (484). Others have read this slur on Canaan as a justification for the animosity between the Israelites and Canaanites.[27] Read as it is, the curse on Canaan could be interpreted as a hyperbolic exercise of authority that is intended more for the *show* of paternal potency than for justice. Crucially, the unfairness of the curse could be explained as the sheer "I can"—the *pouvoir*—of Noah's power. Turner (2009, 50) implicitly sees Noah as the God figure in this scene when he notes the correspondence between Gen 3 and 9, with God doing the cursing in the former passage and Noah doing the cursing in the latter. When he questions "the efficacy of Noah's words" and asks whether "they have the same force as the words of God" (32), he conveys the way in which Noah takes on a divinelike stance. Just as God was described as "overreacting" in the flood-destruction, Evans (1980, 15) suggests, here it is Noah who overreacts.

Of the word *bête*, meaning both "beast" and "stupidity" in French, Derrida argues that to designate a living being either as stupid, lesser, and/or a beast, is a dogmatic, performative gesture, similar, I propose,

---

26. Ambrose and Gregory the Great are two such examples.

27. This is read according to Hebrews being regarded as "Semites," descendants of Shem, and the Canaanites being descendants of Canaan.

to Noah's curse. The "attribution of the attribute *bête*, the attribution of *bêtise*" is "a stratagem, i.e. an act of war, an aggression, a violence that intends to be wounding. It is always an injurious, offensive, abusive insult, always *injurious*, i.e. in the order of right, one that runs the risk of being unjust" (Derrida 2009, 166, emphasis original). Noah's curse is an excessive gesture precisely because Noah is asserting the right of sovereign man as differentiated from the naked, edible beast. As a sovereign figure, he is staged as one who does not have to answer for his actions. Canaan will become a servant to his brothers, a servant's servant (9:25). The freedom of humans given from God, then, becomes construed as sovereign power of autonomy and authority up and against the nonsovereignty of animals as subjected creatures. But Canaan's demotion to servitude as the "lowest of slaves" to his brothers (9:25) reveals the slipperiness of brotherhood and beasts for the sacredness of only human life. With Ham seeing Noah naked and the differentiation made consequently between his son and Noah's other sons, the narrative seems to show that a brother or son can be like Derrida's animal gaze that sees me naked. If human life is not immune from demotion or devaluation, then the line that separates man from beast or brother from nonbrother is fragile. Who, then, is and is not safely immune from killability?

It is pertinent that what is known as the Curse of Ham is linked to the history of race.[28] Noah's sons became models for a "threefold continental schema with a tripartite racial taxonomy" in the world maps of medieval Europe (Livingstone 2008, 6). "Semites, Hamites, and Japhethites inhabited both the physical and intellectual worlds of Christendom's geographical and historical imagination" (6). In debates about humanness and who counted as human, particularly with reference to Gen 1:27 and the idea of humankind being made in God's image, Noah's curse became a port of call for making sense of what was conceived of as deviant from humanity: monstrosity (14). People classed as monstrous were sometimes seen as degraded humans, and other times their humanity was altogether denied (14). Ham was often depicted in these maps as Africa and the forefather of black races. Nimrod, one of Ham's descendants, was in turn portrayed

---

28. David M. Whitford (2009, 77–104) explores the way legitimations of slavery took up the idea of the curse of *Ham* rather than the curse of *Canaan*. Because the division of the earth in Gen 10:6–14 places Ham in Africa and the Middle East, and the transatlantic slave trade required a curse on Africans, the "loss of Canaan" in favor of Ham from the narrative was crucial.

as red-eyed, black-skinned, and misshapen. Such depictions were ways of "coming to terms with any group viewed with suspicion or distaste or hostility" (14). As David N. Livingstone (2008) contends, in the European encounter with America, debates about whether indigenous people were part of the *imago Dei* or not were rife, and this was caught up in a discourse about what kind of species they were, whether they were bestial and barbarian.

In *The Curse of Ham in the Early Modern Era*, David M. Whitford (2009, 3–4) explores how Gen 9 became "one of the most persistent ideological and theological defenses for African slavery and segregation," particularly influential during the sixteenth and seventeenth centuries with the transatlantic slave trade. The idea of the curse in Genesis functioned, as Whitford (140) puts it, as a "noble façade" to gloss the slave trade, an idea that was supplemented by slave ships bearing names such as *Jesus* and *Salvation*. David M. Goldenberg (2005) traces how Gen 9 is understood to justify slavery. "Over and over again one finds Black enslavement justified with a reference to the biblical story of the curse of eternal servitude pronounced against Ham, considered to be the father of black Africa" (3). Questioning whether the origin of antiblack sentiment in the Western world can be traced back to the Bible, he concludes that an increased association of blackness with slavery in the Near East can be located in exegetical responses to Gen 9. While incorrect, a perceived etymology of the name Ham from a root meaning dark, brown, or black had an impact that clung to this text. Such understandings influenced readings of Noah's curse of slavery on Canaan, associated with Ham, since the first century (197). Blackness was sometimes inserted into the story, such as can be found in one fourth-century source, where Canaan is explicitly seen as the ancestor of dark-skinned people (197). The dual curse of blackness and slavery can be found in seventh-century Islamic texts that coincide with Muslim conquests in Africa. This period brought an increasing influx of black African slaves to the Near East. Goldenberg explains how from this time on, "the Curse of Ham, that is, the exegetical tie between blackness and servitude, is commonly found in works composed in the Near East, whether in Arabic by Muslims or in Syriac by Christians" (197). He thus suggests that the increasing emphasis on the curse coincides with the increasing numbers of black people taken as slaves (197).

A similar phenomenon can be observed in sixteenth-century England: "After England's encounter with Black Africans, white and black became the terminology for 'self' and 'other'" (Goldenberg 2005, 197).

Categorizing humans according to skin color was also mapped onto the biblical text. From the seventh century, Jewish, Christian, and Muslim biblical interpretations can be found that pinpoint Noah's sons as different human skin colors (197). Stephen R. Haynes (2007, 87–104) argues that in the nineteenth century, the American proslavery argument used Gen 9 and the idea of the curse to "protect the social order" and instill systems of subordination that upheld such order. Racial hierarchy was a way of understanding "God's careful structuring of the natural world" (89) in a way that could be seen as similar to the ordering of creatures into humans and animals. Black people, Haynes writes, were infantilized and considered "naturally unintelligent" and "morally underdeveloped" and therefore needed to be saved from disorder (89). There are parallels here to the way in which animals are cast as insufficient "humans," or as lesser creatures lacking in morality and intelligence and therefore benefiting from the sovereign ordering of so-called proper humans. Blacks, like animals, were presented as "clearly requiring masters" (91). The story of Noah's curse took on particular power in the perceptions of his postdiluvian world as a utopia, a new beginning that was a pristine world. Ham was what set in motion disorder, so to restore order, his offense must be brought back into order (93). In this light, the idea of Noah and his family as carnivorous creatures is part of the utopia, and the distinction between the killable and edible animals and nonkillable humans must presumably be upheld to ensure the order of this new pristine post-flood world. Ham, or rather Canaan, however loses his status in the order of the (human) family and is demoted to a nonhuman status. The fragility of the brother or the human, then, is not only a matter of edible animals and carnivorous humans but also of the responses to those humans who have historically been deemed other, bestial, nonhuman.

Black liberation theologian James Cone (2001, 23) condemns the logic that determines segregation and slavery in race relations between white and black as the same logic that leads to the subjugation and abuse of animals and the natural world. The use of the curse of Canaan to justify the inferiority of black people demonstrates this in a particularly powerful way. This is not only, however, a matter of a by-now-expired exegetical tradition. In her article, "Unsettling the Coloniality of Being/Power/Truth/Freedom: Towards the Human, After Man, Its Overrepresentation—An Argument," Sylvia Wynter (2003, 266) analyzes the way a conception of human construed as if it were the human proper has been, and continues to be, adapted to subjugate peoples of black African descent "as the ultimate referent of the 'racially inferior' Human Other." Describing this adaptation, she writes that the Judeo-Christian imaginary—in part through racialized readings of Gen 9—projected the "Negro" as "the figure of the human made degenerate by sin, and therefore supernaturally determined" to be "the nearest of all peoples to the ape" (304). With the growing body of scientific discourse, "condemned this time by the malediction of Nature rather than by Noah" (307), this conception morphed into the idea of black people as the "by-nature determined (i.e., caused) missing link between true (because rational) humans and the irrational figure of the ape" (304). This, she argues, is both a continuous and discontinuous process; while the narrative shifted, the descriptive statements for what it meant to be human remained "inscribed within the framework of a specific secularizing reformulation of that matrix Judeo-Christian Grand Narrative" (318). Here, black people are presented as degenerated humans who have taken on nonhuman status in the first instance, or the intermediary link between humans proper and the animal world in the second, and so do not occupy the category of animal per se. But the "space of Otherness" (279), as Wynter calls it, is a space nonetheless overlapping between those deemed subjugatable and those deemed edible and killable. Wynter does not mention animals in her article, but she does make links to "the Poor, the jobless, the homeless" "in their systemically produced poverty and expendability" (325). Much like black slaves as objects in the colonial, economic order, animals are the consumed goods that are legitimately processed due precisely to their nonhuman status. As Lewis R. Gordon (2013, 725) puts it, race is in one sense about who lives and who dies or about "who is supposed to live and who to die." The same could certainly be said of animal species.

What Noah's nakedness and its exposure reveal is that the conceptualizations that divide humans from animals, such as the capacity for nakedness, are strategically constructed. With the particular matter of nakedness, the "nakedness" of the animal as a natural state becomes a way to institute the accepted vulnerability of the animal body as killable and edible. To uphold the clothedness of humans is not, then, merely a matter of custom but also of protection *as* a strong, shielded, sacred species, saved from killability. Such a nonnakedness becomes an aggression against the naked animal, which is perceived as essentially different. As Noah's curse demonstrates, such constructions of difference must be upheld with a spectacle of sovereignty that is a *performance* of the power of the human I am as a sovereign I can. However, if one whose life was protected as a human, a brother, or a son becomes a slave and thus of a closer status to a domesticated or tamed animal, or even a wild animal held in captivity, then the line that divides other humans from animals is less robust and clear-cut. To do as Noah does—asserting the sovereignty of his status as a father, a man, a master—is to refuse the (animal) other who sees him as well as his own potentially vulnerable animal body. Derrida (2008, 18, emphasis original) calls this the violence and asinanity (*bêtise*) of "suspending one's compassion and in depriving the animal of every power of manifestation, of the desire to manifest *to me* anything at all, and even to manifest to me in some way *its* experience of *my* language, of *my* words and of *my* nudity."

Accounting for All Life?

Building on Derrida's reflections on nakedness, animality, and accountability before God, my reading shows that on the one hand, Gen 9 is a prime site for locating the sovereignty of humans given by God to humans, thus ensuring the power of humans over the animal world. On the other hand, Gen 9 stages the tension in such a power dynamic in light of the covenant with *all* life before a justice to come. Because animals are now in principle killable, justice is a space of decidability; animals become a site in which humans must decide how to respond. Such a justice cannot be programmed in advance; it would not *be* a justice to come that demands an ethical relation. With the scene between Noah, exposed naked like a beast in the gaze of his son, and the following curse and demotion of Canaan to slavery, tensions in the differentiation between humans and animals are played out further over the performance of sovereign power. Noah's exposure as naked, resulting in Canaan's demotion to a nonbrother, conveys the fragile, slippery divisions between human life and animal life, showcasing thus the difficulties in delineating who or what is in fact killable and edible and who or what is a brother and neighbor. The repercussions of sovereignly announcing and operating with a boundary between human and animal are powerfully evoked by the long history of interpretation of Gen 9:18–25 in justifying black slavery—treating black people as nonhumans, nonothers, condemned to a position of vulnerable nakedness like animals outside the human and thus ethical realm. In the face of God as a horizon of justice whose covenant is with *all* life, the differentiations and distinctions between humans and animals are more questionable than a simple acceptance of carnivorous, sovereign human power would appear at first glance. Rather, in the face of a horizon of justice to come, a constant vigilance must be practiced as to who or what counts as edible, killable—who or what is deemed animal—and in the name of what sovereignty.

2
ACTS OF EATING

Within the logic of the commandment "Thou shalt not kill," to kill a *human* is generally to commit a crime, namely, murder, whereas to kill an *animal* is not considered murder but rather a lawful killing: hunting, putting down, slaughtering, or sacrificing. The commandment against killing appears in Exod 20:13, Lev 24:17 (24:21), and Deut 5:17. It is qualified in the Hebrew Bible by more detailed laws regarding which animals are killable and edible, along with instructions on methods of killing and eating. These so-called purity laws of clean and unclean animals are expounded in Lev 11 and Deut 14:3–20.[1] Continuing the discussion of the previous chapter about the question of animal killability, I now turn to chapter 10 of the Acts of the Apostles in the New Testament. In this chapter, *all* animals become edible, removing distinctions between clean animals and unclean animals. The scenes of fellowship between Jewish Christians and Christian gentiles are the result of a vision in which animals are at the center. And yet, this narrative has rarely been conceived to be in any sense *about* animals.

In this chapter, then, I address the way in which the animals in Acts 10 have barely been *seen*, let alone been acknowledged as "seeing animal[s]" (Derrida 2008, 14). The category that I propose has been forgotten in the universal fellowship that Acts 10 purportedly promotes is precisely animals. I explore the tension between a universal fellowship whereby animals are simply forgotten and the institution of the indiscriminate killability of animals. The move to *all* animals being edible as it is played out in this narrative—as opposed to only clean animals—could well be seen as a problematic shift toward unmitigated consumption. But even

---

1. For discussions of notions of clean/unclean in the Hebrew Scriptures, see, for instance, Houston 1993 and Schochet 1984.

this is to afford animals in Acts 10 much more attention than is the norm in scholarship on Acts, as the question of animal edibility is raised only in relation to Jewish-gentile relations, not in regard to the animals themselves. Crucially, I argue, the universalism that this passage is so lauded for is undone by the disregard for animal lives; the animal as a general category comes to stand for the acceptable, supposedly legitimate but forgotten zone of otherness, outside the ethical remit. As with Noah's performative speech that turns Canaan from a grandson to a slave—from one who counts to one who does not count—this exclusion of animal lives opens up a space for othering whereby exclusive particularisms operate under the guise of universalism.

Arguably, then, Acts 10 collapses into a human fellowship that limits its universalism in ways that are detrimental to more than animal others. There is, however, another way of reading the implications of Peter's vision in Acts 10 as signaling a universal fellowship founded on the idea of animals as fellows. By paying attention to the animals in the vision and to their potential significance, they might be seen as the precise condition for fellowship with the other.

The Animal Vision

The narrative of Acts 10 stages questions of fellowship, hospitality, and the other who becomes a fellow, but it is also about the laws that underlie or limit fellowship. Following on from my discussion of Noah and the killability and edibility of animals, I show that here too power is oriented around acts of eating in relation to the other.

In Acts 10, Peter has a vision on a rooftop, where a sheet descends before him. "In it were all kinds of four-footed creatures and reptiles and birds of the air" (10:12). In this vision, Peter hears a voice say to him: "Get up, Peter; kill and eat." Peter responds that he cannot do so as he would not, and never has, eaten anything that is "profane" (κοινός) or "unclean" (ἀκάθαρτος) (10:14), but the voice persists a second time, saying: "What God has made clean, you must not call profane" (10:15). This occurs three times. Peter's vision coincides with a visitation from a group of messengers who have come to invite Peter to return with them to meet a Roman centurion called Cornelius, who is a "devout man who feared God with all his household," who also has had a vision and message from "an angel of God" (10:2–3) that has asked him to meet with "a certain Simon who is called Peter" (10:5). Peter goes with these men and, as a consequence of his vision, eats in fellowship with Cornelius and his household despite the prohibition of Jews to eat the "unclean" food of gentiles. Peter declares that he now understands "that God shows no partiality, but in every nation anyone who fears him and does what is right is acceptable to him," that he is "Lord of all" (10:34–36). Acts 10 ends with the gentiles receiving the Holy Spirit and a report that all the "circumcised believers who had come with Peter were astounded that the gift of the Holy Spirit had been poured out even on the gentiles, for they heard them speaking in tongues and extolling God" (10:45–46). The gentiles are then baptized "in the name of Jesus Christ," and Peter stays with them for several days (10:48).

Peter's initial refusal to eat the animals that are presented to him in his vision reflects "the classical Jewish rejection of forbidden food in the face of pressure" (Pervo 2009, 271). But in Acts 10, Peter retracts his refusal to eat unclean animals and comes to accept the edibility, or *cleanness*, of *all* animals. Peter's vision and visit to Cornelius is one of the longest narrative units in Acts, and it is undoubtedly a crucial episode for the main concern of Acts, namely the legitimacy of the gentile mission (Pervo 2009, 264). Early on in Houston's (1998, 18) essay in *Animals on the Agenda: Questions about Animals for Theology and Ethics*, he conveys the relationship between the laws of Leviticus and Deuteronomy and Acts 10. The point of the author of Acts, Houston argues, is opposite of that in God's words in Lev 20:24–6, where God makes a "clear separation" between the Israelites and the non-Israelites (20:24), "and you are to make a clear separation between clean beasts and unclean beasts, and between unclean and clean birds" (20:25). There is here a relation, seemingly, between God's exclusive relationship to Israel and the distinction between clean and unclean animals. Houston (1998, 19) argues that the purpose of this is "to mark the chosen people out as distinctive." Now, in Acts 10, "a major component of the purity code has been abolished" (Pervo 2009, 269), so what Acts 10 seemingly undoes is this major distinction, first between clean and unclean animals and then between Jews and gentiles. It is this undoing that has become connected to the theme of universalism.

Circumscribing Universalism

It has almost become a reflex in scholarship to deem Acts a text that promotes universalism, with its impartial God (e.g., 10:34). Robert F. O'Toole (1983, 2), for instance, argues that the theme of universality weakens "any rigid distinctions between the people of God and the world"; Philip Francis Esler (1987, 34) speaks of Luke's "universalist tendency"; and James D. G. Dunn (2013, 189) refers to the "more universal destiny" Acts 10 appears to foreground as a salvation for all rather than the restitution of Israel.[2]

The setting of Acts is significant, with the early chapters of Acts (1–12) situated around Jerusalem and Judea, that broadens out to Damascus and Antioch, referring also to Phoenicia, Cyprus, and Cyrene (Tyson 1992, 100). This setting highlights a movement that begins in but gradually emerges beyond—toward a larger world—thus placing the origins of Christianity first within Judaism before it broadens out to include gentiles (Tyson 1992, 100).[3] As is clear from the scholarly emphasis on universalism, this is often seen as an inclusive move away from a religious particularism associated with laws that separate people into different categories. With the emphasis in Acts 10 on a "Lord of all" (10:36) and Peter's reference to an "impartial" God (10:34), universalism, in this context, is frequently seen as a breakthrough in terms of equality and fellowship with the other, specifically exemplified by the gentile other. Robert F. O'Toole (1983, 10), for instance, identifies Luke's theme of the mission to the gentiles as "social advance." Martin Hengel (1979, 92) conceives of the figure of Peter as a bastion of tolerance, propagating a form of liberalism that

---

2. There are numerous other examples. François Bovon (2003, 31) discusses the ways in which Luke-Acts is open to "universalism"; David W. Pao (2000, 217) mentions the "universalistic emphasis" of Acts; ; Marion L. Soards (1994, 73) writes that the "universality of God's work and Jesus' lordship are emphasized" in the speeches of Acts; Richard I. Pervo (2009, 277) outlines the "distinctive theme" as universalism in Peter's sermon in verses 34–42, noting that this concern with the mission to the gentiles and its connection to notions of divine impartiality and universalism are reinforced by allusions to Paul's letters (especially Rom 2:11; Gal 2:6; cf. Col 3:25; Eph 6:9); Laura Nasrallah (2008, 538–39) proposes that "Luke-Acts crafts a universalizing narrative of Christian identity that would be attractive or at least comprehensible to philosophical and political minds at the time," thus aligning this sect with a contemporary gentile, Greco-Roman culture; David L. Matson (1996, 86–134) discusses the way this first report of a household conversion in Acts affirms the theme of universalism signified by a move from the temple to the home as the focus of Christian life and worship; in her discussion of early Christianity in the missionary activity exemplified in Acts 10, Clare K. Rothschild (2013b, 1) talks about a "universalizing form of Judaism."

3. For a discussion of conceptions of "world" in the narratives of early Christian missions, see Spittler 2013.

mediates between Jewish and Greco-Roman extremities.[4] Dunn (1996, 141) in turn calls Peter "the liberated Jew."[5] He describes the events from Peter's vision to his encounter with Cornelius as a "transformation," a "decisive breakthrough," "a step forward of momentous significance" (132, 134). However, the animal figures at the center of Peter's vision are forgotten; the text and its reception also seemingly overlook the possibility of more radical implications for an actual universalism of and for all. Richard I. Pervo (2009, 278) points to this when he admits that the concept of divine impartiality is difficult "because it often occurs in contexts that seem to assert partiality."[6]

In her book *Why This New Race? Ethnic Reasoning in Early Christianity*, Denise Kimber Buell (2005) convincingly challenges the ideas of universalism and progress associated with Acts. While early Christianity has become associated with "an inclusive movement that *rejected* ethnic or racial specificity as a condition of religious identity" (1, emphasis original), Buell posits that many early Christian texts in fact can be seen to utilize discourses relating to ethnicity, race, and religion to promote the burgeoning Christianity as authoritative, showing how this often went hand in hand with anti-Judaism (11). She suggests that early Christianity used "ethnic reasoning" (11) to "legitimize various forms of Christianness as the universal, most authentic manifestation of humanity," offering a way for Christians to define themselves up and against others, thus asserting superiority as precisely the universal (2). As she argues, ethnicity was played out in a dynamic of fixed race and mutable identity, arguing that Christianity capitalized on this discourse with the possibility of conver-

---

4. Hengel (1979, 93) writes further of the liberal Peter: "The fact that in Joppa he stayed with a tanner who was despised because of his unclean trade is another indication of Peter's broad-mindedness. It also says much of his 'liberalism' that in the earliest period—when he was still the leader of the Twelve in Jerusalem—he tolerated the relative independence of the 'Hellenist' group by allowing them to have their own assembly for worship without expelling them from the church, and that at a later stage he was involved in mission in Samaria."

5. Dunn (1996, 141) continues: "willing now to recognize that the God-fearer (see on 10.2), the one who fears God, is as acceptable to God as the Jew (cf. Deut. 10.12; Ps. 2.11; Prov. 1.7; Mal. 4.2), without meeting any further stipulation of the law (circumcision in particular)." Circumcision is of course the other crucial "issue" alongside rules of purity concerning animals.

6. He notes as examples Rom 2:11; Gal 2:6; Col 3:25. I will go on to show how there are implicit partialities at play also in Acts 10.

sion as *rebirth* and baptism as *new life*. As I go on to discuss, this idea of
new life becomes also caught up in notions of becoming (more) *human*.
Buell explores the way the emphasis on Christianity as a universal religion
has become a sign of cultural progress that has been important in defining
the difference between Christianity and Judaism "as that of an ideally universal religion versus a religion of a particular people" (24). Further, it "has
also allowed a masking or dismissal of the significance of how Christian
congregations today still often correlate with ethnoracial communities
(Irish Catholics, Greek Orthodox, Norwegian Lutherans, 'Black Church,'
and so on)" (24). Hence, Buell has demonstrated the ways in which references to universalism can form a part of an exclusivity-legitimating discourse and has thereby shown that a closer look at ethnic forms of reasoning is necessary to scrutinize claims of universalism.

Building on Buell, I suggest that part of the problem here is the way in
which scholarship has seen the universalizing theme of Acts 10 in *human*
terms, without regard for what this might mean for the animals that set in
motion the disregard for the Levitical and Deuteronomic laws in the first
place. This entails a logic whereby a space is left open—wittingly or unwittingly—for an "other" to remain outside the so-called universal fellowship
as "animal." In other words, the Christian universal discourse can fall prey
to self-presenting as *more* human/e over against what is seen as animal.
Gilhus (2006, 2–3) discusses the way the Christian relationship to animals was part of such notions of cultural progress, as Christians defined
themselves against Greco-Roman sacrificial cults as well as Jewish animal
sacrifices (I discuss this issue in more detail below).[7] To become Christian
was in some cases, then, construed as passing from a bestial state to full
humanity (150).

Acts 10 appears to divide the animal and the human into multiple
designations. The categories of animal presented in Peter's vision are:
four-footed, reptile, and bird (10:12). In other words, unlike Derrida's

---

7. Mary Douglas (1966, 11) describes this issue of purity and cleanliness as a
criterion for classing religions as either advanced or primitive: "If primitive, then rules
of holiness and rules of uncleanness were indistinguishable; if advanced then rules of
uncleanness disappeared from religion. They were relegated to the kitchen and bathroom and to municipal sanitation, nothing to do with religion. The less uncleanness
was concerned with physical conditions and the more it signified a spiritual state of
unworthiness, so much more decisively could the religion in question be recognized
as advanced."

animal in the general singular, the divisions here are three-fold, suggesting further "all kinds" with the word πάντα preceding four-footed animals (10:12). Human groups are also plural in their designations, as if mimicking the categorization of animals, such as the people (λαός [10:2; 10:41, 42]), the gentile people (ἔθνος [10:45]), man (ἀνήρ [10:5; 10:17; 10:19; 10:21]), human (ἄνθρωπος [10:26]), and kin or relative (συγγενής [10:24]). Such signifiers might well be evidence of what Laura Nasrallah (2008, 535), following Buell, deems the prominent use of commonly available discourses about civic identity and ethnicity as well as notions of correct religious practice in Acts to pose questions of affiliation, belonging, and group loyalties within the Roman Empire, both for purposes of distinction and unification. But the implication of the story of Acts 10 is that while such differences might remain relevant for particular identities and communities, when *all* animals are made *similarly* clean and so enter into a shared state of life, so these human groups and classifications too are *similarly* brought together as "clean," and so able to accept hospitality as Peter does in 10:48.

The universalism seen to emerge from Peter's vision tends to be seen as *for* humans and *about* humans. François Bovon (2003, 32) asserts that the "way to God" is "for human beings," for a "human salvation." Despite seeing Luke-Acts as a demand for radical social reform in the erasure of special treatment for some over others, speaking of the "radically new" entering history with Luke's writing, O'Toole (1983, 3) circumscribes this radical dignity and eternal hope he finds in Luke-Acts only to "human nature." Dunn (1996, 134–35, emphasis added) reads Peter's vision as leading to the recognition "that God does not make distinctions between *human beings in general* as to their acceptability or unacceptability on grounds of their basic identity (ethnic, social or religious)." Clare K. Rothschild (2013a, 298, emphasis added) refers to the "premise" of Acts as bringing people and events together in such a way that "all of *human* life" "is interrelated under the broad auspices of divine guidance." Mostly, however, the specifically human universality is left implicit. It appears to be clear then, as Houston (1998, 18, emphasis original) argues, that Peter's vision "is not really about animals." Rather, it is about calling "no *human being* profane or unclean."

The text itself to some extent supports this emphasis on the specific relationship between two humans and the groups they represent. As such, it is perhaps not strange that this fellowship has become generalized to a human universalism. In Acts 10:25–26, Cornelius falls before Peter, worshipping him, and Peter raises him from the ground, saying: "Stand up, I too am a man," thus emphatically asserting the similarity and even fraternity between him and Cornelius in the aftermath of his vision. Justin R. Howell (2008, 27, emphasis added) proposes that Peter's response in correcting Cornelius "implies that they are both *humans* under the authority of another, namely Jesus." Further, in his speech Peter explains the shift that is taking place: "you yourselves know that it is unlawful for a Jew to associate with or to visit a gentile; but God has shown me that I should not call anyone profane or unclean. So when I was sent for, I came without objection" (10:28–29). This scene precedes the hospitality Cornelius extends to Peter. It stages the equality between Jews and gentiles to make the point that hospitality is now possible, and the distinctions previously separating them are erased.[8]

It is clear, however, that Peter's vision refers to the distinction between clean and unclean *animals*. From the actions that follow this vision and Peter's own comment about no longer considering "anyone profane or unclean" (10:28), evidently when he utters these words to Cornelius he is referring both back to his vision and to the gentiles with whom he is in company. Pervo (2009, 274) highlights that the revelation to Peter is not simply given; rather, the "revelation is an interpretation of the vision" that unfolds in Peter's encounter with Cornelius: "that interpretation is the moment of decision." This, Pervo stresses, is *Peter's* moment of conversion, which is presented not as a direct command—although this is implied in the vision itself—but as the result of Peter's reflection (274). Gentiles are conceived as analogous to the now universally clean animals. *Like* animals, the gentiles must similarly not be considered profane or unclean. The NRSV translation of Acts 10:28 states that Peter has learned he must not call "anyone" unclean, but in the original Greek, the word that is used is ἄνθρωπος, that is, a human. Peter has understood his vision as: he must call no *human* unclean. This is the crucial interpretive leap that takes place in this text. Acts implies that the impetus for the gentile mission is a consequence of the decision to interpret the vision in a figurative way (Pervo 2009, 274–75). Hence, the vision is understood as being about gentiles or humans more generally than about animals per se. Dunn (1996, 134–35)

---

8. In Gal 2:11–13, Paul has a rather different account of Peter and his eating habits. Paul accuses Peter of being a hypocrite for eating with gentile believers but then backtracking in fear of "friends of James" who are in favor of the continued requirements of Jewish law.

spells this out in two stages; first, Peter recognizes God makes no distinctions between "human beings in general as to their acceptability or unacceptability on grounds of their basic identity (ethnic, social or religious)." Second, "on the basis of that recognition," Peter sees that God accepts Cornelius and his fellow gentiles in the outpouring of the spirit in 10:44–46 (135). Peter thus tacitly constructs an analogous connection between the animals once considered unclean and the gentiles once considered not to be the people of God.

The vision could of course be read as referring *only* to food laws and the dismissal of such laws regarding animal distinctions. In this case, the hospitality accepted by Peter from Cornelius would merely be the consequence of foregoing such divisive laws. There is thus no practical, ritual obstacle to their eating together any longer. But if that was the case, Peter's comment to Cornelius would appear strange, where he refers back to his own vision about animals but replaces the animals with humans, thus mapping the meaning of the vision onto gentiles. Peter clearly makes a connection between the now universally clean animals and the gentiles he encounters, now no longer to be considered "unclean" or "profane" in 10:28, the same words used of the animals in the vision (10:14).

Kill and Eat

What appears to have taken place in the narrative is that the animals that were once considered unclean or profane are now—after the vision— deemed clean. Peter, already described as hungry (10:10), can kill any animal in order to eat the previously prohibited animals shown in the sheet—and so *all* animals are indiscriminately killable and edible. Linzey and Cohn-Sherbok (1997, 4) write about this passage: "the implications for the moral status of animals are … not encouraging." Seen in this light, this is a biblical text that might furnish an example of the Bible and the Christian tradition as desanctifying and demoting animal life by turning animals from distinct and differentiated creatures into the catch-all concept of the animal in general singular. It is a matter of what Gross (2014, 139), drawing on Derrida, describes as a "sacrificial" mode of being in the world "that both necessitates a 'nonviolence' synonymous with the inviolability of the human, and, in the name of this restraint, justifies violence of potentially unlimited scale, making war against the nonhuman possible and perhaps inevitable."

If notions of clean and unclean are not arbitrary designations but concerned with the *ordering* of ideas, or a way to map out moral analogies on the bodies of animals, as Mary Douglas (1966, 41, 43) has suggested, what sort of reordering takes place here? What happens in the analogical leap from animals being clean to gentiles being clean? What happens to the command that accompanies the vision of the animals to "Get up, kill and eat" (10:14)? Derrida (2009, 14) proposes that analogies designate "the place of a question rather than that of an answer." An analogy, then, "is always a reason, a *logos*, a reasoning, or even a calculus that moves back up toward a relation of production, or resemblance, or comparability in which identity and difference coexist" (14). What reasoning is taking place in the analogy Peter makes between clean animals and clean gentiles? The haunting command to "kill and eat" given to Peter in his vision remains a tacit remainder in the encounter with the gentiles in Cornelius's home. Instead of retaining the specialness of God's people as the people of Israel with laws of clean and unclean animals, this new commandment undoes such distinctions, correlatively contracting any regard for the specialness of some life forms into the killability of *all* life as "clean" and thus edible and killable. Now that *everything* is clean, is everything also edible and killable? It is clear that this logic is detrimental to animal welfare in the sense that all animals are unquestionably up for grabs. But is there not also something detrimental to more than animals, as gentiles too are conceived within the category "clean" and are therefore also technically, or at least figuratively, killable?

Here, Derrida's reading of the command not to kill as connected to the story of Cain and Abel is instructive. With the commandment forbidding murder, seemingly in line with God's commandment in Gen 9, Derrida is eager to probe the underpinnings of a regard for *some* life and at the same time disregard for *other* life. The point of his emphasis on this commandment is to think about the ways in which distinctions between humans and animals become enshrined in laws that signify the sanctity of life, but with exceptions that desanctify or demote other life. Essentially, Derrida is suspicious of qualifications and legitimizations of murder based on classifications and categorizations of calculated otherness. He critically questions how to determine such absolute distinctions regarding the purported killability of nonhuman life forms and the determination of who is a who and who is a what for the inclusion and exclusion of ethical consideration. The refusal to recognize the animal other as a fellow, exemplified in the commandment not to kill (humans), is, for Derrida, tantamount to an automated dogmatism in the ethical order that eschews an awakened responsibility.

The biblical example Derrida uses to explore further the "Thou shalt not kill" in relation to the question of who is and who is not killable—the fellow, brother, and animal other—is the story of Cain and Abel in Gen 4. As I discuss in chapter one, Derrida (2008, 112–13) reflects on God as a figure of justice who waits to see, who repents—as he could be said to do after the flood in Genesis, too—of his preference for the sacrificial animal and who sees the animosity this creates between the two brothers. What happens to the fraternity of brothers, Derrida asks, when an animal comes on the scene (12)? In his allusion to Cain and Abel, Derrida suggests that the otherness of the animal, understood as an animal rather than a brother or fellow, ensures a fraternity based on exclusion. Cavalieri (2009, 3) discusses this attitude of "perfectionism," where attributes thought to belong to some beings are higher or better and are used to exclude others thought to lack such attributes. This attitude "accepts degrees in moral status," where some individuals matter more than others (3). Animals are at the bottom of such a system. The competition of mastery between Cain and Abel leads from the killing of an animal to the killing of a brother; Abel offers an animal sacrifice to the Lord, but Cain, seemingly jealous of the favor shown Abel, kills his brother.

The murder of Abel (Gen 4:8) follows the sacrifice of the animal that Abel offers to God and that God prefers to Cain's "fruit of the ground" (Gen 4:3–5). By killing his brother, Derrida (2008, 44) suggests that Cain falls into a trap ("sin is lurking at the door" [Gen 4:7]), having become prey to evil in the competition between the brothers and awoken by Abel's animal killing. If the animal can be killed, then why cannot the brother who has shown Cain—and his offering—to be lesser before the Lord also be killed? Derrida reflects on the God who then extends his protection to Cain after all, as if God, again, had repented: as if "he were ashamed or had admitted having preferred the animal sacrifice. As if in this way he were confessing and admitting remorse concerning the animal" (44). The significance of this interpretation in *The Animal That Therefore I Am* appears to be that the killing of an animal is part of a competition of power that foregrounds the killability of *more* than the animal; a brother, too, may be(come) an other who is killed for the performance of power. As such, it is perhaps the animal who must become a brother before a relation to every other can be founded in a regard for life and fraternity. How does one recognize a fellow?

Is the "fellow" only what has human form, or is it anything that is alive? And if it is the human form of life, what will be the criteria for identifying it without implying a whole determinate culture, for example European, Greco-Abrahamic culture, and in particular Christian culture, which installs the value of "neighbor" or "brother" in the universality of the world, as totality of all creatures? (Derrida 2009, 106)

Derrida (2008, 48) proposes that the "confusion of all nonhuman living creatures within the general and common category of animal is not simply a sin against rigorous thinking, vigilance, lucidity, or empirical authority, it is also a crime." He qualifies this by denying the generality of the term animal and emphasizing the plural animals, or the neologism *animot*[9]: "Not a crime against animality, precisely, but a crime of the first order against the animals, against animals" (Derrida 2008, 48). Humanity and human rights, Derrida implies, are terms that have been admirable attempts at universal, inclusive concepts of equality, freedom, and compassion based on principles of protection but are founded in a fundamental distinction between the human and the nonhuman. This is crystallized most forcefully perhaps in the distinction between a *permissible* killing of animals and the *impermissible murder* of humans.[10]

One source of such a distinction could be traced to the passages in the Hebrew Scriptures, the Decalogue (or more popularly Ten Commandments), that refer to "Thou shalt not kill" in terms of a prohibition against killing *humans* (Exod 20:13; Lev 24:17 [21]; Deut 5:17). The Hebrew verb רצח in Exod 20:13 is in the NRSV translated as "murder" rather than "kill" or "slay," avoiding in advance any confusion in the word "kill" as to

---

9. To reiterate the meaning of *animot* from the introduction: *animot* is a term Derrida coins to signify (in sound) *animaux*, animals in plural, rather than the animal in general singular, to mark the absurdity of what such a general singular animal could possibly mean. But it also refers to *mot* ("word") and his emphasis on this *word* animal, the violence and generality it denotes, the attention paid to what a word means, and what powers words can have for cramming such a vast multiplicity of living beings into this verbal enclosure and allowing violence on a mass scale to take place in the name of this word, as a negligible nonfellow or neighbor to humans.

10. Midgley (2004, 175) too uses the language of crimes in response to the utilization of nature and its creatures: "The painful words WE WERE WRONG must not only be spoken but spelt out in action, and this needs to be action with a strong symbolism that bears on the offences that have been central to our crimes."

whether it also includes nonhumans. In Lev 24:17, נכה is used, meaning "to strike, slay, hit, kill" in regard to the *life* or soul, נפש, where this life/soul seems distinctly tied to humans, אדם, as a crime by humans against humans. Leviticus 24:17 reads in the NRSV: "Anyone who kills a human being shall be put to death," and is followed in verse 18 with: "Anyone who kills an animal shall make restitution for it, life for life," repeated in verse 21: "One who kills an animal shall make restitution for it; but one who kills a human being shall be put to death." In the corresponding Decalogue, or Ten Commandments, רצח is translated like Exodus in Deut 5: "You shall not murder" (Deut 5:17). But are these crimes only against humanity, Derrida asks? Is "Thou shalt not kill" for humans alone (Derrida 2008, 48)? It is in the catch-all concept of the animal, thus perceived as distinct from the human species, that a separate ethical order with its logic of difference between killing and murdering can continue to be upheld. Masking the inanity of such a forced concept of the animal in general, Derrida indicts this confusion of all nonhuman living creatures as a collapse of critical thought and crucially, a crime. The killing of animals cannot continue to be conceived as an acceptable "crime" comfortably external, or alien, to the ethical realm. As well as being a polemical gesture to draw attention to the somewhat arbitrary and hypocritical distinction between humans and animals, Derrida's insistence that such a dogmatic line-drawing is a crime is not a call for a homogenization of humans and animals as the same but an attention to and respect for irreducible difference and complexity, a call for *more* responsibility in ethics regarding *all* life (34).

Derrida's aversion to an ethics founded in the exclusion of animals as too other is based on the belief that there is a thin line between a fraternity based on the exclusion and othering of a group of living creatures (animals) to other forms of exclusion and legitimized violence. Such an exclusion of animals from the realm of criminal killing on the grounds that animals are nonfellows opens up an outlook whereby my neighboring people are not neighbor enough, my brother is not brother enough. This is what Elizabeth Weber (2007, 336) calls "the specter of eugenics, the determination of belonging via blood and the corresponding bloody exclusion of the other" that haunts human group dynamics. Weber explains that Derrida challenges legacies in terms of "how to address ourselves to the other, not just to the ghost, but to the other *tout court*. It requires defending justice not only for the known 'other,' the familiar and related 'other,' but also for the *other* other" (340).

The question of what happens to the family of humans when an animal comes on the scene foregrounds Derrida's proposal that it is imperative to rethink an ethics that has been programmed toward *human* subjects. For Derrida, this is about the conditions of ethics itself as a radical opening to the other. But for ethics to be such a radical opening, this other cannot be calculated in advance as *this* or *that*, the other cannot be preprogrammed as human or "like me" because what this does is to specify in advance what the other can or cannot be. Thus the other is no longer conceived as other but merely a reflection or construction of myself. Such an ethics is precisely what Derrida indicts as a dormant ethics. The condition for ethics is one that situates me *after* the animal other, who goes before, whom I come after. He writes that a thinking of the other cannot first and foremost privilege the one conceived of as a family member, but that "the infinitely other who looks at me" should:

> privilege the question and request of the animal. Not in order to put it in front of man, but in order to think that of man, of the brother and the neighbor from the perspective of an animal request, of an audible or silent appeal that calls within us outside of us, from the most far away, before us after us, preceding and pursuing us in an unavoidable way. (Derrida 2008, 113)

Referring to the biblical commandment "Thou shalt not kill," Derrida takes Levinas to task for accepting this as "You shall commit no murder": not on the grounds of an error in interpretation of the biblical text— Derrida does not comment specifically on the biblical passages in this instance—but as an indictment toward Levinas himself as a prominent and powerful thinker of the ethics of the other, unable to question this distinction between the *human* face of the other and an animal (113–17).[11] This commandment not to kill "forbids murder, namely, homicide, but doesn't forbid putting to death in general, no more than it responds to a respect for life, a respect in principle for life in general" (110). Derrida makes use of words such as genocide and holocaust in his discus-

---

11. Derrida addresses here Llewelyn's question to Levinas at the 1986 Cérisy conference as to whether animals have a face. For a further discussion of Derrida and Levinas on animality, see Gross 2009 and Stone 2014.

sion on animal abuse, because it can no longer be repressed "that men do all they can in order to dissimulate this cruelty or to hide it from themselves; in order to organize on a global scale the forgetting or misunderstanding of this violence, which some would compare to the worst cases of genocide" (26). As Stephen Morton (2013, 120) sees it, "Derrida's point is that the violent logic of manufactured death that was first exemplified in the Nazi death camps has become normalized through practices such as the factory farming of animals." Derrida (2008, 26) proposes that we should neither abuse the term genocide nor refuse to use it altogether, precisely to cause unease at the mass killing and suffering of animal life for the putative well-being of humans.[12] What is worse, this is a matter of common knowledge, a permitted killing, in what Morton (2013, 121) calls "the necropolitical forms of sovereignty that continue to kill particular forms of animal life—whether human, subhuman or non-human." This is why Derrida insists on an *awakening* to the horrors of animal suffering.

Altogether, then, Derrida argues that if the animal can be killed without it being murder or even killing properly speaking—in other words, without the "Thou shalt not kill" coming into play—it is because the animal is considered alien to protection on the grounds of sanctity, the sanctity of life. Alluding to Levinas (Derrida 2008, 111), he shows that the way in which ethics and metaphysics relate to the "Thou shalt not kill" become construed around the person as the *human* face, thus making responsibility toward humans proper and anomalous to animals. With its forgetting of animals and its regard for the face of the gentile other, is Acts 10 a crucial part of the legacy that has dreamt of a universal discourse of impartiality but remained in many ways in an ethnocentric and anthropocentric discourse? Is this, moreover, something that happens with the emergence of Christianity?

---

12. When Derrida uses the word *genocide* in connection with animals, the point he is trying to make is that ways of imagining and treating nonothers have also taken place in regard to humans. Cavalieri (2009, 35) discusses this explicitly in regard to the "Aktion T4" example, where a Nazi elimination program killed disabled children and adults (6000 children, 180,000 adults): individuals lacking certain cognitive skills. If to have full moral status requires one to be "human" and to be human is to have certain cognitive skills, this is clearly problematic in more instances than those concerning animals. Derrida (2004, 62) also discusses similar issues in relation to Cavalieri and Singer's "Darwinian" project, which advocates not animal rights but human rights to nonhumam great apes. See Cavalieri and Singer 1995.

Christian Anthropocentrism?

In *Animals, Gods and Humans*, Gilhus (2006, 4) suggests that the emergence of Christianity corresponded with a sacralization of the human and a desacralization of the animal. The concomitant move from sacrificial cults to cults without animal sacrifice became associated with cultural progress, while animal sacrifice became considered primitive (2–3). The laws and rituals around purity and animality could also be perceived in this light as becoming associated with the primitive as opposed to progress, with notions of universalism becoming connected to social advance and to what became identified as Christianity. Along the way, animals became seemingly—for better or worse—insignificant. Acts 10 could be seen as one site in which such a shift from animals to humans is played out.

Gilhus (2006) suggests that in the early formation of Christianity, there was a gradual shift of emphasis from animal bodies in sacrificial rituals to the human body. Grant (1999, 8) draws attention to Paul's critique of Egyptian worship of animals in Rom 1:23–28 and how Christians continued to denounce such worship of animals:

> The apologist Aristides complained about worship of no fewer than twenty-three of them, while Justin denounced "Greek" worship of trees, rivers, mice, cats, crocodiles, and many other "irrational animals"; Athenagoras decried Egyptian worship of cats, crocodiles, snakes, asps, and dogs; and Clement attacked Egyptians for worshipping cats and weasels or, in another place, cats, crocodiles, and indigenous snakes.

Animal sacrifices were also critiqued. Emphasizing the importance of animal sacrifices in the Roman Empire and the cult of the emperor, Gilhus (2006, 123) explains how multitudes of animals were sometimes slaughtered in orgies of ritual killing. By the end of the first century, Christian polemic against blood sacrifice was presented, she argues persuasively, "in an apologetic context and was an ingredient in standard Christian counterattacks against paganism" (148).[13] Hans-Josef Klauck (2000) argues that it

---

13. Gilhus (2006, 147–59) describes how pagan gods were imagined as demons and blood sacrifice was seen as feeding such evil demons. This can be seen in Athenagoras's *A Plea for the Christians* (from the second half of the second century) and Origen's *Exhortation to Martyrdom* (from the late second to mid-third century). Such arguments grew in the third and fourth centuries. In *The Preparation for the Gospel*, Eusebius follows Porphyry in criticizing animal sacrifices as a degeneration of human-

is striking that Christianity nonetheless took on a sacrificial culture. "Not only does sacrifice remain alive in Christianity as a theological and spiritual category; it even achieves a stable position in the heart of Christian thought and Christian piety" (12). While animal sacrifice became linked to barbarism, much sacrificial language can of course be found in the New Testament (Gilhus 2006, 156, 158). But the animal body is replaced by the human body, most prominently "in the master body of Christ" (148). "Real animals were excluded from Christian rituals, but animal imagery was still used, for instance when Christ was identified with the sacrificial lamb" (160).

The human body essentially took the place of the animal body. To become Christian was also sometimes construed as passing from a bestial state to full humanity (Gilhus 2006, 150). Baptism was one important trope for being reborn and receiving true life, and it has a prominent place in Acts 10 as the pinnacle of the fellowship portrayed (150). As Buell discusses the idea of mutable identity being possible in the "death" and "rebirth" of baptism, such discourse can also be seen as a rebirth into becoming human or becoming less animal. Through the ritual of baptism, humans could become "real" humans, while pagans remained animals: "to be an animal implies not being fully alive" (Gilhus 2006, 151). This seems rather ironic in relation to Acts 10, considering Cornelius could be seen analogically precisely as *(a clean) animal* who now can be "eaten" (with). Essentially, then, Greco-Roman sacrificial discourse was continued but combined with the spiritualizing and personalizing religious trends associated with early Christian groups. In the Eucharist, the sacrifice of the body and blood of Christ was celebrated and seen as a higher form of sacrifice, thus implicitly trumping animal sacrifice with not only human or human-divine sacrifice but a death considered to be *the* sacrifice as such (Gilhus 2006, 151). Thus, for Christians, Gilhus goes on, "the animal sacrifice was a significant cultural borderline between themselves and pagans" (155).

Discussing the Christian reaction to dietary laws, Gilhus (2006, 165) mentions Acts. She makes the connection between the reaction against dietary prescriptions and animals fading out of focus, becoming thus less relevant to what became Christianity in contrast to their important place

---

ity. He holds up the Eucharist as the proper form of ritual, celebrating the only proper sacrifice, that is Jesus. Tertullian's *Apologeticus* from the turn of the third century and Arnobius's *Against the Gentiles* from the turn of the fourth century expand on such critiques. At the end of the fourth century, animal sacrifice is banned by Theodosius I.

in the Mosaic laws. This subject is most vividly described in Acts 10:10–16 and Acts 11:5–10. In the narrative of Peter's vision, the verb θύω—"to offer or sacrifice"—is now used for the *killing* of animals rather than the special sacrifice of some selected animals. Animals fulfil "their true destiny as food for humans" (Gilhus 2006, 166), and Christians need reject no food.[14] According to Gilhus, the New Testament more generally reflects this move away from animals (167). With its emphasis on the human instead of the animal body, she describes a hermeneutic movement in many New Testament texts that point away from literal toward allegorical meanings (167–68). "When differences are wiped out, sameness abides, and from now on the internal differences between animals were made subordinate to their fundamental difference from man" (166). This could also explain why Peter's vision is seemingly not about animals; they are merely figures that signify the lack of distinctions between *humans*. However, I suggest that Acts 10 could be read otherwise, namely as a radical opening of hospitality to animals as fellow creatures. In fact, if any kind of human fellowship is to be made possible, such a possibility rests on an altered relation to animals as fellows.

Facing Animals

As I discuss above, a limited universalism can open up "the worst kinds of abuses toward those beings who are left outside the scope of moral concern" (Calarco 2008, 72). If, as Calarco suggests, universal consideration entails "being ethically attentive and open to the possibility that anything might take on a face" (73), it might be conducive to reflect on what Acts 10 means if a universalism in which animals also count were to be imagined. This is not, I suggest, a plea for *adding* another other to the universalist group hug, so to speak, but rather to take critical heed of the foundation of fellowship in Peter's vision *about animals*. Crucially, if the emphasis on universalism in scholarship is to be followed, then the cessation of distinctions between animals is precisely the ground upon which distinctions or discriminations amongst humans cease.

Arguably, if the gentiles are conceived as equals under an impartial Lord of all, it would seem the animals too—now no longer perceived as unclean—are clean, given to the gentiles *as fellows*. Pervo (2009, 269–70)

---

14. See also 1 Cor 8:8; 1 Tim 4:4; Matt 15:11–19.

draws attention to the evocation of Gen 1:24–25, 6:20, and 7:14 in the animal categories of Peter's vision as a form of gentile Christian apologetic that is arguing against Mosaic regulations by appealing to "the original intent of the creator, in this instance, the goodness of creation." Hence, the vision—with its different kinds of animals that mirror the groups of animals in Genesis—is revealing the goodness of *all* creation, without separation between animals as clean or unclean. Difference is preserved without qualitative distinctions. If the link between gentiles as clean and thus fellows is so clear, then why is the relation to animals as those who first became clean not equally clear? Is not the vision of animals as clean the precise ground upon which an understanding of clean gentiles is founded? The transformation of the category of gentile to be considered clean and thus included in Peter's mission and fellowship *is founded on* the transformation of animals from partially clean to completely clean. Thus, animals too are to be considered fellows, included in this hospitality. Flipping the figurative reading of clean animals as really about human gentiles, it might be claimed that Peter's vision is about all—be they human or non-human animals—as clean animals. As all animals *and* Cornelius are now considered clean, there is a cessation of any stark and absolute distinction between the human and animal. While I suggest this could imply the killability and edibility of all, it could also imply the possibility of hospitality and fellowship with all.

The animals of the vision arguably form the foundation of fellowship and hospitality. Rather than an indiscriminate killability, then, the vision could be said to entail an unconditional hospitality. In this sense, Acts 10 could indeed be read as a universalizing move, not in the exclusively human terms usually assumed or merely in regard to the Jewish-gentile and Jewish-Christian-Roman relationships but in a larger embrace of animals as fellows. This expansive inclusion might not be simply a utopian dream. There appear to be glimpses of such possible inclusive practices among the early followers of Jesus. Despite influential figures such as Augustine who argued against any community shared by animals and humans, there were Jewish Christians who saw Jesus as a vegetarian (Grant 1999, 11). Grant writes that there are reports of James the brother of Jesus avoiding meat, and some claimed that the apostle Matthew ate seeds, nuts, and vegetables. Later, the Manichees and the Marcionites were to reject the eating of meat (11). In the so-called apocryphal Acts, there are multiple animals that play central roles, testifying to a potential in early Christianity for a greater regard for animals. In her study *Animals in the Apocryphal Acts of the Apostles: The Wild Kingdom of Early Christian Literature*, Janet E. Spittler (2008) discusses the significance of animals in all five of the major apocryphal Acts of the Apostles: the Acts of John, Acts of Peter, Acts of Andrew, Acts of Paul, and Acts of Thomas. It is striking that animals do not appear merely as anecdotes or metaphors there (Spittler 2008, 6). Spittler argues that the apocryphal Acts, "in their prominent and often positive portrayal of animals, offer an untapped opportunity to flesh out and generally enrich our understanding of early Christian conceptions of the natural world and the Christian's place within it" (9). In these texts there are friendships between humans and animals; there are animals that recognize the divine; and there are even animals that are baptized (156–89).

Like the hospitality now open to gentiles in Acts 10, the animals in Acts 10 too could be seen as possible subjects of hospitality, open to a fellowship and recognition in difference but not domination or demotion. Opening up the idea that there might be more to Peter's vision than a technical debate about food laws and a figurative dream for human fellowship means rethinking the boundaries of hospitality when it comes to the performances of power. Who or what sits *on* the table awaiting to be eaten—as life that is categorized as fundamentally killable and edible—and who are privileged to partake and participate *around* the table in this spectacle of power, human over beast, humans over nonhumans, or as this text shows, between different groups of people? What happens when species meet, to borrow Haraway's (2007) title? If this is in a sense what is asked when Peter and Cornelius meet one another, why should it not also apply to other animals, other "species"? As I allude to, for instance, in the apocryphal Acts of the Apostles, considering animals more seriously is not an absurd notion. Although the idea of a wild ass giving a speech, as in Acts Thom. 4, easily looks like an anthropomorphic absurdity, such speech prompts the idea Derrida (2008) explores throughout *The Animal That Therefore I Am*, namely, the animal response. To reflect on the way an animal might respond is already to begin questioning the right humans have to deny animals the ability to respond, to express, to communicate, and to form relations.

Haraway (2007, 18) urges a way of life that is lived in intersectionality, which might be a more constructive way of thinking of universalism. To live in such a way requires a particular regard:

> To hold in regard, to respond, to look back reciprocally, to notice, to pay
> attention, to have courteous regard for, to esteem: all of that is tied to

polite greeting, to constituting the polis, where and when species meet. To knot companion and species together in encounter, in regard and respect, is to enter the world of becoming with, where *who and what are* is precisely what is at stake. (Haraway 2007, 19, emphasis original)

Living in intersectionality demands recognizing animals as creatures that also *see*. It is a matter of seeing otherwise than "the objectivizing staging of the animal of theory, the animal as it is seen" and recognizing "the animal that sees" (Derrida 2008, 82). The world of "becoming with" that Haraway describes is one in which stark distinctions between entities are scrambled without being eradicated or erased. Identities emerge, but they remain relational, "in entangled species" (Haraway 2007, 32). In *When Species Meet*, Haraway is interested in emphasizing the necessary relatedness of different species as social subjects that are mutually communicative, or at least recognizing the other as a social subject in order to learn anything about the social habits of the other species. To make this point, she discusses an incident where Barbara Smuts, a bioanthropologist, attempts to observe a group of baboons. Haraway comments that Smuts's tactic of pretending she was not there in order to observe the baboons did not work. Known as the "rock act," the idea was to simply observe the baboons as an outside presence. It was not until Smuts entered into a relational, responsive engagement with the baboons, however, that *she* took on a "face" and therefore could enter into their lives and be accepted as a presence (25). There are, of course, no baboons to be seen—or that see—in Acts, not even any "real" animals, only visionary ones. But the vision, portraying animals in silence and passivity in the sheet that descends, having become killable and edible animals, might prompt a different thinking regarding acts of eating, despite the command to kill and eat. Paradoxically, if Cornelius is to be recognized as an other who has gained a "face" in this new universal world Acts is trying to make, then we might have to recognize the faces of animals as precisely not killable, but as potential companions. The whole scene is about rethinking acts of eating and the implications of these acts for a universal hospitality and opened fellowship, free of hierarchical divisions between self and other.

The automatic assumption that violence and murder are only prohibited between humans by law might be opened to a law that—on principle— forbids deliberate and unthinking violence toward and killing of animals. In this sense, the change in the status of animals as now all *clean*—"what God has made clean you shall not call profane" (Acts 10:15)—would not be a death sentence to the animal but rather a call to see animals also as companions in creation. It is not a matter of simply expanding universalism by *also* including animals, and thereby losing the warning of scholars such as Buell that exclusive reasoning can still function despite a rhetoric of inclusion. It is perhaps, rather, in the spirit of Derrida and even more so of Haraway, a matter of recognizing the relational and responsive movements that constitute one's being in the world. There are no preexisting identities that can simply be eradicated—by, for instance, undoing the opposition clean/unclean—only, as Haraway (2007, 32) offers, "cobblings together that give meaning to the 'becoming with' of companion species in naturecultures." Such a relational "becoming with" can take a violent form—a carnivorous relation, for instance, where the animal becomes an object to be consumed as humans become carnivorous consumers. But it can also be nurturing and affectionate, even world-changing in the upending and undoing of such distinctions between the consumers and consumed, the subject and object, the seeing and the seen, the clean and unclean.

For Haraway (2007, 36), "caring for, being affected, and entering into responsibility are not ethical abstractions; these mundane, prosaic things are the result of having truck with each other." Touch, regard, becoming with, "make us responsible in unpredictable ways for which worlds take shape" (36). The possibility of a universalism—or intersectionality—also for and with animals might be opened up by having truck with them, even if they cannot be touched or even really seen in the vision of this text.

All Life

If there is in much scholarship on Acts 10 a tendency to map an emergent Christianity onto concepts of universalism and openness to the (gentile) other, then the failure to perceive of the idea of animals as fellows in Peter's vision has resulted in a universalism embedded in an embryonic anthropocentrism. In other words, the universal conceived of as Peter's Lord of all would only be partial in fact to human life, a Lord not to "all" but to all *humans*—in whichever ways the human is then imagined. One of the points is, following Buell, that the human here is not simply given. The idea of the human too is subject to judgements about what it is to count as precisely human, as opposed to the barbaric, for instance, the uncivilized, the pagan, the nonuniversal, the killable, the animal.

In this chapter, I suggest that the universalism of Acts 10 is undercut by the tacit exclusion of the animal lives that are at the source of this so-called universalism. A more generous interpretation of the universalism of Acts 10 (seeing in it more than anti-Jewish, pro-Christian propaganda) might conclude that it represents a dream for universal hospitality, fellowship, and liberation from entrenched separations between groups of people, but that remains problematically limited. A less generous interpretation would propose that, at the foundations of the emergent Christianity in Acts and its universalism, there is a forgotten violence in the command to kill and eat that accompanies the "cleanness" of all life. In any case, whether the idea of *all* as clean animals under an impartial Lord is an opening to a carnivorous relation to the other or to companionship with the previously conceived other is, surely, the crucial question, and one to be posed time and time again.

3
POLITICAL ANIMALS

The book of Daniel hosts a variety of animals. There are the well-known lions in the pit, the king who becomes an animal, and the bizarre beasts that have become popularized in the apocalyptic imagination.[1] In the first two chapters of this book, I examine the notion of permissible killing in the Bible and the way it relates to animality and acts of eating. I suggest that the commands that allowed for animals to be killed and eaten are less straightforward than they might seem, as they are inextricably caught up in the relational covenant with all life and universal fellowship so central to Genesis and Acts, respectively. Although eating continues to be a theme, in this and the following chapter I shift the focus somewhat to the political animals of the book of Daniel and the book of Revelation. I explore why it is that kings and empires are depicted as animals; why we might read Daniel as a political animal; and what significance such animal figures might have for sustaining adverse conceptions of animality or for shoring up sympathy for, and solidarity with, animals. As I argue in the introduction, the theme of sovereign power is key for reflecting on how the idea of animals as inferior subjects is upheld in relation to the idea of the sovereign human as set apart from, and above, animals. Whether animals are killable or not depends on who deems them killable and by what (sovereign) right. The question of power, and who holds power—human or divine—is played out in Daniel with reference to the question of who is animal.

Both the book of Daniel and the book of Revelation depict the political order as beastlike: political regimes and figures are characterized as beasts that capture and conquer like wild predators. Is this a case of the way the

---

1. Additionally, in the apocryphal additions to the legends about Daniel, "Bel and the Dragon," there is the story of a great snake.

animal, or beast(ly), has come to signify what is bad in and about humans, such traits as a propensity to violence, to ferocity, to lack of compassion? Is it a case of the "human" denoting the civilized and the humane, and the "animal" the barbarous and bestial in the political order? I argue that closer attention to the animals in these texts will help us to think about other ways in which animality is played out in relation to the political. Starting with the book of Daniel, I show how human sovereignty is critiqued because it involves an exclusion of the divine and the cutting up of life into the human and the animal. The book of Daniel, I argue, undoes the human/animal distinction by showing all to be animals under a God of all the living. Daniel does this by establishing the proper hierarchy as that of divine/animal. In other words, I suggest that the human/animal binary is radically destabilized, even undone, but the structure of a (divine) sovereign master over its pet/prey is left intact.

Beastly Politics

Daniel is a multifaceted book in the biblical archive, normally divided into two parts, chapters 1–6 and 7–12. The first six chapters are commonly described as court legends, while the last six are usually classified as apocalyptic literature.[2] Jan-Wim Wesselius (2005, 242) calls it "a kaleidoscopic work" because of its variations in genre, style, and language. The book is pseudepigraphal, antedated, and bilingual (Hebrew and Aramaic).[3] Daniel is a text that is rife with diverse influences[4] and has a long and influential

---

2. These two parts are often read separately, or at least classified differently, but Jan-Wim Wesselius (2005, 255) puts forward an interesting argument for its unity, calling the book a "linear literary dossier." Wesselius's argument is based on the correlation he traces between the language (particularly the Aramaic) and structure of Daniel with two other biblical books, Gen 37–50 and Ezra, which Daniel mirrors.

3. David M. Valeta (2008, 330–40) sums up the four positions generally proposed in scholarship regarding the mixture of Hebrew and Aramaic: "(1) a single author composed the book in two languages; (2) the entire book was composed originally in Hebrew, with subsequent partial translation into Aramaic; (3) the entire book was composed in Aramaic, with subsequent partial translation into Hebrew; and (4) older Aramaic material was redacted into a work being composed in Hebrew." Theories two and three have few adherents, and it is generally agreed that one or four are more plausible. Hebrew tends to be seen as the more elite language, with Aramaic being more commonly spoken, an element some scholars identify with the content of Daniel.

4. John J. Collins (1977, 102–3) argues that the ancient mythological motifs used

trajectory on the genre of apocalypse, particularly on the book of Revelation, to which I turn in the next chapter.[5] It is a collection of stories that have been popular especially among children, particularly known for its lions.[6] Despite this benign association, Daniel is a highly political book, something that might be useful to flesh out briefly before engaging with what I call its political animals.

The book of Daniel places the eponymous hero of Daniel in the Babylonian and Persian courts in the sixth century BCE. Daniel is presented as one of the Judean exiles in Babylon along with other noble Jews. Daniel's narrative setting in the Babylonian exile signals a context after the Babylonian king Nebuchadnezzar destroyed Jerusalem in 587 BCE. The Babylonian exile that followed 587 BCE is a time of crisis, of submission to foreign powers. But the book of Daniel was written around the time of the Maccabean revolt (167–163 BCE). Assmann (2012, 39) calls the Maccabean revolt "a unique historical phenomenon, the influence of which has reverberated down through the centuries to the present day." During this period, the Greek king Antiochus IV Epiphanes of the Seleucid empire issued a decree that prohibited the practice of Judaism in what Martha Himmelfarb (2012, 33) calls "a rare instance of religious persecution in Greco-Roman antiquity," suspicious of the worship of foreign deities "masking political conspiracy." Gabriela Signori (2012, 1) explains that the idea of defending faith through violence took shape under Antiochus IV Epiphanes (175–164 BCE) as a result of his prohibiting Jews from living according to their customs, his violation of their temple, and his violence against those who resisted his rule. John J. Collins (1981, 3) conveys how the Maccabean revolt against this decree and its implications has "stood through the centuries as a striking paradigm for recourse to armed, violent revolution in the name of religion." Assmann (2012, 41) highlights that this war was seemingly about resistance to the Seleucid persecution, but it

---

in Daniel must be understood in light of the interest in such traditions in the Hellenistic age. He suggests that in the Hellenistic Near East, such ancient material was drawn from an interest that was complementary to an increased use of pseudepigraphy: "antiquity was thought to be superior to the present. Therefore writings and traditions which either were or claimed to be ancient enjoyed special prestige."

5. For more on the Daniel imagery and its influences in apocalyptic texts, see, for instance, Beale 1984.

6. See, for instance, Pyper 2012.

was also a Jewish civil war between a "modernizing reformist faction and an orthodox faction of those faithful to religious law."

The story of Daniel, then, can be seen to reflect both a past crisis and a present crisis (Davies 1985, 13). Phillip R. Davies (1985, 13, emphasis original) relates how the characters of the Babylonian king Nebuchadnezzar and the exiled Jews in Daniel "are both the *predecessors* and the *prototypes* of the persecuting monarch Antiochus IV and the persecuted Jews of Palestine centuries later." Daniel L. Smith-Christopher (2001, 280) argues persuasively for the organic nature of this folding of past and present in the book: "memories and traditions regarding the hubris of Babylonian rulers that formed the 'raw materials' for the Daniel tales would not need extensive 'revision' to be flexible enough to apply with equal cynicism to the pretensions of rulers throughout the Persian and Hellenistic eras." He argues that despite the differences between the political and ideological regimes from 587 to 164 BCE, the Daniel tales reflect an understanding of empire building in the ancient Near East as a recurrent display of, and battle for, power (Smith-Christopher 2001, 280). The political themes in the book of Daniel are those of foreign occupation and resistance, of how to live—and how to live religiously—under foreign rule. In particular, the text is about the hubris of human power. A useful way of understanding how such hubris works and how it is critiqued, I suggest, is by reflecting on the ways the divine and the animal operate as categories in relation to the idea of human power.

As I have already noted, in many ways the human political order is presented as beastly in the book of Daniel. The second half of Daniel more emphatically displays the terror in facing life under a foreign political order that is depicted as a carnivorous, violent force. Daniel abides as if in a "magic zoo of fearsome and fabulous beasts" (Porter 1983, xi), unknowing who is foe or friend, envisioning only ferocious animals in a world ruled and fought over by competing beasts. In Dan 7–12, human power is made synonymous with the jaws of beasts. In 7:17, a confused Daniel is told that the beasts he sees in dreams are kings to come. In 7:3, Daniel dreams of four great beasts, where the first is like a lion and becomes like a man (7:4) on two feet and with a human mind, emphasizing the beastlike nature of such a human. Daniel 7:5 presents the second beast like a bear which is told to devour much flesh. A leopard too appears, with dominion, and is a hybrid creature—partly bird and with four heads—as if to emphasize the disorder of human power in its beastly guise. The fourth and final beast is described in 7:7 and is "terrifying and dreadful and extremely strong. It had great iron teeth and was devouring, breaking in pieces, and stamping what was left with its feet." This description is emphasized by the repetition in 7:19 of the beast, "exceedingly terrifying, with its teeth of iron and claws of bronze, and which devoured and broke in pieces, and stamped what was left with its feet." Despite the beast being predicted to be put to death and burnt in 7:11 and the others being deprived of their dominion in 7:12, Daniel admits "my spirit is troubled within me, and the visions of my head terrified me" (7:15).

In Dan 7:23, the fourth beast is said to devour the whole earth and crush it and break it to pieces. Again, the promise is made that the holy ones of God shall prevail eventually, but by 7:28 Daniel is alarmed at the political animals he has seen and continues to see. Daniel 8 continues with a violent battle between a ram and a goat, representing kings fighting one another, and the destruction of the holy ones is predicted in 8:24. Daniel 9 is dominated by Daniel's pleas to his God to help. But the visions continue relentlessly, with a flood in 9:26, another terrifying vision in 10:8, and anguish in 10:16. Here, seemingly, the hybrid, ferocious animals of Daniel's visions signify a political future of terror; animality is portrayed as carnivorous, predatory, and terrifying. Koosed and Robert Paul Seesengood (2014, 12, 14) argue that evil becomes consigned to the image of the animal as beast in the book of Daniel and therefore can and must be killed. Animality is consigned to "the worst," "radical evil" (Derrida 2002, 56). In other words, human tyrants are conceptualized as animals in order to make them killable (Koosed and Seesengood 2014, 12–13). The image of animality in Daniel could be seen to rely on the killability of animals (12). The political critique of human rulers in the book of Daniel would in this sense also be caught up in a logic that demonizes animals, a logic whereby all that is evil in the human political realm becomes mapped onto the animal, the beastly. In order to resist foreign rule, to critique and overthrow it, this human order must thus be imagined as animal; as animal it can also be hunted down and killed.

There are two other instances in the book of Daniel that seem to corroborate the idea of human power as beastlike, namely, the scenes where King Nebuchadnezzar quite literally becomes animal and Daniel is in the pit of the lions. In Dan 4, Nebuchadnezzar looks out over his "magnificent Babylon," which he has built "as a royal capital by my mighty power and for my glorious majesty" (4:30). With the words of self-admiration still in his mouth, he hears a "voice from heaven" (4:31) telling him that his kingdom will be taken away from him. "You shall be driven away from human society, and your dwelling shall be with the animals of the field" (4:32). This fate, "made to eat grass like oxen" until "seven times" have passed over him, is so that he will learn "that the Most High has sovereignty over the kingdom of mortals and gives it to whom he will" (4:32). Immediately this takes place: "He was driven away from human society, ate grass like oxen, and his body was bathed with the dew of heaven, until his hair grew as long as eagles' feathers and his nails became like birds' claws" (4:33). Although Nebuchadnezzar here is a rather benign animal, the lesson could be seen as a display of his true "bestial condition" (Ricoeur 1979, xxii). Making him animal shows that he is vulnerable and mortal rather than an infinitely powerful (human) ruler.

When Daniel is punished by being thrown into the lion's pit in Dan 6, the lions could be seen as representations of the carnivorous sovereign force of the human political order that sentences Daniel to death. Karel van der Toorn (2001, 43) emphasizes that references to lions in the Babylonian tradition are not real animals: "they stand for human adversaries. The single time that a pit of lions is mentioned in a cuneiform scholarly text, it serves as a metaphor for the hostility and competition among the court sages." In light of this, he suggests that a literal understanding of the lions is a "misrecognition" and "misunderstanding" (43). The entry on the lion in *An Encyclopedia of Bible Animals* by Peter France (1986, 100–101) notes that lions were so much a part of mythology that almost all contexts in which they are used in the Hebrew Bible are metaphorical, referring to human qualities as lion-like. France explains that lions are a figure for "the power of evil," but as *human*, and so the "wicked ruler," for instance, is seen "as dangerous as a prowling lion" in Prov 28:15 (100–101). In one of the psalms, cries for help are expressed because "my soul is among lions" (Ps 57:4) as if trapped and subjected to vicious powers (France 1986, 100–101).

The lions in Daniel are clearly associated with human wickedness, particularly political court conflict. Jealous of Daniel, the "other presidents and satraps tried to find grounds for complaint against Daniel in connection with the kingdom" (Dan 6:4). When they cannot find any grounds for complaint, they realize that their best option is to use "the law of his God" (6:5) against him. Appealing to the king's vanity, "O King Darius, live forever!" (6:6), the presidents, satraps, prefects, counsellors, and governors "all agreed that the king should establish an ordinance and enforce an interdict, that whoever prays to anyone, divine or human, for thirty days, except to you, O king, shall be thrown into a den of lions" (6:7). The document is duly signed, and when Daniel is later found praying as usual to his God (6:10–11), the conspirators tell the king and remind him of the impossibility of revoking the law (6:12, 15). The king does not want to charge Daniel but is foiled by his own law, and he has Daniel thrown into the pit of lions to be eaten and killed (6:14–17).

As the king is tricked into this position from his vanity, however, his law and his political aides could be seen as precisely lion-like in their politics when Daniel stands before the law in the form of the lions' mouths. The lions are a way of showing the human political order as malevolent, signifying human power as carnivorous animality. Animality is used to convey the worst aspects of human political rule: the beastly, the carnivorous, the predatory. Consequently, Koosed and Seesengood (2014, 12) suggest that "Daniel is replete with the Animal as symbol," as "part of the strategy of the apocalypse to construct a great divide between humans and animals, one that allows humanity to be divided into the good and the evil where the evil is consigned to the category animal and slaughtered accordingly." But as they themselves affirm, "the borders of God, human and animal are repeatedly blurred" (3). I go on to argue that it is this *blurring* that is significant in Daniel, and that in fact, the great divide between humans and animals is undone in the critique of human sovereignty as an empty charade.

Human Sovereignty

Arguably a stronger current in the book of Daniel than the depiction of human power as beastlike is the critique of *human* sovereignty. Human sovereignty is critiqued in its exclusion of the divine, or rather the mapping of the divine onto human sovereign figures. But also, crucially, critique could be seen as levelled at the reliance on a category—animals—to be ruled over in a performance of sovereign power. I first discuss the idea of a human sovereignty that is constructed in relation to animals before going on to show how in Daniel this is coupled by the exclusion of the divine, or of the folding of the divine into the human sovereign figure. What is critiqued here, as I analyze in more detail in the next section, is the cutting up of life into the human and the animal. All the living are shown to be *animal*; the only proper hierarchy is that between divine and (human and nonhuman) animals. This is not, as I suggest above, to display the worst aspects of the human political order, or at least not only that. Rather, the animality of all is a way of fostering solidarity amongst the living under a God who is the only sovereign ruler, in this way radically undercutting the power of human sovereignty.

Returning to the lions that I suggested might represent the beastly power of the human sovereign, their role in the text might be rethought by seeing them not as representational of human power but as quite simply the role they are made to play as lions. The lions in Daniel arguably signify the animal subjection to human power that props up the latter as sovereign. André Lacocque (1979, 50) conveys how Babylonian kings are often shown as ruling over wild beasts and birds. Keeping captured animals for hunting in menageries as "symbols of their universal domination" (50) is a prime way of ensuring the show of mastery. What underlies such a practice, he argues, is an enactment of the myth of "man as dominant over the animals" (50). Van der Toorn (2001, 51) points out that Assyrian kings kept wild animals; but for this purpose, lions were not kept in pits but in zoological gardens. He argues that the motif of lions goes back to Babylonian wisdom literature; in the Babylonian tradition, however, the lions are not real lions but usually stand for human adversaries (43). Van der Toorn suggests that the author of Daniel must have been aware of such stories about lions and taken the imagery literally, making the lions real. "The image of a group of lions in a pit, therefore, evokes the idea of famished animals fighting one another for the slightest morsel of food" (51). Whether this is a misunderstanding on the part of the author or not, the fact that the lions are real lions is, as I go on to discuss, pertinent. The power to capture living wild creatures, withhold food, and determine the life or death of such creatures is a testament to the power of the sovereign owner of such animals: the one who is the strongest, most powerful, who can even capture and subdue lions.[7]

When Derrida (2005b, xi) wonders whether "the very concept of law, that juridical reason itself, includes a priori a possible course to constraint or coercion and, thus, to a certain violence," the captured lions might indeed point to a human power and law that involves a carnivorous force and logic.[8] This is Derrida's (1995b, 280) sovereign subject as "phallogo-centric," characterized by "carnivorous virility," desiring to eat well. Here,

---

7. For further discussion of leonine imagery see Strawn 2005; for royal hunting practices throughout history see, for instance, Allsen 2006.

8. France (1986, 102–3) argues that the biblical authors had not necessarily actually seen a lion. Israelite culture "was shot through with the myths of Egypt and Babylon, both of which celebrated the regal majesty of Lions."

to eat well means to eat flesh, to have power over the other as a weaker subject, categorizing such subjects as animals. To perform human sovereign rule, then, the category of animals provides the prey that allows for a performance of such carnivorous virility via the lions. Adams (2010, 48) starkly proposes: "people with power have always eaten meat," relating such power to patriarchal structures. Derrida (1995b, 282) too poses the question: who could be Head of State and declare himself, publicly, a vegetarian? To what extent is the question of human power and its relation to the other caught up in a carnivorous logic? Eating well is what is at stake. But what is it to eat *well*? Is it to consume voraciously, carnivorously, unboundedly? Or is it to eat cleanly, without being defiled by participating in social practices of consumption that are based on domination, subjugation, and violence? And who has the power to put to death, to determine who or what can be sacrificed in order to eat well? To decide who or what is animal and who or what is divine? Calarco (2008, 131) explains that Derrida's term "carnophallocentrism," or "carnophallologocentrism" (Derrida 2004, 68) suggests a subjectivity structured by *sacrificial* (carno), *masculine* (phallo), and *speaking* (logo). In this context, the lions are sacrificed for the masculine domination of the sovereign whose speaking is synonymous with the power to condemn or put to death, the power or voice of the law.

The specific crime Daniel has committed when he is thrown to the lions is to respond not exclusively to his human master—the king as the single, sovereign, and sole power—but to destabilize this dominion by disregarding the law and to continue responding to a nonhuman power, his God. On the surface of it, Daniel's crime is merely to be successful, provoking jealousy amongst his fellow courtiers. But in light of the focus on human power in opposition to Daniel's God in the book in general, the underlying element here is the issue of competition between human and divine powers, the latter trumping human domination. Hence, Daniel refuses to act as if the human king is the highest power. Jan Willem Van Henten (2001, 151) calls this a "fundamental relativization of state authority," which could be read as a questioning not only of Babylonian or Seleucid rule but of the *human* right to master and rule over nonhuman others.[9]

---

9. Van der Toorn (2001, 52) suggests that the author of Daniel has drawn on other biblical images for the punishment of being thrown in a pit of lions (Ezek 19:4, 8; Jer 48:43–44) or a cistern (2 Sam 23:20; 1 Chr 11:22). There are also other parallels to such cavities being used for humans (e.g., Jer 38:6), and King David claimed Yahweh

Daniel eschews such mastery from the beginning of the book by referring to himself as a "servant" (1:12, 13) and resisting the food of the king, refusing thus to eat well.[10] Eating only vegetables and drinking water (1:12) rather than the delicacies of the king, Daniel is both emphasizing his non-belonging to the king's court and a resistance to participate in the privilege and power of human mastery.[11]

The hungry lions and the emphases more generally on the acceptance or rejection of food in Daniel evoke the power related to food and eating. The theme of eating and captivity is brought up also later when Daniel fasts (Dan 9:3) and in the fasting of King Darius when Daniel is sentenced to the lions' pit (6:18). These are examples of chosen acts of not eating which point to the way that acts of eating (or not eating) are tied up in dynamics of power and of resistance. Resisting the "sovereign mastery over the beast" characterized by "having possession, appropriation, and the property of beasts (through capture, hunting, raising, commerce, enclosure)" (Derrida 2009, 283), Daniel's position is one alongside, and in solidarity with, the enclosed lions. The lions too could be said to fast when Daniel is presented to them as food, seemingly choosing not to eat. In this sense we might, like Stefan Beyerle (2001, 225), say that the book of Daniel does indeed envisage "a radical replacement of social organization."[12]

---

delivered him from lion (and a bear in 1 Sam 17:37): "The author of the Daniel story, then, bred on the Bible, knew that victims of jealousy and royal disfavor might expect to be cast into a pit; that many a lion had ended up in a pit as well; and that God had delivered his servants from the attacks of lions before" (Van der Toorn 2001, 52).

10. John Walton (2001, 69) connects this refusal in eating to Daniel's powers of prophecy and knowledge. In refusing the king's diet and accepting only the "seeds" or "crumbs," "so the divinatory and mythological literature of Babylon provided but the raw materials for Daniel's career as a sage and prophet in the court of Babylon."

11. John C. Trever (1985, 90) argues that the author(s) of Daniel represents a peaceful version of opposition to Hellenization during the time of Antiochus IV. Trever links this amity specifically to the Qumran community and calls the authors behind Daniel "a pacifist faction of the Hasidim" who refused to follow militant Jews in the Maccabean revolt beginning in 167 BCE.

12. Beyerle (2001, 224–26) proposes that this comes more to the fore in the second part of Daniel, in Dan 7:3–8, 11–12, with the war of the "horn" against the "holy ones," which he sees as representing two realities of a corrupt and lost world, on the one hand, and an everlasting world of salvation, on the other. This, he says, spurs on a "hope for salvation within a transcendent reality that only comes to light through the visionary context of Daniel." Such a hopeful view could be argued to rather be

A further example of the relationship between power and eating well can be found in Dan 5 with King Belshazzar and his feast. Belshazzar's self-possession is disturbed, his face going pale, thoughts terrified, limbs giving way, and knees knocking together (5:6) at the disembodied "fingers of a human hand" writing on the wall (5:5). Daniel is called upon to interpret, and he criticizes Belshazzar's spectacles of power and mastery in not seeing, hearing, or knowing "the God in whose power is your every breath, and to whom belong all your ways" (5:23). Part of the critique is levelled at Belshazzar's father, whom Belshazzar is following, in killing those he wants to kill and keeping alive those he wants kept alive, degrading and honoring according to his whim (5:19). The point is to challenge the power and mastery enacted by the human ruler.

Danna Nolan Fewell (1988, 37) proposes that "eating from the king's table is symbolic of political covenant and compromise,"[13] a contract Daniel is clearly unwilling to enter. His refusal is a matter of not defiling oneself (1:8 [גאל]); this "defilement," however, is not inherent in the foreignness of the rulers to which Daniel finds himself subjected but is primarily linked to their misplaced hubris and self-aggrandizement as godlike. Davies (1985, 84, emphasis original) draws attention to the fact that the tension is not between Daniel's god and other gods, "but to political powers, be they kings or courtiers. Indeed, the problem of all the stories is not whether Judaism is *theologically* acceptable to gentile rulers, but whether it is *politically* acceptable." As is clear from the decree pronounced against praying to other gods except the king, the divine must be expelled from the human sovereign reign to ground exclusive power to the sovereign. Divinity must in that sense be mapped onto the human ruler. Fewell (1988, 15) too points out that in Dan 1–6 "the most basic opposition" and the source of tension is between divine sovereignty and human sovereignty. Notably, the Seleucid ruler at the time Daniel is written called himself Antiochus IV Epiphanes—"God made manifest"—and as Himmelfarb (2012, 34) points out, "his peculiar behavior led some of his contemporaries to refer to him instead as Antiochus Epimanes, 'mad man.'" Daniel is keen to assert that it is God who is a higher ruler than any human king

---

present in the first half, whereas in the second half, violence appears to be a possible trait of a carnivorous sovereign divine master.

13. Fewell (1988, 37) draws attention to another biblical example, namely, when David stops eating from Saul's table and Saul thinks David has rebelled against him in 1 Sam 20:30–34.

when in Dan 2:37 he slips in that it is "the God of heaven" who has given "the kingdom, the power, the might and the glory" to Nebuchadnezzar. All "who live must know that the Most High is sovereign over the kingdom of mortals" (4:17). In this way, a clear distinction is made between human power and divine sovereignty.

Lacocque (1979, 119) interestingly compares Daniel's lions to another animal figure, namely, Balaam's ass in Numbers: "like the ass who was more clairvoyant than its master the 'prophet,' the lions had more sense than the king." Hence, there is something of a nonhuman alliance between animals and God. Daniel becomes a near-martyr, fully expected to be eaten alive by the lions, becoming himself "a morsel of food" (Van der Toorn 2001, 51) as a result of breaking the law and addressing a nonhuman other. The judgment scene thus moves from human faux-divine mastery over life and death to a divine-animal power that interrupts and overrules because Daniel is *not* killed and eaten. Daniel survives *with* his fellow subjects of human power.[14] Because he becomes (like) the nonhuman other—the lions and God—Daniel destabilizes and thus delegitimizes the power of the human rulers.

Animals under God

What the book of Daniel conveys is the way all the living are animals under God. When Daniel is turned into "food" for the lions, he is essentially shown to be the (animal) flesh he already is, even if he is spared from being eaten in this instance.[15] I suggest that viewing Daniel as animal lifts up the themes of political subjugation and political critique in this text in helpful ways. Sharing a space with the lions points to the way he too is an "animal" captive under foreign rule, brought into a foreign court, and made subject

---

14. Grant (1999, 17) tells of other narratives with friendly lions (in addition to Daniel's), the most famous one being about Androclus and the lion. Androclus is saved by a lion because the lion refuses to eat him. Another features an old man who lived in a Palestinian cave where he gladly received lions, and in another, a lion helps a monk dig the grave of Mary of Egypt. In the third century, Hippolytus of Rome insisted that the lions in the story of Daniel "rejoiced by shaking their tails as if submissive to a new Adam; they licked the holy feet of Daniel and rolled on his footprints in their desire to be trodden by him" (17).

15. Unlike those who are gobbled up by the lions in Dan 6:24; there are also those who are "cooked" in the furnace—Shadrach, Meshach, and Abednego in Dan 3:19–30—but whose flesh turns out not to be burnable in this instance.

to the rule of a king who feeds and keeps him, as pet or prey. Thinking of real, living, wild animals trapped in a pit is crucial for understanding how subjection to foreign powers—whether Babylonian, Persian, or Seleucid rulers—could be configured as an animal state, being domesticated, caged, captured, and removed from one's territory. Such a position opens up the possibility of a nonhuman alliance between the animal and the divine, an alliance with the God who destabilizes human powers of subjection.

Daniel and his companions are given new Babylonian names (1:7) and a new education (1:5), as if to tame them and demonstrate their status as trained animals. In *The Religion of the Landless: The Social Context of the Babylonian Exile*, Smith-Christopher (1989, 40–41) argues that although it has become common to assume that the Jews were not slaves in the Babylonian empire, it is still pertinent to reflect on modes of slavery that might be appropriate for the subjects under Babylonian power in this context. He mentions social "death," demotion, and removal of identity markers and name changes (40). Just as the captured lions could be seen as a marker of human sovereign power, then, Daniel and his fellow Jews could be read similarly as animals in their status as subjects of foreign rule. Like an animal, a foreign species to the Babylonians, Daniel becomes the domesticated subject that lives within the confines of his master's house and becomes the master's favored pet. But in suggesting that *all* are animals under a God of all the living, human sovereignty is radically destabilized.

The most forceful example of the animality of all is in the famous narrative of Nebuchadnezzar, already discussed briefly above. In Dan 4, King Nebuchadnezzar's dream comes to fulfilment, and he is turned into an animal. The king symbolizes the power and mastery of the human subject who plays at being a god. Placing Daniel in the context of court narratives in Jewish literary traditions more broadly, Lawrence M. Wills (1990, 11) argues that the figure of the king in such legends varies but that it essentially performs the function of "absolute power." Nebuchadnezzar's name, from *nebo*, means "to protect the boundary." The word for "besiege" (צוּר) used for Nebuchadnezzar's entrance to Jerusalem at the beginning of the book means literally to cramp, confine, or bind (Dan 1:1; Strong 2001, 765), as if his entire character is marked by protection and mastery over the other's freedom through restriction and subjection. But it is precisely the boundaries that guard the human as exclusive master from both animality and divinity that are challenged in the king being made an animal. In this way, the depiction of all the human rulers as beastlike is not only, or primarily, a demonization of the animal aspects of humans as signs of evil in the political order, but a comment on the animality of humans under a higher power that flattens the hierarchical distinctions at work between sovereign and subject. But even when Nebuchadnezzar comes back to himself and speaks in the first person, having recovered his reason or power of knowing (4:34), he has arguably learned his lesson about the true order of things. He has awakened to "the Most High," his "sovereignty as an everlasting sovereignty," who does what he wills "with the host of heaven and the inhabitants of the earth" (4:35). While King Nebuchadnezzar's "majesty and splendor" are restored to him, and while he is reestablished over his kingdom and more greatness is added to his rule (4:36), he is put in place as to the proper hierarchy whereby the divine trumps human power: "Now I, Nebuchadnezzar, praise and extol and honor the King of heaven, for all his works are truth, and his ways are justice; and he is able to bring low those who walk in pride" (4:37). Nebuchadnezzar is judged by the law of this God to become animal, in order to reveal the king as ultimately without mastery. A human sovereign is no higher or grander than a grazing animal; they are essentially similar, near one another, while God as the highest is irreplaceable as *the* sovereign power.[16] As Koosed and Seesengood (2014, 7) put it: "kings are, at best, a simulacrum and must remain mindful of the real power, God."

Humans are in this way shown to be animals, sometimes glorified animals that give themselves (or are given) power to rule as divine-like masters who are attempting to subjugate their subjects (nonhuman and human animals) and exclude God from the political in order to ground this position of power. In the foreword to Lacocque's *The Book of Daniel*, Paul Ricoeur (1979, xxii) comments that King Nebuchadnezzar "condemned to graze like a beast, is Adam and every other Master whose inhumanity leads back to a bestial condition." But arguably, it is the king's *human mastery* in playing God that is the problem and that has to be altered, to be shown as what it essentially is. The "bestial condition" is the condition of *all* in the face of God's power. What is emphasized is that *all* the living

---

16. Lacocque (1979, 54) relates how Alexander the Great and his successors generally held tolerant attitudes to religious practice, so the God of Israel was thus accepted amongst other gods. But, in a parallel development, attitudes to deities turned also in the direction of a divinization of Hellenistic rulers. The worship of emperors as divine figures is widely discussed as to its import and significance. Daniel, then, might be seen to grapple with the challenges to ideas of divinity when human sovereign figures—also considered enemies—claimed worship for themselves.

are animals in the hands of God. This is intimated in the beginning of Daniel, when it is written that the Lord gives King Jehoiakim of Judah "into his hand" (Dan 1:2; again, the NRSV translation is "power," but the word used is that for hand [יד]). It is also shown in the address of Daniel to the king: "you, O king, the king of kings—to whom the God of heaven has given the kingdom, the power, the might and the glory, into whose hand he has given human beings, wherever they live, the wild animals of the field, and the birds of the air, and whom he has established as ruler over them all" (2:36–38). A king may be established *as if* a ruler, but essentially, he is no different from the animals of the field and the birds of the air in their *all* being in the hand of God. Whereas previously Nebuchadnezzar is addressed with the greeting to "live forever," the scene in Dan 4 is a lesson as to his finitude as a mortal animal.

King Nebuchadnezzar must thus recognize that the Most High is master over the realm of humankind (Dan 4:25); the human king does not rule: heaven rules (4:26). When King Nebuchadnezzar does come to this realization, he calls God and his kingdom everlasting, his dominion lasting forever (4:34), an echo of the greeting previously addressed to *him*: "O king, live forever!"[17] This greeting to human sovereignty as "living forever" (2:4; 3:9; 5:10; 6:6, 21) is a denial of mortal life, as if human kings are nonhuman and could live ad infinitum. In Dan 4:35, Nebuchadnezzar expounds how all who dwell on earth are in God's hands—no one can question this mastery. The point would be, then, that Daniel's god is more than a tribal deity (Young 1949, 18) and thus cannot be replaced by other human or pagan gods. This nonhuman other is a singular and superlative power. If, as Lacocque (1979, 26) puts it, "Daniel finds himself in the very center of idolatrous power, par excellence, Babylon," then what is idolatry or misplaced mastery is not merely a particular king and his gods but rather the centering of power in a *human* subject that is constructed from the exclusion of the divine and a cutting up of life into human and animal. What is undone in Daniel then is a boundary between humans and animals. God is the only and ultimate sovereign master—all the living are his pets or prey. The proper hierarchy is that between divine and animal, not human and nonhuman. All are in God's hand (4:35); the breath of life is in God's hand (5:23);

---

17. Lacocque (1979, 38) points out that this greeting is frequently used in Akkadian and is used at the Persian court up to the Islamic period.

men are to fear and tremble before this God, he is the living God and he rules the kingdom (6:26).

The idea of God as the proper sovereign master could be said to merely shift the problematic elements of human sovereignty to the divine and to map the beastly associations with human sovereign power onto God. Is the "voice from heaven" in Dan 4:31 God's voice? If God has a voice, does he also have a mouth? Does he need to eat? Is he carnivorous? Is this imagining of all the living as animal a way of fantasizing, as Koosed and Seesengood (2014) suggested, about the killability of one's political oppressors as beasts for slaughter? In many ways, then, God could be seen as a potentially ferocious humanlike ruler, living and participating in the political world of warring carnivorous creatures, simply higher up in the hierarchy. With his "hand" in whom all the living find themselves, this God may enact violence, condemn or sentence with his voice, and devour with his mouth. On the scale of mastery as the superlative power, this God too may be *like* a carnivorous, predatory master. The anthropomorphic elements of his hand and superlative position as a higher power to the human mark the divine out as a potentially violent force also competing for power.

This God figure could also be seen as both beastlike and as a tyrannical (human) keeper and destroyer of beasts (Koosed and Seesengood 2014, 9). Hugh S. Pyper (2014, 63) points out that lions in the Hebrew Bible are sometimes represented as God. "Yahweh can be represented as the roaring lion that opposes Israel's enemies," but part of this is that "he is also depicted as turning on Israel itself, regarding it as prey." As Pyper puts it: "what is strong and fierce enough to protect me can also threaten me, and the image of the lion uncannily ties together this duplicity of protector and threat, ruler and unruly" (64).[18] This is indeed the case with the lions in Daniel too, who refrain from eating Daniel but who show a rather different attitude to "eating well" when it comes to Daniel's accusers ("they, their children and their wives") in breaking all their bones in pieces (Dan 6:24). Pyper wonders whether a wider metaphor of lions may be at work in the Hebrew Bible, seeing the world and its politics as God's hunting park "where the nations can be either his quarry or his hunting beasts," where Israel is either witness or victim (67). With the border being redrawn in the critique of human sovereign power, no longer between human powers and the animals

---

18. Pyper (2014, 66–67) provides examples of Yahweh using lions to punish people, such as in 1 Kgs 20:35–36 and 2 Kgs 17:25.

ruled over but between the divine and animals, the image of God's hunting park is apt. God is both the protector but also potentially a predator.

Derrida argues that noncarnivorousness is perhaps the impossible. Speaking of vegetarianism, he says that "a certain cannibalism remains unsurpassable" (Derrida 2004, 67). Derrida (2004, 68) states: "it is not enough to stop eating meat in order to become a non-carnivore." There are other carnivorous processes in living with, near, besides, on, and off one's others. It is always possible to "incorporate, symbolically, something living, something of flesh and blood—of man and of God" (68). Eating the other always remains a temptation and a possibility. This, Derrida writes, is not merely an admission of potential violence in every other but also the temptation of love in proximity to, and possession of, "my" other, my "pet" (68).[19] As Derrida (1995, 282) states, one must eat, and one lets oneself be eaten. There is no possibility of avoiding violence toward the other whole-sale. But as Ruth Lipschitz (2012, 562) suggests, this might be a call for self-critical attention to boundaries and representations that come to constitute "hierarchies of conquest," as well as opening up the ethical imperative of "eating well." The moral question, as Derrida (1995b, 282, emphasis original) poses it, is: "since *one must* eat in any case … *how* for gooodness' sake should one *eat well*?"

In Daniel, to eat well seems to consist in refraining from eating the food of one's master, thereby becoming complicit in the logic of the master who feeds his subjects, and in resisting eating one's fellow subjects under sovereign rule, as the lions resist eating Daniel. As the lions also show, however, to eat well might also be to eat one's enemies, along with their wives and children. On the one hand, solidarity with one's fellow animals is promoted in a resistance to the human sovereignty that denotes carnivorous power over those deemed animal. On the other hand, the temptation of carnivorous power remains as all are shown to be essentially animals under a sovereign God, and thus all are potentially prey.

Pet or Prey

Cutting up life into the "human" and the "animal" is depicted as an erroneous strategy to support a performance of human sovereignty that is,

---

19. Derrida (2009, 210) is drawing on Hélène Cixous here; see particularly Cixous 1998.

ultimately, a spectacle to cover over the animality of the living, human and nonhuman. To further sustain such human sovereignty, the divine must be excluded, and the place of the "divine" mapped onto human sovereignty as the superlative power. Such an exclusion and mapping of the divine onto the human is the order that the book of Daniel critiques with its political animals. Undoing the distinction between the human powers and their "animal"/animal subjects allows for a resistance to the "reason of the strongest" as grounded in a conception of the sovereign human *over* the subject animal.

Being animal under the God of all the living, however, is somewhat different depending on one's status as pet or prey in the hands of a deity who might, like the lions, sometimes eat (meat) and sometimes refrain from eating (meat). While the human/animal divide might be said to be eradicated in the book of Daniel, the divine/animal hierarchy is in place in a way that might impel a continuance of the model of the sovereign master over his pets or prey. Although this text shores up sympathy for, and solidarity with, the animals under human sovereign rule (be they nonhuman or human) and undermines such rule by demonstrating the animality of all, it does not undermine the logic of such a hierarchy itself between sovereign and subject. Proper power should be located in the divine, and the living are mortal creatures in the hand of God, without distinction as to human or animal. The problem here is that the remaining hierarchy between a sovereign divine and the animality of all allows for a fantasy of a divine—or divinely driven—carnivorous machine that can kill and eat what is thus presented as its rightful prey. In this sense, the animal and the political become tied to the equality of all the living at the same time as animals remain connected to the edible, and the political retains at least the temptation of a carnivorous logic. The sovereign God may or may not, after all, be vegetarian.

4

BODIES OF THE BEAST

The book of Revelation is a significant text in the Western cultural canon that has been mapped onto political scenes, struggles, and situations, with its animal figures and zoo-powers as prominent examples of the religio-political. In this chapter, I focus on the figures of the Lamb and Beast in chapter 17. Revelation 17 could be seen as a key moment in the book—as well as in the Christian imagination. Here the victory of the victim over the colonial oppressor is heralded, when the Lamb is announced as Lord of lords, King of kings, and a conqueror of the Roman Empire, represented by the Beast and Whore. Revelation 17 might be read as a triumph of the weak animal against the tyrannical master.

As a specific animal figure, the Lamb could be said to represent a particularly liberating force against colonial structures and the domination of animal lives—human or nonhuman. I argue, however, that as Koosed and Seesengood (2014, 12–13) suggest in relation to the book of Daniel, the narrative of Rev 17 ultimately relies on the killability of animals in the destruction of Rome-as-Beast. Paradoxically, perhaps, for a text that holds up the weak Lamb as an emblem of early Christianity, the enemy is portrayed as *nonhuman* in order to represent the brutalized evil of Roman rule that must be defeated. Packaged into this imagery of the Beast is the body of the female-as-animal, a body that represents a threatening, ferocious, and wild other. The Lamb that triumphs plays into a logic of sovereignty that relies on the idea of the Beast that must be mastered; the Lamb triumphs by becoming the ultimate sovereign figure that must do violence to the wild animal other in order for a new political order to be imagined. Rather than focus on the Lamb as the key animal figure, I suggest a reading in which the imagery of the Beast is unpacked and critiqued, including the way the Whore as a body is folded into that of the Beast. These animal bodies have been frequently obscured by the immediate connotation of the Beast with political evil. I unpack this imagery in order to destabilize the logic whereby evil, and particularly political evil, is consigned to the imaginary space of the beastly. Such imagery problematically perpetuates associations between animality and brutality, associations that naturalize the idea that animals must be confined to safe human-controlled spaces (such as zoological parks, cages, or arenas under human control) or outright killed in justified acts of slaughter.

Animals at War

Thought to be written late in the first century CE and set in Asia Minor (modern-day Turkey), John's Revelation is a text in the Christian biblical archive that caused and still causes controversy with its competing animal figures. Nonetheless, or perhaps because of this, it is one of the most influential books of the Bible. Christopher Rowland (2001, xvii), for instance, suggests that the text of Revelation "has probably had more effect on Christian doctrine, art and literature than almost any other." Positioned at the end and edge of the Christian Bible, its style and symbolism have commanded much attention. As Cohn (1999, 41) articulates, this text has "proved extraordinarily adaptable and long-lived." Revelation has been reinterpreted "again and again to fit ever-changing circumstances" and has "continued to affect the perceptions of millions of both Christians and non-Christians right down to the present day" (Cohn 1999, 41). Moore (2014b, 197) calls Revelation "an animal book extraordinaire, a bizarre bestiary, more thickly populated with nonhuman animals than any other early Christian text." Like Daniel's animals, these too are distinctly political animals. But what is implied in the politics of the Lamb and Beast, where the one appears in the guise of the good and the other of evil? What are the implications of the way these animal characters figure in the political imaginary of Revelation and beyond?

In Rev 17, an angel takes the writer of this revelation, John, to see a scene in the wilderness in which a woman is "seated on many waters" but who also sits on a many-headed, many-horned Beast (17:1, 3). The woman is seen to be "drunk with the blood of the saints and the blood of the witnesses to Jesus" (17:6). John is amazed at this spectacle (17:6), but the angel swiftly explains "the mystery" of the Beast and woman (17:7). The Beast "was, and is not, and is about to ascend from the bottomless pit and go to destruction" (17:8). The angel explains the seven heads as seven mountains on which the woman is seated, and as seven kings, some who reigned, some who reign, and some who will reign (17:9–10). The ten horns also represent ten kings, united with the Beast (17:12–13). The text says they will make war on the Lamb, "and the Lamb will conquer them"; those with the Lamb "are called and chosen and faithful" (17:14). The waters on which "the whore is seated" (17:15) and that John has been shown are said to represent "peoples and multitudes and nations and languages" (17:15). The kings and Beast are eventually predicted to "hate the whore; they will make her desolate and naked; they will devour her flesh and burn her up with fire" (17:16). This is said to be God's purpose, agreeing to give over power to the Beast "until the words of God will be fulfilled" (17:17).

The Beast of Rev 17 is a key figure that has been used to symbolize numerous powers in the human political world.[1] In the historical context of the book of Revelation, however, it is commonly agreed that the Beast with its heads and horns refers to the Roman Empire and/or Roman emperors. The Beast of Rev 17, θηρίον, is a hyperbolic hybrid creature that picks up on the reference to a Beast in Rev 13:2, "like a leopard, its feet were like a bear's, and its mouth was like a lion's mouth," and likewise to the Beast of Rev 11:7 that comes up from the bottomless pit to make war, conquer, and kill witnesses to God. In 17:3, the Beast is described as "scarlet," "full of blasphemous names," with "seven heads and ten horns" (17:3), the heads representing kings "of whom five have fallen, one is living, and the other has not yet come" (17:10). A belligerent figure, with "power and authority" (17:13), it is warmongering, making war on the Lamb and those that are "called and chosen and faithful" (17:14). In some ways it is unclear whether the Beast described in 13:2 is the same as the scarlet Beast in Rev 17; they are explicitly connected by both being described as having seven heads and ten horns, so in this sense I treat them as one Beast. But there is also the second beast mentioned in 13:11 (that pays obeisance to the first), with two horns like a Lamb and speaking like a dragon, as well as the great red dragon, with seven heads and ten horns (12:3). Here I focus on the description of the Beast and Whore in battle with the Lamb in Rev 17 and relate it to the description of the Beast in 13:2, but essentially the whole array of beastly imagery participates in the logic of evil animal (Beast) against the good and divine animal (Lamb). The assemblage of beastly figures throughout Revelation could be seen as one hybrid multi-Beast:

---

1. For discussions of how the various figures and images of Revelation have been interpreted and appropriated, see, for instance, Koester 2001, Kovacs and Rowland 2004, and O'Hear and O'Hear 2015.

an enemy assemblage of wild animal imagery.[2] This multi-Beast plays the part of ferocious enemy to be defeated. The mythlike beast-assemblage conveys, as Leonard L. Thompson (1990, 185) puts it, "the Roman order as demonic." However, it is rather that the Roman order is portrayed as *beast-like*, as hyperbolically ferocious, threatening, carnivorous, violent, and powerful, whereas the Lamb is set up as its innocent, weak counterpart.

To denote the evil of Rome, Rome is likened to wild, carnivorous animals (leopard, bear, lion), to multiple horns and heads, making a negatively perceived political domination synonymous with the animal as monstrous beast. Craig R. Koester (2001, 29) notes that Revelation is not unique in using animal images to depict nations and political powers. Naturally, he mentions the book of Daniel and the vision of empires as animals (Dan 7:1–8), proposing that the author of Revelation amalgamates properties from Daniel's four beasts into the single seven-headed beast (Koester 2001, 29). Interpreters also customarily link the Beast who "was, and is not, and is about to ascend from the bottomless pit and go to destruction" (17:8) to the emperor Nero and his persecution of Christians (Koester 2001, 5)—a haunting figure in the political imagination of Revelation, possibly to return after surviving his fatal wounds (13:3, 12, 14).[3] Like with Daniel, the destruction of the Beast in Revelation can be read as a reassertion of the proper sovereign power, that is, of *divine* sovereignty. Steven J. Friesen (2005, 352) suggests that the anti-Roman rhetoric of Revelation is a means to bind communities together against imperial cults.[4] This was, he argues, a prominent part of Roman imperial society: "emperors were worshipped in their own temples, at temples of other gods, in theatres, in gymnasia, in stoas, in basilicas, in judicial settings, in private

---

2. This enemy assemblage draws on the beastly, hybrid-animal imagery of Daniel, particularly Dan 7–9.

3. George H. van Kooten (2007, 207) explains the "complex of beliefs surrounding the figure of Nero Redivivus, who was supposed by many not to have died in 68 [CE], but to have fled to the East, from whence he was expected to return." He suggests that this influence on Revelation has been understated and argues that many passages in Revelation bear "Neronian overtones," although most New Testament scholars opt for a date under Domitian (91–96 CE). One way of doing justice to these overtones in the light of this dating is to suppose that in the mind of the author of Revelation Nero was thought to return "in the guise of Domitian" (208).

4. Friesen argues this was a rhetorical ploy rather than a reflection of crisis and persecution relating to imperial cults in the author's own time. Imperial cults were a way of criticizing Roman imperialism more generally.

homes and elsewhere" (Friesen 2005, 363). Friesen (370) argues that the passages in Rev 17 in which Rome is portrayed as a beast-riding prostitute, committing fornication with kings and inhabitants of the earth, can be interpreted as emperor-worship or the worship of other deities than John's sovereign Lord. In this sense, the narrative can be read, like in the book of Daniel, as a critique of Derrida's (2009, 50) model of sovereignty as tied to an all-seeing, all-powerful godlike power, the "I can" imagined as a human sovereign power. The Beast, in Koester's (2001, 159) words, "is the great mimicker of God, for if God is the one who 'was and is and is to come' from heaven (4:8), the beast 'was and is not and is to ascend from the bottomless pit' (17:8)." As such, the figure of the Beast becomes a decidedly adverse metaphor for the human political order.

The Beast is thus associated with Roman human sovereignty that imitates divine sovereignty, while the Lamb is presented as the true divine sovereignty. Arguing that this text was part of a larger context of criticism against the Roman Empire, Peter S. Perry (2007, 476) too proposes that "divine sovereignty" is pitted against "Rome as a city of excess, luxury and conspicuous consumption" in this passage.[5] Thompson (1990, 174) calls the Beast a "superhuman" figure, revealing the way in which this figure represents the human political power modelled on the logic of "more than" that puts human power in the seat of ultimate sovereignty. As Perry (2007, 493) puts it, the problem the author of Revelation appears to present is that "the Roman Empire does not appropriately imitate divine rule." Matthias Reinhard Hoffmann (2005, 105) argues that the apparent synonymous sharing of the throne and worship between God and the Lamb in Rev 4 and 5 conveys the tight connection between sovereign divinity, Christ, and animality. Richard Bauckham (1993, 66) notes that the word *Lamb* referring to Christ occurs twenty-eight times. Seven of these refer to God and the Lamb together (5:13; 6:16; 7:10; 14:4; 21:22; 22:1, 3), emphasizing the way the Lamb stands both as a small, weak animal and as a sovereign divinity. The throne of God in heaven figures frequently as a Hebrew Bible motif, reappearing here as a "symbol of divine sovereignty" (Harrington 1969, 41). As Hoffmann (2005, 105) argues, Lamb and God are "on par." The aim is for the "kingdom of the world" to become "the kingdom of our Lord" (Rev 11:15) "for you have taken your great power and begun to

---

5. Perry specifically compares the author of Revelation to Dio of Prusa, showing a larger context of criticism against Rome existing across class and social status.

reign" (Rev 11:18). It is God who will be "King of the nations" (Rev 15:3), not the Beast and Whore.

The Lamb seemingly stands in stark contrast to the description of the wild Beast, like a leopard, with bear feet, and a lion-like mouth. Using the image of the Lamb is a way of grounding sympathy in an innocent counterpart to the Beast who, with the Whore, is linked with ferocity and prostitution. In opposition to the ferocious sovereign figures of the Beast and Whore, the imagery of the Lamb denotes innocence and sacrificial, saving powers. Rowland (1993, 75) emphasizes the significance of such a "weak creature" as an "agent of God's purposes." This suffering lamb figure is often linked to the Passover lamb from the Exodus narrative as a sacrificed and saving animal.[6]

The conflict described in Rev 17 has often been seen as a critique of Rome specifically as an imperial power that oppresses its human and non-human animal subjects. In this sense, the Lamb is a savior figure against imperial structures of domination. Wes Howard-Brook and Anthony Gwyther (1999, 225) discuss the claim in Revelation that the empire belongs to the followers of Jesus rather than Rome, suggesting that the text constructs a "mythic challenge to imperial power." They argue that Revelation redefines the idea of victory: "Is it the fruit of imperial conquest, or is it the faithful rejection of empire and embrace of the way of God? Revelation's answer is crystal clear: it is only by rejecting empire and by maintaining loyalty to God and the Lamb that victory is won" (230). As a fantasy of victory against the colonial other, the Lamb rises up triumphantly. In 17:14, the Beast and its kings "will make war on the Lamb," but "the Lamb will conquer them, for he is Lord of lords and King of kings" (17:14). This is presented as a theatrical staging of animal sovereignties at war, or indeed, as a spectacle. The emphasis on witnessing and spectacle in Revelation is commented on by Christopher A. Frilingos (2004, 6), who suggests that the monsters and martyrs of Revelation act as spectators in the text, with the Lamb as the most important spectator figure. But at the same time, in Rev 17 the Lamb is a *spectacle* at the center of Revelation (88). The invitation to *see* is also for the readers of this book as spectators. Following Frilingos, Seesengood (2006, 74) deems Revelation to be more like a spectacle than a vision. He argues that the "repeated pattern of combat scenes

---

6. In Exodus, followers of God are saved by the blood of the Passover lamb while the Egyptians are punished. See for instance Hoffmann 2005, 250 for more on the significance of the connection between Revelation and Exodus.

and exotic displays found in the Apocalypse may be deliberately evocative of the spectacles of the Roman arena" (75).[7]

I argue that the language of animality and sovereignty in Rev 17, drawing on the spectacle of the Roman arena, is paramount for constructing sympathy and antipathy for the opposing sides the Lamb and Beast represent. Seesengood (2006, 71) explains this dynamic of competition by emphasizing the use of words connected to νίκη, in verb form νικάω ("to conquer, prevail, be victorious"), which attests to the language of warfare but with an increasing association with the spectacles and violence of Greco-Roman sport. He writes that when νικάω is used in the New Testament, it generally refers to the victory of Jesus and the early Christians over pagan culture. In other words, early Christian discourse was making use of Greco-Roman culture to articulate its own claims about "a triumphant Jesus" (Seesengood 2006, 71). When this verb form is used in Revelation,[8] it tends to conform to this pattern, Seesengood suggests. He makes reference to the Lamb described as the "Lion of the tribe of Judah" that has *conquered* (Rev 5:5; Seesengood 2006, 71). The many-headed "great red dragon" that appears in 12:3 is conquered "by the blood of the Lamb" (12:11). The martyrs of the church who have "endured to the end" are the victorious ones over the Beast (Rev 15:2; Seesengood 2006, 71).[9] Just before the Lamb is described as "Lord of lords and King of kings," he is said precisely to *conquer* the kings and Beast who yield their power and authority (17:14). As Seesengood puts it, "Revelation casts the Lamb (and his super alter-ego, 'one like a Son of man'), the image of the all powerful God (*pantocrator*) in battle for the beleaguered Christians. They will, John assures us, conquer" (71).

In the battle staged between the Lamb and Beast, Revelation provides a textual theater that narrates spectacles for its ancient Christian audience and does so by drawing on available discourses in the Roman Empire (Frilingos 2004, 40). Frilingos suggests that such spectacles were a "particularly effective mode for the production of authoritative knowledge about other and self under the Roman Empire" (11). The idea of

---

7. For more specifically on martyrdom as spectacle, see also Potter 1993, Perkins 1995, and Shaw 1996.

8. As Seesengood testifies, Revelation contains nearly two-thirds of its use in the New Testament.

9. The rider on the white horse in Rev 6 also marches out "conquering and to conquer" (6:2).

a violent battle and sacrificial figures martyring themselves was part of such a discourse. Gilhus (2006) writes of the ways martyrs were turned into cultural performers in much early Christian discourse. These martyr figures conveyed how fighting and dying for God as "lambs" became both a proper and noble sacrifice and a triumph against Roman power (186).[10] Eusebius, for instance, suggests that John, the author of Revelation, had been persecuted and exiled to Patmos because of his testimony to the word of God—despite lack of evidence—so Revelation too becomes caught up in a discursive cultural performance of victimhood and victory (Knight 1999, 21).[11] There is in Rev 17, then, a spectacle of animals at war, where the Lamb denotes the victim of the Beast, that is, colonial Roman rule—but a victim that becomes victorious. What kind of animal victory against the master tyrant is this, however?

The Struggle for Sovereignty

Arguably, the Lamb is not a wholly different or opposing power to the Beast but is an increase of the powers of the Beast, presented as *more* sovereign: "Lord of lords and King of kings" (17:14). Derrida (2009, 290, emphasis original) argues that in discourses on sovereign power it "is not only an alternative between sovereignty and nonsovereignty but also a struggle *for* sovereignty, transfers and displacements or even divisions of sovereignty." The Lamb participates in Derrida's concept of sovereignty as a logic of competition: an I can of violence that is continuously played out as higher, a continuous *pouvoir*. "What counts is the *more*, the economy of the *more*, the economy of the surplus or the economy of the supplement, the smaller able to be more powerful or even larger than the largest" (259, emphasis original). This is, as David F. Krell (2013, 28, emphasis original) puts it, an order of knowledge that "operates as the hubris of the *more*, the

---

10. Gilhus (2006, 159) recounts how Ignatius, martyred in Rome early in the second century CE, wrote a letter in which he describes himself as God's sacrifice and as the bread of Christ, while Polycarp describes himself as a ram and burnt offering.

11. Eusebius, *Hist. eccl.* 3.18.1, cited by Knight 1999, 21. Knight discusses Eusebius's claims to first-century persecutions by the Romans but suggests these are difficult to verify and clearly caught up in a mixture of legend and history. Gilhus (2006, 188) cites the Martyrdom of Polycarp, the Martyrdom of Perpetua, and the anonymous second-century Christian apologia Letter to Diognetus in using such sacrificial discourse in the face of martyrdom and specifically also in being thrown to animals in Roman arenas.

sovereign *plus que* that is never satisfied." The Lamb thus plays into what Derrida (2009, 257) describes as "essential and proper to sovereignty," "not grandeur or height" "but excess, hyperbole, and excess insatiable for the passing of every determinable limit: higher than height, grander than grandeur."

The Lamb as a weak figure of domestic animality and sacrificial victim in Rev 17 is proven capable of fighting back—and winning. Accordingly, the Lamb participates in the power games of the Roman order, in "a mimicry," adopting the actions of the enemy (Seesengood 2006, 78). Wilfrid J. Harrington (1969, 37) emphasizes the lamb as a "striking antithesis" to the Beast. However, in fact, the Lamb and the Beast are *like* one another in striking ways. Like the Beast, the Lamb is a sovereign force. It is described in analogous ways to the Beast, marking them side by side as oppositional forces but that, significantly, mirror each other. In his chapter on Revelation in *Empire and Apocalypse: Postcolonialism and the New Testament*, Moore (2006) argues that while Revelation appears in the guise of an antiimperialistic text, it to a great extent reinscribes rather than resists Roman imperial ideology. Drawing on Homi K. Bhabha, he teases out the ambivalence between the idea of colonial power and subject. With its "language of war, conquest, and empire," Revelation is undercut by "covert compliance and attraction" (Moore 2006, 114). It is parasitic on the structures of imperial ideology. This is perhaps particularly the case with the notion of sovereignty and the Lamb as the ultimate sovereign.

In the first volume of *The Beast and the Sovereign*, Derrida (2009) explores the idea of "sovereignty" as a dominant conceptualization of the human in relation to the subjection of those it deems animal. Sovereignty, Derrida writes, "has often been represented in the formless form of animal monstrosity" (25). Sovereignty becomes linked to a godlike power in being placed above the law, but this is also construed as Beast-like in the potential power of the sovereign outside-the-law to enact any imaginable violence (17). As I touch upon in chapter 3, sovereignty has, Derrida argues, been translated into a "reason of the strongest," that is, a *reasoning* or logic in which what is construed as the exclusive *powers* of the human—such as precisely reason—constitute a sovereign strength in the face of those that are deemed animal. On the one hand, then, the human as a political animal is "superior, in his very sovereignty, to the beast that he masters, enslaves, dominates, domesticates, or kills, so that his sovereignty consists in raising himself above the animal and appropriating it, having its life at his disposal" (26). On the other hand, conceptions of the human political realm are frequently characterized *as* animal or beastlike (26). Both could be seen in Revelation, where the human political realm is imagined as beastlike, and where the Lamb raises itself above the Beast that he masters when it becomes a political animal that triumphs in becoming the most sovereign force.

Whether one thinks violent struggle against colonial powers is necessary or not, my point is to signal what is problematic about operating with the image of the Beast as political evil. I do so not only because of the ambiguities that might be involved in determining the enemy or because the figure of the enemy so easily becomes linked to an imagined, simplified other that stands in contrast to a properly human/e subject, but also, more specifically, because it involves a facile collapse of violence and brutality with animality, whereby animals become the nonhuman that must be kept at bay, subjugated, or killed to ensure peace. In colonial literature, the colonized other quite often becomes animalized as either a violent and uncivilized subject that must be tamed, or as a domestic creature that ought to be governed properly by the colonial master. Similarly, in cases of torture, the victim of torture is dehumanized as part of the techniques of subjugation. Darius Rejali (2007, 290), for instance, recounts practices of torture that force the victim to adopt animal positions, such as the "Lizard," where victims are forced to crawl and twist on the ground for long distances.[12] In Revelation, the animal Lamb as the victim triumphs over the colonial master, but a logic remains whereby the enemy other—in the form of the Beast—must be destroyed. In fact, the idea of the enemy as animal is reinforced by references to eating "the flesh of kings, the flesh of captains, the flesh of the mighty, the flesh of horses and their riders—flesh of all, both free and slave, both small and great" in Rev 19:18. The fate of the Beast is to be captured and "thrown alive into the lake of fire that burns with sulfur" (19:20). Animals are still connected, then, with the brutal, with what must be killed for a new political order to be imagined.

Rather than merely posit that the Lamb participates in the logic of sovereignty by mimicking the Beast, however, I suggest it is necessary to critically examine the imagery of the Beast more closely. Resisting the tendency to jump to discussions of who or what the Beast *represents* is as much about seriously attending to animality as it is about refusing to

---

12. Rejali recounts multiple torture methods related to particular animals such as duck, rabbit, dog, and frog.

accept the beastly imagery at face value. Revelation stands in many ways loosely within the fable tradition, with its fantastic animal metaphors (Moore 2014b, 197). Rather than simply accept the idea of the Beast as a fantastical and fabulous image of the Roman Empire, or indeed, as a parody of it, the Beast could be understood in relation to the Roman arena to uncover the ways in which the imagery is assembled from the more literal (and real) albeit long-expired lives of animals in the Roman Empire.

Animals in the Roman Arena

To critically examine the imagery of the Beast, I suggest a closer look at the Roman arena and the way the imagery of the Beast could be seen as an assemblage of animals in the imperial spectacles of Rome. Seesengood (2006, 75) posits that there is no reason to presume that the author of Revelation would be unable or unwilling to write about the arena. "Arena combat was common in Ephesus, Pergamum, Sardis, and the other cities of eastern Asia Minor" (75). The popularity of arena sports has been demonstrated by the variety of excavated mosaics depicting scenes of combat discovered in Antioch, a city key to the emergence of Christianity in the first century (75). In *Animals, Gods and Humans*, Gilhus (2006) explains two particularly pertinent performances of Roman power involving animals, namely, *venationes* and *damnio ad bestias*. The former were essentially hunting spectacles that took place in arenas, often involving large numbers of animals being killed. The *venationes* were a form of mass entertainment in antiquity (31).[13] In contrast to animal sacrifice which was an age-old institution, the arena was relatively new, and its popularity increased with the growth of the empire (31).[14] Constructing stone amphitheaters in the first century CE made it easier to control animals and offered more room for spectators. Such spectacles were a version of hunting, but in controlled spaces and dependent on an imperialistic state system that made it possible to catch, keep, and deliver the animals to Rome or other areas in

---

13. The first such known hunting spectacle, involving lions and panthers, was in 186 BCE organized by Marcus Fulvius Nobilior (Gilhus 2006, 31, citing Livy, *Hist. Rom.* 39.5.7–10; 39.22.2). For more on this, see Balsdon 1969 and Coleman 1990. For animals in Rome more generally, see particularly Toynbee 1996.

14. Gilhus (2006, 32) describes how such spectacles developed into large-scale massacres under the Roman Empire, as is described by Pliny in his *Hist. nat.* 8.20.53; 8.24.64.

the Empire (32). Gilhus recounts how this use of wild animals in relation to spectacles of power could be seen in Mesopotamia and Egypt, where conquering lions was a royal sport and where aristocratic elites hunted big game. A zoo with exotic animals, for example, had been proof of Pharaoh's claim to rule the ordered world (32). In the Roman arenas, animals were imported and indigenous, carnivorous, wild and domestic; they had to be captured, put in menageries, and kept in cages in lower levels of the Colosseum and special areas outside the city (32). For the fights, animals were brought into arenas in Rome: "bulls were set against panthers, rhinoceroses against bears and lions against tigers, as well as all types of animal against humans" (33).

The *venationes* can be seen as a display of power through the use of animals to showcase and enjoy a "spectacular event" (Lindstrøm 2010, 313). As Gilhus (2006, 33) explains: "the hunt had become a spectacular show over which the emperor presided as its patron and all classes of people participated as spectators." In a sense, these were hunts that had been democratized, not just for those in power but now also for a mass audience. Here, numerous animals were killed. While domesticated animals were already under human control through agriculture, such entertainment including wild animals showed them too as under human domination (34). "The *venationes*, as well as the gladiator contests, contributed to demonstrating the authority of the emperor as well as the extent of the empire and the wealth of those who paid for the shows" (34). Roland Auguet (1994, 112–13) recounts the killing of a lion in Rome that was considered by Romans a symbol of their total power over the universe.[15] Such accounts testify to the symbolically important and real exercise of power of human controlling animals and Rome controlling the world through the lives (and deaths) of animals (Gilhus 2006, 34). The diversity of animals in the Roman arenas showed off the geographical expansion of Rome's power and influence (34). Torill Christine Lindstrøm (2010, 312) gives examples of *venationes* with hundreds, sometimes thousands, of animals killed. As she puts it, the "Romans' use, or misuse, of animal lives in extravagant carnage is probably unsurpassed in human history" (312). Lindstrøm goes on to argue that two messages were put forward to spectators: "a warning not to oppose the state, and a reassurance of the state's strength and protective powers" (318).

---

15. Gilhus (2006, 30) also describes how some emperors kept lions as pets, such as Elagabalus and Caracella, who thought of them as status symbols.

Probably from the time of Augustus (63 BCE to 14 CE), the *venationes* also included the execution of criminals and gladiator fights (*munera*) (Gilhus 2006, 32). Gilhus explains the *damnatio ad bestias* as the sentencing of humans to beasts as punishment for severe crimes (33).[16] These killings were staged in amphitheaters of the great cities at the celebration of feasts and for general entertainment of spectators: "Humans being killed by animals, together with arena performances, were part of the mass entertainment of antiquity, viewed by virtually everyone, even if not everyone appreciated it" (183).[17] Parading the wildness and ferocity of the animals thus demonstrated the ferocity and power of Roman rule but also portrayed the animals as puppets, dying for the entertainment and law of human rulers and citizens. The Beast of Rev 17 who is leopard, bear, and lion could be read as an amalgamation of such animals used for Roman spectacles, representing quite literally the *beastly* powers of Rome. These animals might well be ferocious, but they are also exploited, captured animals deprived of their habitats and might be seen as other than merely brute beasts; or, indeed, these animals might be seeing, responsive creatures rather than merely seen as this or that.[18] The imagery of the Beast as political evil masks the real animal lives that are assembled to form this imagery—animals that are capable of suffering and of responding. The conflict and alternative vision of power embodied by the Lamb still relies on the killability of the animal as beast. The killable animal has shifted from the early Christians as martyrs—as lambs—to Rome-as-killable-animal-beast. A logic of sovereignty is upheld whereby animals remain a political category that signifies the other to be mastered and destroyed, as if the Lamb has merely swapped places with the Beast. Is it the case, then, that the author of Revelation is not critiquing violent sovereign power but

---

16. The *damnatio ad bestias* was introduced for deserters in the middle of the second century BCE by Scriptio the Younger and took on increasing popularity as a form of punishment. See Robinson 1994.

17. Gilhus (2006, 183) cites Cicero's distaste for such spectacles in *Epis. Fam.* 7.1.3.

18. Lindstrøm (2010, 319) recounts an exception to the enjoyment of cruelty and violence to the arena animals in 55 BCE, when twenty elephants fought against men with javelins. The suffering of the elephants aroused pity among the spectators, who rose to their feet, weeping and cursing Pompey. She argues that identification between the spectators and the elephants could have taken place as the elephants tried to escape and the spectators felt afraid and vulnerable—sharing the vulnerability of the animals. She concedes this could be simply the death anxiety of the spectators rather than genuine compassion with the animals.

is rather caught up in a discourse that aims to identify "the proper colonizer," that is, the Lamb (Seesengood 2006, 78)? "Might John be 'staging' his own arena event to articulate visually his own propaganda of kingdom and domination?" (79). In that case, God, as Tina Pippin (1999, xi) articulates it, "is as much a power of domination as any other power."

Furthermore, examining the imagery of the Beast necessarily involves making sense of the way the imagery of the Beast is assembled with the Whore as a key part of its animal bodies. I suggest that the idea of the female here is caught up in the imagined animality—or rather, the beastliness—of the enemy other. To dominate and destroy the enemy sovereign, then, the enemy is imagined as a Beast, where the truly beastly is a vision of the female-and-animal as the wild, brutal, and evil other that must be killed and eaten. As I unpack the imagery of the Beast with regard to the animals of the Roman arena, it is also necessary to unpack the "beastly" imagery in regard to the Whore of Babylon.

Abject Womanimality

It is not of course insignificant that the female body of the Whore is attached to the hybrid Beast. Like the Beast, the Whore too is a sovereign power in opposition to the Lamb, equally if not more bellicose; simultaneously described as a "whore" (17:1), "woman" (17:3), and "queen" (18:7), she rides the Beast, rules "over the kings of the earth" (17:18), and manages to do all this while being drunk on the "blood of the saints and the blood of the witnesses to Jesus" (17:6). This "great whore" (17:1) "with whom the kings of the earth have committed fornication, and with the wine of whose fornication the inhabitants of the earth have become drunk" (17:2) is "clothed in purple and scarlet, and adorned with gold and jewels and pearls, holding in her hand a golden cup full of abominations and the impurities of her fornication" (17:4). The Whore of Babylon is a significant part of the image of Rome in Rev 17. In the last verse of the chapter, she is described as ruling "over the kings of the earth" (17:18); in 18:7, the word *queen* is used of her. She is the rider of the Beast, and so when the Lamb triumphs it is by laying her bare through turning the Beast against her, making her desolate, eaten, and burnt (17:16).

Along with the Beast, the Whore of Babylon symbolizes Roman power as well as the ancient symbol of an enemy superpower in the Hebrew Bible, Babylon. She is thus a layered and hyperbolic symbolic figure of tyrannical political power. As Koester (2001, 31) points out, seated on seven hills, connecting her to the seven hills of Rome, the Whore could be seen as a representation of Rome as the destroyer of the Second Temple and Babylon as the destroyer of the First Temple. She can be understood as the goddess Roma, *dea Roma*, who, as David E. Aune (1998, 920) attests, is depicted on a Vespasian sestertius minted in the Roman province of Asia in 71 CE. On this coin, the goddess Roma is clothed in military dress and seated on Rome's seven hills with the river god Tiber reclining at the right and the she-wolf with Romulus and Remus at the lower left (920). Aune suggests that the author of Revelation might have utilized this popular image as a way of framing his attack on Rome (920–22). The fact that Roma is holding a parazonium—a small sword—on the coin might be seen as a reminder of Roman military might, which is amplified in the violent image of Rome in Rev 17 (927). Koester (2001, 155) emphasizes the caricature at work in this figure as an exaggerated political fable with a clear moral: this figure of evil will fall to destruction, but meanwhile, followers of the Lamb must avoid affiliating with the Roman powers associated with her (31).

In order for Roman authority to be polemically portrayed as an arch-enemy, it is thus represented as an amalgamation of wild animals (the Beast) and a specifically female radical evil, conveyed, to use Kristeva's (1982) concept in *Powers of Horror: An Essay on Abjection*, as *abject*. Kristeva's concept of the abject is primarily characterized by revulsion at food, corpses, and female sexual power, all qualities embodied by the figure of the Whore. Further, abjection is tied to ambivalence, particularly to the ambivalence of female sexuality as both a threat to male potency and a desirous object. As a sovereign, the Lamb that battles for power could be read as fantasy for a virile sovereignty, as I discussed earlier with reference to Moore as mimicry of and desire for imperial power. Kristeva (1982, 4) suggests that what causes abjection is "what disturbs identity, system, order. What does not respect borders, positions, rules. The in-between, the ambiguous, the composite." Abjection is above all ambiguity, Kristeva argues, and this ambiguity of abjection is tied to perpetual danger and risk (9). Abjection is a "composite of judgement and affect, of condemnation and yearning, of signs and drives" (10). Further, a certain logic of prohibition grounds the abject (64).

The imagery of the great Whore draws on many texts of the Hebrew Bible that liken prostitutes to cities, such as Tyre in Ezek 27:3 and Isa 23:17, and Nineveh (capital of Assyria) in Nah 3:4 and 2 Kgs 16:5–16 (Koester 2001, 159). By characterizing the figure of the Whore of Babylon as Rome, but also such cities as Tyre, Nineveh, and Babylon, Koester (159) suggests, she is a figure for human evil power more generally. However, Koester fails to note the specifically *female* association with evil. Elisabeth Schüssler Fiorenza (1991, 96) argues that because Revelation draws on the prophetic language of the Hebrew Bible, with its traditions of gendered imagery and language, the Whore of Babylon should not be thought of as an actual woman. She suggests that just as the Lamb should not be thought of as an animal, the Whore's symbolism for "human culture and political institutions" does "not tell us anything about the author's understanding of actual women" (96). This may well be the case, but that does not mean that her specifically female characterizations and context can be set aside as irrelevant or arbitrary.[19] Her femininity is integral to the construction of political evil that she denotes, just as the more literal animality of the figuration of political evil is and needs to be attended to more closely, as I suggest above.

The debates in animal studies over the animal as an other to the human of course mirror Simone de Beauvoir's (2010) famous characterization of woman as the other to man. Just as she commented on Aristotle's understanding of women as *lacking* certain qualities reserved for man and the Genesis story where Eve is created from Adam's rib (de Beauvoir 2010, 5–6), the animal debate has similarly located such discursive sources as detrimental for animals. The Whore is such an other to the male figure of the Lamb, and thus Rome as evil is associated with a particular kind of woman, the prostitute, as well as the carnivorous brutal animal. Political evil becomes, in other words, associated with a sexualized woman and the beastly animal in opposition to the Lamb's divine sovereignty. Pippin (1999, x) argues that we must refocus readings of Revelation on the gender-specific violence in this text and that scholarly readings have too easily eschewed such images of violence. I contend that such a refocusing needs to include the way violence is justified implicitly by the idea of the Whore as female and beast. The Whore of Babylon is certainly one such image of violence *of* a woman and violence *toward* a woman, with her drinking of human blood (17:6) and then the later devouring of her own naked flesh (17:16). In the same way that the Beast of Rev 17 has been mainly connected to Roman emperors rather than seen in the light of animals suffering in the Roman

---

19. Caroline Vander Stichele (2009, 106–7) makes this point, arguing that the Whore cannot be taken purely as a metaphor.

arenas, the Whore is also all too easily eschewed as a symbolic emblem of Rome, of political corruption, and indeed evil more generally.[20]

In *The Woman Babylon and the Marks of Empire*, Shanell T. Smith (2014, 130, emphasis added) argues for the "simultaneous duality" of the Whore's characterization as "a brothel slave woman *and* an empress/imperial city." The Whore is on both sides of the colonial divide as both colonizer and colonized (127). Smith argues that the reinscription of empire that the author of Revelation participates in does not preclude the possibility of solidarity for the oppressed in this text (131). However, from a womanist point of view, in which the "well-being of *all* peoples" is paramount, the destruction of the *woman*—and we might add *animal*—Babylon must be countered (131, emphasis original). The text may indeed be a minority report, but it is a *"masculinist* minority report" (15, emphasis original). "When one considers the devastating and horrid manner in which the woman Babylon is rejected and ultimately destroyed, the masculinist logic that pervades John's supposedly anti-imperial agenda becomes readily apparent" (150). I would add here that a particular understanding of the woman as animal is folded into this masculinist vision of the enemy other as a particular womanimal, whose flesh is "being ripped from her body to be consumed as if she had a sign on her that said, 'This is my body. Take. Eat all of it'" (Smith 2014, 132). As an *edible* embodiment of evil, she is flesh that stands outside ethical consideration. As Smith herself states, she becomes "just the flesh upon which her former clients feed" (152), without making the connection between the gendered description of the Roman Empire and the animalized logic of this feeding scene.

John W. Marshall (2009, 32) draws attention to the specifically sexualized violence in the scene with the Whore of Babylon of Rev 17, in that she is a distinctly *female* figure, made naked and also, as he puts it, cannibalistically eaten (29). As such, she is both woman and animal. Indeed, the woman Babylon could be said to be continuous with the Beast as a joint body, and not only because they both represent imperial Rome; the Whore's appetite for human blood likens her to a predatory beast. She is the tempting image of female sexuality to be voyeuristically viewed as a specifically female sexual seduction but ultimately a subject of destruction or annexation as Rome. The Whore of Babylon is to be burned like

---

20. There are many connections made between gender studies and animal studies. See, for instance, Donovan 1990, and more recently Gruen and Weil 2012, as well as Donovan and Adams 2007.

the remains of a sacrificial animal carcass and "devoured" or consumed (17:16). Stripped of the marks of her seductive power, her flesh will be made naked, like an animal or a raped woman. Roman power is associated with female powers: sexually seductive, gloriously "clothed in purple and scarlet, and adorned with gold and jewels and pearls" (17:4). The great wonder proclaimed at the first sight of the Whore in 17:6 could be read as curious allure or as abhorrence, with the wondering or marveling at her signaling amazement or admiration.[21] But she is also construed as repellent force and bestial unrestrained power, breaking taboos relating to blood as if she/Rome were a carnivorous animal. Returning to Kristeva and her writing on abjection, it is pertinent that the abject is associated with the feminine. This association "does not succeed in defining itself as *other* but threatens one's *own and clean self*, which is the underpinning of any organization constituted by exclusions and hierarchies" (Kristeva 1982, 65, emphasis original). To represent Rome as evil, then, the strategy is seemingly to depict it as that which can be seen as abject, namely, a female prostitute and wild animal(s), which thus "becomes synonymous with a radical evil that is to be suppressed" (70).

Related to a mother of whores and to blood in 17:5–6, the Whore of Babylon becomes a prime image of an abject woman-animal. She is explicitly associated with what is unclean in 17:4 over her abominations and fornication. As Jennifer A. Glancy and Moore (2011, 566) state, "the monstrous spectacle of a sexualized woman utterly out of control serves as a trope for imperial autocracy—absolute power exercised to excess, entirely without restraint." But this trope is crucially dressed up in the apparel of animality. Like the blood the Whore drinks, blood here connotes also animal blood, in animal sacrifices and prohibitions against drinking blood. The Whore is thus associated with improper, boundless sexuality, the unclean, taboo, *and* animal carnivorousness, but remains a vital

---

21. Beale (1999, 862–63) too suggests that admiration could be considered a plausible element to the seer's reaction, although he explains that shock, fear, and confusion are more likely. He argues that even if the author of the vision temporarily admires what he sees, the visions of the Whore on the beast are "too horrific" to continue such admiration. He admits in the end (having given several reasons to the contrary) that despite these considerations, they "do not nullify the likelihood that John was also attracted in some way to the Babylonian woman." He suggests a good translation might be "awestruck," which would contain the ambiguity of abjection and admiration.

and powerful figure of such abjection. A "Terrible Mother" figure (Collins 2009), the Whore is allied to the female prostitute as faithlessness or impurity as well as the animal wildness and carnivorousness of her beast-like power. As a "mother" of whores *and* prostitute, she is portrayed as Kristeva's (1982, 77) "excessive matrilineality" in relation to male power—that is, an organization of power traced and inherited from the mother, and thus in competition with a male sovereignty. Rome thus becomes the excessive woman-animal to the Lamb's male sovereignty. The woman is *too* potentially (and potently) generative, uncontrollably so, and in domination over the male kings she seduces (Kristeva 1982, 77). The Whore is made an abject sign of the improper woman situated in the wilderness (17:3) as if she was an untamed (and perhaps untamable) beast. In this sense, the Whore becomes inextricably bound up with the wild animals of Revelation's Beast as Rome, and Roman society becomes metonymic with unbounded promiscuity and wild animality.

The Whore of Babylon's ambiguity, and therefore abjection, is in part related to her particularly female sexual powers. With the description of her luxury, she is also an alluring figure, seductive and tantalizing. As the prohibited other, the Whore is the power the Lamb desires to usurp and the power it is repelled by as unclean. Perhaps what she represents here is not only the sheer brute force of Roman power embodied in the Beast she rides, but also the temptation to and of power: the seduction of sovereignty as an imagined space of unrestrained potency projected onto the female body in the wild, as if a free, untamed, unrestrained animal. The Whore of Babylon thus presents a dangerous boundary between the desired power of Rome and the rejected and despised Roman power: what must be killed and destroyed as too beastly and what is *desired* in consumption as satisfaction of desire. She is a dangerous boundary between desire and threat embodied in "the paradox of an enthroned prostitute" (Glancy and Moore 2011, 565).[22]

Food, Kristeva (1982, 75) writes, "becomes abject only if it is a border between two distinct entities or territories. A boundary between nature and culture, between the human and the non-human." Kristeva discusses the way in which corpses too are a typical example of abjection. The Whore is imagined as both food and a corpse in the description of her fate (17:16).

---

22. Glancy and Moore (2011, 565) suggest she can be understood in comparison to the Roman empress Messalina, *meretrix augusta*, whom Juvenal labels a "whore-empress."

For Kristeva, as Lipschitz (2012, 556) explains, "nothing is more abject, and hence more dangerous to the autonomous self, than the raw literalness and materiality of the corpse," which is both seen as part of the finite mortal creature and as other to its proper living body. "It is this abject return of the dead animal body and the embodied threat of the 'becoming-corpse' of the subject" that the signs of a dead animal evoke in relation to the human form (556). Corpses and food are related in the animal body when the animal goes from life to flesh to be eaten. The Whore's abjection is conveyed as an uncontrollable threatening female power which must be destroyed, but as a destruction that is legitimized as the Whore's body is made nonhuman animal flesh, eaten and burnt like the carcass of a beast. As a woman-animal, her status as food is ambiguous and haunting, on the boundaries between what is edible and what is not, what is clean and unclean, desirable and disgusting. The burning of the flesh is also significant in resembling something like a sacrificial ritual where the animal is turned from a living creature to become sacrificed flesh and edible meat.[23]

Caroline Vander Stichele (2009, 114–15) argues that the Whore of Babylon represents an other in colonial terms, "viewed as alien territory to be conquered and eventually destroyed." She proposes that this rhetoric is founded in the female body of the Whore, thus presuming "an analogy between military and sexual invasion, the colonizer presented as male, the colonized as female" (114–15). The Whore's body, as Rome, is thus what is desired to be conquered, to be possessed like a rape in a tension between desire and aversion toward the woman-animal other and the power of Rome. However, while the abject is conceived of outside or apart from the "I," Kristeva (1982, 2) argues that "from its place of banishment, the abject

---

23. Gilhus (2006, 17) writes about the way sacrificial rites involved a religious elevation before being reduced to objects of consumption as well as prediction. The sacrifice thus "transformed" parts of the bodies of animals to food for the gods, food for humans, and "texts" to be read as their intestines were used to read the future. See also Gilhus 2006, 114–38 and Jameson 1988. Rather than refer to sacrifice this might well, as Koester (2001, 161) points out, refer to Nero, as under Nero the city set on seven hills was devastated by fire once before as described in Tacitus's *Ann.* 15.38. At the same time, the burning of naked flesh that is not only killed but also eaten strongly suggests the mixture of sacrifice as an offering of the body and as flesh to be eaten. As such, the images of the destruction of a city by fire and the sacrifice of a female body to be eaten come together to portray the magnitude of the destruction, and thus the power of the city/woman, as well as the power *over* this woman symbolized in laying her bare and eating her body.

does not cease challenging its master." Stichele (2009, 118) notes the stereo-type of the woman out of control, demanding mastery, reinforced by the image of the Whore as drunk (17:6), associated with the wine and drunk-enness of the kings and inhabitants of the earth seduced by her (17:2).[24] Jean K. Kim (1999, 72) connects the Whore to the references to whores in Jeremiah, particularly Jer 3, as a metaphor for the relationship between the faithless people of Israel and the Lord. Kim points out that Jeremiah uses animal sexual imagery that could be compared to the lustful woman in Rev 17, with the "restive young camel interlacing her tracks" (Jer 2:23), the "wild ass at home in the wilderness" who is also licentious (Jer 2:24), and the "lusty stallions" (Jer 5:8). She argues that both "female imagery and animal imagery are used here to convey disgusting behaviors" (72), but the implication is that women are accountable for this behavior, while animals are not. But there is more going on here than a simple distinction of accountability. The abject confronts us "with those fragile states where man strays on the territories of *animal*" (Kristeva 1982, 12, emphasis origi-nal). Just as the question is asked in Jeremiah about the "wild ass"—"Who can restrain her lust?" (Jer 2:24)—the connection made between these ani-mals and the woman of Rev 17 as Rome is perhaps rather one of similar subjection to sovereign power as male, virile, and carnivorous. The desire and wildness of such a woman-animal is thus an otherness that potentially escapes suppression and that poses a challenge, in that she also evokes the fragile state of male sovereign power.

The link between female prostitution and animality is interwoven also in the figure of the *dea Roma*. As already mentioned, the image on the coin in which the goddess of Rome is depicted also shows the well-known Roman legend of the infants Romulus and Remus being nursed by a she-wolf. Aune (1998, 925) explains that the Latin term *lupa*, she-wolf, had the connotation of prostitute. Revelation's figure of the Whore could thus be toying with Roma's proximity to the she-wolf as a prostitute-cum-animal. Further, her appearance in Revelation, colorfully clad and laden with jew-elry, draws on stereotypical descriptions of prostitutes in ancient literature (925). Glancy and Moore (2011, 552) propose that readings of Revelation have been too "bookish" in their dealings with the Whore of Babylon, thus failing to take account of the Whore *as a whore*. Just as the image of the

---

24. Both Robert Knapp (2013, 248) and Paul Chrystal (2013, 160) note the fre-quent association in the Roman Empire between barmaids and prostitutes.

Beast masks the colonized animals of the Roman arena that are depicted as merely a violent synonym with Rome, the image of the Whore could be seen to mask the suffering of prostitutes in Roman society. Seen simply as beastly, she is intended to evoke antipathy, where the body of the Whore is unquestionably evil and repellent. Like with the image of the Beast, I suggest it is necessary to question and unpack this image of evil by refusing to simply accept it at face value. Instead, an attention to the bodies of the Beast as colonized animals in the Roman arenas and the Whore's relation to prostitutes can destabilize the facile connection between the Beast, brutality, and female sexuality that covers up precarious bodies that suffer by being demonized as nonhuman.

Glancy and Moore (2011) focus on the way in which the Whore is akin to a brothel or street prostitute rather than a courtesan. They argue that the references to πορνεία "would have conjured up first and foremost in the minds of the urban Christians addressed in Revelation a certain category of flesh-and-blood person" rather than a figure of high class literature and art in the form of a courtesan (557). Because prostitution was not illegal nor seen to be breaking moral laws, as it was not considered adultery, prostitutes in the Roman Empire were generally left alone, unprotected (Knapp 2013, 239). In his *Ancient Women in Rome*, Paul Chrystal (2013, 160) discusses the ways in which images of the phallus were popular throughout Rome, emphasizing the dominance of male virility in the social order. Chrystal relates how female prostitutes and slaves were perceived as objects for men who desired to satisfy their sexual appetite or to "demonstrate their virility and prowess over women: the prostitute allowed the client to assert his manhood and virility through serial penetration" (160). In Roman literature, prostitutes are predominantly represented as marginalized, second-class citizens, vulnerable to male desire and the real and symbolic powers of the phallus (164). As Robert Knapp (2013, 261) testifies in his book *Invisible Romans*, with limited protection for prostitutes and a frequent conflation of prostitutes with slaves, these women were considered "fair game" when it came to social and physical abuse. While prostitution was a source of income and was recognized by the law in being a taxable trade (Pomeroy 1975, 201), it frequently fell to the vulnerable as a form of survival. Sarah B. Pomeroy, for instance, notes that baby girls and daughters were sometimes sold into prostitution by their parents (192), and it can be assumed that dire poverty led many women into prostitution, a status lower even than slaves, whose welfare was at least maintained according to their value in a household (202). It goes without saying that this was frequently a dangerous life, most often located at the bottom of the social order.

As Smith (2014, 127) remarks, markings on the body such as tattoos and branding were commonplace in antiquity; in the case of the woman in Rev 17 the inscription on her forehead is a "mark of ownership" that is linked to the profession of prostitution (127, 136). Smith (138) discusses the way such tattooing and branding was a sign of degradation and usually inflicted as punishment on the foreheads of slaves. Characterizing the Whore of Babylon as a brothel slave, then, "intermingles issues of gender, ownership, profession, and the negative social implications in Roman culture" (139). Bringing race, ethnicity, and class to bear on the description of the Whore, she reads the woman Babylon's identity as a brothel slave in the light of African American history. While ancient slavery is not commonly presented as racialized (128), the reference to slaves and human lives in Rev 18:11–13 functions for African American readers as a "mirror" into their own history (Martin 2005, 83). But the gender and slavery issues here are also arguably caught up in the distinct animalization of the Whore as a nonhuman entity, owned like the animals of the arena the Beast represents, and therefore not a worthy candidate for any solidarity the author of Revelation may or may not have for the oppressed. The Beast, for Smith (2014, 143), can be seen as the pimp of the Whore and her client. While the Whore can be seen as a woman, a slave, and a prostitute—a "victim" (148)—deserving sympathy, the Beast remains unquestionably the embodiment of evil.[25] This is not to imply that Smith's discussion of the pain and trauma of American slavery is the *same* as the plight of animals as killable objects set apart from "humans" or human-favored pets. Rather, it is to expose the logic whereby an African-American slave becomes seen as *nonhuman* through pernicious processes of dehumanization and demonized as a disposable form of life (166). The "animal" thus provides a space in which the slave can occupy and, like the Whore, be disposed. Holding on to an unquestioned depiction of the enemy other as

---

25. While Smith (2014) does not discuss the ambivalence in the imagery of the beast, she is attentive to the ambivalence of the Whore and does not cast her exclusively as a victim. She also examines the way the woman Babylon is on the side of imperial power and how this might mirror the complicity and complexity of the politics of the text as well as the politics of readerly engagement in the context of global capitalism (Smith 2014, 167). As she puts it, she employs a hermeneutics of "ambivei-lence" to hold these tensions together (171).

"beast" is a way of refusing the ambivalence that is granted to the Whore as a representation of evil.

Lindstrøm (2010) draws a connection between the animals of the arena and prostitution explicitly when she explores the way aggression and sexual arousal could be seen as linked in the spectacle of the staged hunts of the arenas. She raises the point about the "*venationes* spectactors' lustful experience of agitation" (Lindstrøm 2010, 315) and the fact that some spectators engaged in sexual intercourse with prostitutes who waited outside the arena (Bruch 2004, 4). Some animals, and some people, it seems, could be "*used* as articles of consumption" (Lindstrøm 2010, 317, emphasis original); the animals of the arena and prostitutes both fall into such a category.

In Rev 17 the Whore of Babylon as a symbol of Rome taps into this imagery of prostitution, and, I argue, is crucially reinforced by the animalization of the Whore to exploit the most efficacious mode of conjuring up antipathy. Closely affiliated with the Beast, she too is deemed beastly. Her blood-drinking denotes a predatory ferocity; as if an animal carcass, she is to be burned (17:16), or perhaps the burning is a form of cooking preparation before she is devoured, as if her body has become meat (17:16). Stripped of the marks of her personhood, her clothes and jewelry, her flesh will be made naked, as if an animal. These materials are, after all, proper to humans. Accepting the Whore as a repellent woman tied to the beastly obscures the way political evil is inscribed on the bodies of vulnerable and suffering women. The suffering of these women becomes instead caricatured as a political evil that must be eradicated, even devoured. Such imagery reinforces the idea of animality as that in human life that must be controlled, captured, or consumed. Such a category of animality is not only applicable to nonhumans but to all those who become associated with the beastly, such as here the idea of wild female sexuality. If, as Schüssler Fiorenza (1991, 117) puts it, "Revelation's central problem and topic is the issue of power and justice," a reading that draws attention to the prostitutes and animals of Roman society uncovers the modes of constructing sovereign power and justice at the expense of others—the female and the animal.

Shared Finitude

In this chapter, I suggest that, like the book of Daniel, the battle of sovereignties between the figures of the Lamb and Beast in Revelation can in part be seen as a critique of human political power as beastly, asserting divine sovereignty as the proper power. Casting the victorious Lamb in the role of this divine sovereignty could be read as the triumph of the weak animal against the colonial powers of Rome. But as Rome is cast in the figure of a hybrid Beast, I suggest this text relies on notions of proper sovereignty and the killability of animals in a problematic way. The proper sovereign, the Lamb, is established in the destruction of the enemy, whereby the enemy is pictured as the animal and female as a wild Beast that must be conquered, killed, and (at least partially) eaten. Primarily, the idea of political evil in the guise of a Beast perpetuates an easy association between animality and brutality that legitimizes violence done to animals. As part of this beastly package, the idea of the female as wild and brutal is similarly commandeered to evoke antipathy against Rome as a figure of political evil. Instead of focusing on who or what the Beast and Whore *represent*, I argue that this imagery for political evil should be critically examined to uncover the bodies that are hidden from view by the quick connotation between beast and evil.

These bodies—the animal bodies of the Roman arena and the prostitutes of Roman society—can only be glimpsed through this conscious effort to destabilize the imagery the narrative relies on to construct good and evil. The point is not, however, to excavate such bodies in order to expose their corpses and evoke exclamations of pity at the lives they lived. The point, rather, is to dismantle the imagery of political evil that relies on facile associations between animality, female sexuality, and evil, by refusing to allow such imagery to signify a brutality and wildness that is set up in order to be conquered by the proper sovereign power. As Gayatri Chakravorty Spivak (1987, 205) suggests, strategic essentialism is useful to offer up political critique in this regard. But to perpetuate imagery that relies on the animal and the female as beastlike and therefore needing to be conquered, tortured, and eaten is to be complicit in preserving a violent logic of sovereignty where the human is justified in mastering, enslaving, and killing animals, be they human or nonhuman, but particularly if they are nondomestic animals or women.[26]

---

26. For a discussion of similar themes in Rev 17 from the perspective of reception history, see Strømmen 2018.

CONCLUSION: ANIMAL AFTERLIVES

In this book, I chart biblical terrain from Genesis through Acts, Daniel to Revelation, exploring the way animality plays out in relation to the themes of killability and sovereignty. I suggest that the themes of killability and sovereignty are key for orienting the way the human and the animal become hierarchically delineated as distinct entities. Sovereignty is a way of designating human dominion over animals, where animals become subjected to human sovereignty as killable, consumable others. When God says, in Gen 1:26: "Let us make humankind in our image, according to our likeness; and let them have dominion over the fish of the sea, and over the birds of the air, and over the cattle, and over all the wild animals of the earth, and over every creeping thing that creeps upon the earth," it would seem that God quite straightforwardly posits humans as sovereign above nonhumans. But such a sovereign status slips throughout the biblical archive, just as the state of animality shows itself to be changeable, where the human can be(come) animal and the animal human. Naturally, modern conceptions of "human" and "animal" are foreign to the ancient biblical texts. The Bible is, as Gen 1:26 exemplifies, full of specific animals, wild creatures, beasts, creeping things, living things, beings, and flesh. Nonetheless, separations between human and nonhuman animals do operate in biblical texts, as can also be seen in the Genesis passage; they additionally operate in the interpretive trends and trajectories that have followed biblical texts. In this book, I set out to trouble the certainty with which such separations are secure and solid. Notions of human sovereignty and animal killability, I argue, are more fraught with ambiguity than has been admitted.

In this conclusion, I draw together the arguments from the different chapters in order to reflect on their significance as a whole. Building on these reflections, I go on to address critical questions about the stakes of such a project on animals in the Bible, pointing to its potential limits. Ultimately, I conclude with the suggestion that posing the question of the animal through delving into the biblical archive after Derrida can open up instructive new interpretive trajectories that set in motion more caring and more curious relations between human and nonhuman animals both inside and outside archives such as the Bible.

Animals in the Biblical Archive

In the first chapter, "The First Carnivorous Man," I examine the way Gen 9 plays out a decisive moment in the biblical archive over the relations between animal, human, and divine. I argue that the scenes of Gen 9 are more complex than a mere permissibility of carnivorous power. On the contrary, I propose that the proximity between God's permission for humans to eat animals and his covenant with *all* life evokes a tension in the text over killability and accountability. God's promise to account for *all* life marks the power given into human hands to consume animals, but simultaneously the response and responsibility that will be demanded of them. Further, Noah's nakedness in the second part of the chapter points to what is at stake in the covering up of vulnerability shared amongst living animals—human and nonhuman—namely, the changeability of status regarding brotherhood and the human, where a brother and a son or grandson can become relegated and subjected to a lower status as a nonbrother, a nonhuman.

In the second chapter, "Acts of Eating," I suggest what has been forgotten in the (interpretation of the) universal fellowship of Acts 10 is precisely the animals that are so central to Peter's vision. I explore the tension between a universal fellowship in which animals are simply forgotten and the institution of the indiscriminate killability of animals. The move to *all* animals being edible as it is played out in this narrative—as opposed to just clean animals—could well be seen as a problematic shift toward unmitigated consumption. Crucially, I argue, the universalism that this passage is so lauded for is undone by the disregard for animal lives; the animal as a general category comes to stand for the acceptable, supposedly legitimate but forgotten space of otherness, outside the ethical remit of a universal fellowship.

In the following chapter, "Political Animals," I propose that human sovereignty is critiqued in the book of Daniel for involving an exclusion of the divine and the cutting up of life into the human and the animal. In the performance of human sovereign power, the subjects to such power are in an animal state, tamed and mastered, from Daniel and his fellow Jews to the lions in the pit. But the book of Daniel arguably undoes the human/animal distinction by showing all to be animals under a God of all the living. Undercutting the misplaced hubris of human sovereignty that gives and takes life, sovereignty is revealed as a mere spectacle that covers up the animality of all. This text undoes the human/animal distinction by establishing the proper hierarchy as that of divine/animal. Accordingly, I suggest that the human/animal binary is radically destabilized, even undone, but the hierarchical structure of a sovereign master over its pet/prey is in place. The divine might be seen as the only proper sovereign master, and his subjects are in the mercy of such a master as the vulnerable, mortal animals they are.

In the final chapter, "Bodies of the Beast," I make the case that the narrative of Rev 17 relies on the killability of animals in the destruction of Rome-as-Beast. Paradoxically for a text that holds up the weak Lamb as an emblem of early Christianity, the enemy is portrayed as *nonhuman* in order to represent the brutalized evil of Roman rule that must be defeated. Packaged into this imagery of the Beast is the body of the female-as-animal, a body that represents a threatening, ferocious, and wild other. Rather than focus on the Lamb as the key animal figure, I suggest a reading in which the imagery of the Beast is critiqued, including the way the Whore as a body is folded into that of the Beast. The animal bodies of the Roman arena and the prostitutes of the Roman Empire have been predominantly obscured from view by the immediate connotation of the Beast with political evil. I critically examine this imagery in order to destabilize the logic whereby evil, and particularly political evil, is consigned to the imaginary space of the beastly.

What can be concluded from these chapters? Obviously there can be no simple conclusion about the biblical treatment of animals, whereby a line like "the Bible says ..." can be finished either with an animal- or a human-centered agenda. The Bible, as Yvonne Sherwood (2004b, 5, emphasis original) puts it, is not "some solid *arche*, given once and for all (like the image of the Bible epitomized in the 5200 pound granite monument of the ten commandments erected outside an Alabama courthouse), *nor* some newly discovered, exotic (dis-Orientating? Hebrew? Jewish?) other, come to seduce a Greco-Christian West." The biblical archive is a complex compendium fraught with tensions and ambivalences that can, with its animals, only be held in abeyance. There can be no final ownership proclaimed of this archive and its animals, nor can this conclusion unsuspend them from such an ambivalent state.

However, any notion of a settled identity or established concept for the "human" as a superior, separate, and sovereign subject in the biblical archive is, as I argue, impossible to maintain. The idea of the sovereign human is frequently played out and just as frequently destabilized, or shown to make animals of humans and humans of animals. Sovereign manhood is performed by Noah in Gen 9 but ends up deeming his own grandson a nonhuman, a slave, demonstrating the slippery nature of the "animal" as a separate and simply given category of otherness. Sovereign humanity trips up also in Daniel when King Nebuchadnezzar becomes animal, designating the way all the living are essentially animals under the only proper sovereign figure: God. The categories of human and animal become jumbled as they are both expanded and contracted. Despite the apparent preference for humans in Genesis, God's covenant in Gen 9 is with all the living; in Acts 10 there is a glimpse of a universal fellowship that is, arguably, founded on animals as fellows instead of killable objects of consumption. In Daniel and Revelation, human political figures and empires are depicted as beasts, which in some ways makes such political figures eminently killable as predatory enemies to be slain. But they also spell out the similitude of the living as mortal animals and the possibility of solidarity amongst creatures, where no living being can be granted a higher position as a sovereign human above those who are deemed "animal."

Despite the fact that the idea of the human as completely set apart from animals might be unsustainable, it is not a matter of being stuck with the shards of a broken-down concept. It is a matter of critically interrogating how spaces of "human" and "animal" are occupied, of analyzing the tacit exclusions such spaces can entail, recognizing the constant need to reexamine the stakes of our intellectual and ethical enterprises. Such enterprises thus become a means of gathering ideas that multiply impressions of the staid spaces of the "human" that add, grow, and provide places to think with others, with otherness and not merely the self-same. In this sense, it is imperative to question the way the universality of Acts 10 is an opening that is at the same time a closure; the gentile might be a category now included in the universal fellowship, but the figure of the other shifts and maps onto the forgotten animals of Peter's vision. It is necessary to interrogate the figures for political evil that operate in the popular imagination, where the image of the wild beast becomes a way of picturing a political evil that is associated with wild women and animals as embodiments of evil, thereby foreclosing the possibility of seeing such women and animals otherwise.

Further, destabilizing the idea of the human is a matter of bringing, as Derrida (2008, 28) puts it, the "suffering, fear, or panic, the terror or fright that can seize certain animals and that we humans can witness" to bear as an injunction and imperative to our thinking. What is human cannot be divorced or theoretically untangled from such a witnessing. When animals are utilized to denote political evil, or to create a space for a killable other outside the ethical remit, this witnessing ought to be activated also in practices of reading, where such ideas become normalized and normative. It is a matter of facing up to the "perspective of an animal request, of an audible or silent appeal that calls within us outside of us, from the most far away, before us after us, preceding and pursuing us in an unavoidable way" (113). If such a perspective is indeed brought to bear also on our reading of animals and the relationship between the human, animal, and divine, then the biblical archive becomes a prime space to grapple with the dynamics of sovereign mastery and mortal vulnerability that structure engagements and encounters with animals.

Another Apocalyptic Shibboleth?

In *The Illusion of the End*, Jean Baudrillard (1994, 21) proposes that the modern world has lost "the glory of the event" and that history has become "cannibalistic and necrophagous," constantly calling for new victims and new events "so as to be done with them a little bit more." His contention is that modern history is dominated by an apocalyptic presentiment, that we live in age of *ressentiment* and *repentance* (22). "Rather than pressing forward and taking flight into the future, we prefer the retrospective apocalypse, and a blanket revisionism" (22). My own starting point—reflecting on Derrida's last work, his legacy as an important and instructive intellectual thinker, and my focus on the Bible—could be classed as such a revisionism. Thinking about animals and the acute problem of animal suffering, with two of the biblical texts characterized as "apocalyptic," merely reinforces Baudrillard's point as to a certain tone of repentance. I could indeed be accused of "trawling over our own culture" (Baudrillard 1994, 25), "rifling through its own dustbins and looking for redemption in the rubbish" (26). Apparently with some scorn, Baudrillard diagnoses the current intellectual context the latest stage of colonialism as a "New Sentimental Order," with ecological concerns for nature as a subject of pity and sympathy (67).

In line with my introductory remarks regarding a sense of disillusionment marking current intellectual attitudes toward the human, including the place of humanity in the world, Francis Fukuyama's (1992) infamous end of history thesis also comes to mind. He writes:

> We in the West have become thoroughly pessimistic with regard to the possibility of overall progress in democratic institutions. This profound pessimism is not accidental, but born of the truly terrible political events of the first half of the twentieth century—two destructive world wars, the rise of totalitarian ideologies, and the turning of science against man in the form of nuclear weapons and environmental damage. The life experiences of the victims of this past century's political violence—from the survivors of Hitlerism and Stalinism to the victims of Pol Pot—would deny that there has been such a thing as historical progress. (Fukuyama 1992, xiii)

Does the question of the animal in fact veer between guilt and a desire for repentance that manifests itself in an anxious and desperate revisionism, a deflated disillusionment at human progress and civilization (or the lack of them, thus the necessity of ironizing them in inverted commas), and a saccharine sentimentalism as a quick-fix solution to heal the wounds? Calarco and Atterton (2004b, xv) suggest that the "death of the author," the "death of God," the "end of philosophy," the "end of humanism," and the "death of man" are all apocalyptic shibboleths that have become self-defeating pronouncements in a modern and postmodern discourse that has barely said anything about animals. But what is the question of the animal if not another such shibboleth that could equally be termed "the death of the animal" and be added to the above list?[1] It could already be said to persist as an apocalyptic "death of ..." announcement in the ecological anxieties over animal extinctions, or, indeed, the urge to proclaim the death of the human.

The animal as a subject of intellectual study in the humanities is caught up in a discourse that flits between the idealistic and the cynical. Animals are appropriated as intellectual currency in reams of words that appear to have little to do with actual animal lives and deaths. The subject reveals a glimpse of the hideous reality of the material conditions for millions of animals outside what now sounds like the cozy enclave of animal studies. With the sometimes implicit, sometimes explicit references to slaughter, factory farming, and/or the bleak conditions of so many animals in the

---

1. Cavalieri's (2009) book is named precisely: *The Death of the Animal: A Dialogue.*

world today, a reality of pain, suffering, impossible living, and grotesque death haunts this area of study. A gruff inertia at the impossibility of *doing* anything is difficult to resist for those who want to address these issues within institutional academic spaces today. And so, the different tones of animal studies range from polemical, pious, moralizing, persuasive, self-righteous, beseeching, incensed, defeated, hopeless to hopeful.

Explaining why animals ought to be taken seriously is sometimes met with a palpable sigh: not another marginalized group who demands academic attention! As if ethnic minorities, black people, women, homosexuals, and animals are all victim groups queuing to get their due done in intellectual circles and be redeemed from the invisible margins. And, as if academics cannot wait to cash in on such victim-groups, scoring intellectual advantages from the smug vantage points of virtuous abhorrence at how anyone could possibly have failed to face up to such an outrage before, thus settling further into the arm-chair-throne of self-righteousness. This is what Graham Huggan (2001) identifies in relation to postcolonialism as the postcolonial exotic. As he suggests, it would be easy to be cynical "in an era of academic over-production" where "commodified terms used largely for academic purposes" (1) become fashionable and help to keep people in careers. To emphasize the reality of pain and suffering that is the impetus of such studies, ought one to insert images of the horrors of factory farms? Ought one add links to YouTube clips of suffering animals? Or of one's cute pets at play? Of clever creatures surprising us with their human-likeness? Ought one to exhort people toward vegetarianism or veganism or asceticism?[2] To throw red paint at the fur-clad fashionistas? Is there not something insufferably superfluous about reams of *words* on animal suffering? Or elements of unbearable sluggishness about an academic approach to such current issues? And why limit oneself to animals? As many scholars now testify, *things* are also deserving of attention as active or vibrant "agents."[3] Further, there might be something problematically exoticizing in perceiving the animal as other, both strange and familiar. As Huggan (2001, 13) discusses, exoticism is about a perception that "renders people, objects and places strange even as it domesticates them," and animals could easily also be added to the list.

---

2. Lawlor (2007, 105), for instance, advocates ascetism.
3. See for instance Bennett 2010.

At this juncture I would like return to Haraway's critique of Derrida's writing on animals. She argues that Derrida identified some of the key questions in regard to animals, but only came "to the edge of respect" before being sidetracked by his philosophical interlocutors, never returning in curiosity to the pet cat that sets in motion his thinking in *The Animal That Therefore I Am* (Haraway 1991, 20). It could be said that if I began by announcing an interest in animals and animal studies, it is noteworthy that not only have few "real" animals appeared—rather, textual animals, animal characters, or figures—or been sought after, and further, much of the discussion has centered around the role animals have as placeholders. In many ways, I have been asking what the consequences are for *humans* in terms of an erasure or blurring of stark boundary lines between humans and animals. Further, could it not be said that Derrida's distraction from his cat into the world of philosophy is exacerbated by my own distractions into his thinking and into the biblical archive? Haraway (1991, 21) asks why Derrida did not enquire further about the possibilities of animal responses, turning for instance to anthropologists Gregory Bateson and Barbara Smuts or ethologist Jane Goodall, scholars who have done ground-breaking work on cybernetics, animal behavior, and social, psychological, and neurological studies of animals. This would seem a promising move to avoid exoticizing animals as either a familiarized human product of taming or a strange spectacle only seeable in contrast to a human world. Haraway acquiesces that animal suffering is important, but unlike Derrida, who in turn draws on Bentham, she resists such suffering being the decisive question. Pity is important, but what about curiosity, and joy in the mutual response and engagement with animal others? What if such curiosity and joy are what changes everything about the relationship between those starkly delineated categories "human" and "animal," recognizing both multiple differences and similarities (Haraway 1991, 22)? What if this is what avoids exoticization of animal life and a transformation of "animality" into intellectual currency as fashionable academic jargon? Haraway is interested in forging a "world of becoming with, where *who and what are* is precisely what is at stake" (Haraway, 2007, 19, emphasis original). She is undoubtedly right about the necessary forays into anthropology and ethology, about encounters with real animals beyond the feeling of pity. However, arguably, what is simultaneously necessary in a world of "becoming with" where who and what is at stake is a critical confrontation with powerful legacies and ideas that solidify hierarchical distinctions between humans and animals that perpetuate violence against the latter.

The significance of the expansions and contractions of animality that I outline might be understood in light of a larger "turn to religion," particularly in continental philosophy in the last decades. As Moore and Sherwood (2011, 128) point out, "the Bible is coming to be seen as a key site where foundational, but unsustainable, 'modern' separations were made." Particular understandings and interpretations of biblical texts could, for instance, be seen as foundational for modern conceptions of the state, for the relationship between politics and religion as well as for the human. Hent de Vries (1999) diagnoses this important shift in modern philosophy, particularly exemplified by Derrida's later work. Recent scholarship within this turn to religion holds that citations from religious traditions are "fundamental to the structure of language and experience" in a way that has been obscured by the "genealogies, critiques, and transcendental reflections of the modern discourse that has deemed such citations obsolete and tended to reduce them to what they are not" (de Vries 1999, 2). Rather than dying and disappearing from the public scene, religion seems to live on in one guise or another (3). The biblical archive becomes an urgent source of critical study as it appears, on the surface, to be less relevant, known, or read in a modern Western world. If biblical citations and legacies become all the more blurred and less overtly discussed, the Bible risks becoming a locus no longer critically explored and mapped out.

A driving force for scholarly debate is, as de Vries (1999, 6) puts it, the "resurfacing of religion as a highly ambiguous force on the contemporary geopolitical stage." De Vries suggests that "*retracing* the religious means also—and, perhaps, first of all—*tracing it otherwise*, not allowing it to take on one particular—that is, universal—meaning once and for all" (1999, 31, emphasis original). In renegotiations of "the Bible as a symptomatic cultural space," Moore and Sherwood (2011, 128–29) argue that the Bible has become a site in which "settled identities" and "established concepts" might be disrupted. Building on their insights into such disruptions, I have demonstrated the way settled identities of human and animal are, and certainly can be, disrupted in revisiting the biblical archive after Derrida. But as de Vries attests, there is an ambiguity at play in the diverse and sprawling corpus called Bible that does not offer simple answers or getouts. While taking heed of Haraway's warning not to get embroiled in the mires of textuality, forgetting the animals and animal encounters that can radically alter anthropocentric structures, it is clearly necessary to remain vigilant about how religion and the Bible come to play strategic—and often reified—roles. The Bible cannot save animals or become *the* vehicle for animal rights. But exploring its archival spaces critically and with an attention to the places where the human is both done and undone, and where animals become something other than killable, consumable objects, might at the least disrupt the desire for a legitimating or a blameworthy canon at the heart of Western culture. Rather, a more multiple and complex biblical archive might give rise to a consciously less anthropocentric interpretive trajectory, one that is open to recognizing animals as companions.

Turning to the biblical archive with Derrida provides a prime position for thinking today. As I already mentioned, the question of the animal challenges a neat division between theory and practice, or between intellectual discourse and moral action. Derrida's insistence on tradition, legacy, and hauntologies[4] is a testament to the ongoing, often obscured and implicit significance of classics and canons and the vitality of texts and traditions. Weber (2007, 340) describes how such a hauntological focus is a challenge to proclaim not merely apocalyptically the death of various concepts but to face up to their powerful and persistent legacies. They live on. In a similar way to the critique of the word animal as a performative construction leading to practices that frequently condemn living beings to death, so, too, intellectual discourse can keep grappling with legacies conceived as archetypal as well as those conceived as extinct (sometimes the same legacies). Paul Strohm (2000, 80) suggests that "the archive does not arrest time, but rather exists as an unstable amalgam of unexhausted past and unaccomplished future. Open toward the future—that is, toward activities of future interpreters—the archive consists of texts that await meaning." Thus, even "when we try to stop time, to freeze a moment for synchronous investigation as a part of a literary cross-section, that moment nevertheless turns out to bear within itself intimations of past and future that amount to a form of implicit diachrony" (80). This is "an unruly diachrony, referring in the most surprising and unpredictable ways to what has been and what is not yet, to the residual and the emergent" (93). Derrida is a thinker who orients us toward a past that can always be rethought—which is always already rethinking itself—and thus is never fixed as an immovable inheritance. Accordingly, Royle (2000, 11) describes deconstruction in the following way:

---

4. That is, the way in which intellectual specters—such as the legacy of humanism—are neither a form of being or nonbeing but haunt philosophical ontologies in elusive ways.

a logic of destabilization always already on the move in "things themselves": what makes every identity at once itself and different from itself:
a logic of spectrality: a theoretical and practical parasitism or virology:
what is happening today in what is called society, politics, diplomacy,
economics, historical reality, and so on: the opening of the future itself.[5]

The Bible abides in a tension between being thought of as the most popular
and widely read "book"—found in hotel bedsides; quoted in films, political speeches, and literature; used for popular rites and rituals—and with
an impression of its heaviness, its impenetrability, as an obscure, weird,
or dreary artifact. The Bible is both archetypal and archaic, marked by
ubiquity and extinction. It is crucial that scholarship intervenes in this
tension between "what we all know the Bible is about" and what appears to
be shrouded from general view in the esoteric enclaves of biblical studies.
Who can measure exactly what impact the biblical archive had, has, and
will have for current attitudes to animals? It seems clear, however, that if
textual traditions have any influence whatsoever, then the Bible would be
an obvious and essential archive to explore more closely and critically for
conceptions of animal, human, and divine.

Derrida (2004, 64, emphasis original) exhorts that the "relations
between humans and animals *must* change." And this "both in the sense
of an 'ontological' necessity and of an 'ethical' duty" (64). Ontology and
ethics are in quotation marks because both will have to be rethought with
this question of the animal in mind. While human rights have undoubtedly brought much that is beneficial, their foundations, implications, and
exclusions must nonetheless be "relentlessly analyzed, reelaborated, developed, and enriched (historicity and perfectibility are in fact essential to it)"
(65). Not to "destroy the axiomatics of this (formal and juridical) solution,
nor to discredit it, but to reconsider the history of law and of the concept
of right" (74). Derrida (1995b, 266) asks, "can one take into account the
necessity of the existential analytic and what it shatters in the subject and
turn toward an ethics, a politics (are these words still appropriate?), indeed
an 'other' democracy (would it still be a democracy?), in any case toward
another type of responsibility that safeguards against" what he calls the
worst kinds of violence taking place today? This, he concludes, "can only
take place by a way of a long and slow trajectory" (266). He also invites

---

5. This last part of Royle's quote, "the opening of the future itself," is a citation of
Derrida (1992, 200).

"a slow and progressive approach" (Derrida 2004, 74), akin to the "slow motion" reading, following Sherwood, I suggested in the introduction with regard to the biblical archive. There is then a sense of urgency in the imperative for change but also for an interminable patience in ongoing critical thought as to the structures that underpin social, political, and ethical relations in the world when it comes to the other and how this other is conceived, welcomed, or excluded. There is, then, arguably a necessary corollary to animal rights activism, namely a critical attention to the ways cultural legacies and archives subtly, implicitly, and often unconsciously inform contemporary practices of violence against animals. No conclusion about animals in biblical texts can directly change the relationship between humans and animals. But such critical engagement can perhaps help build toward Derrida's other "type of responsibility" that works against violence toward animals.

Balfour (2007) conveys how Derrida has been accused of relativism, skepticism, irresponsibility. But, he states, "the opposite is far truer: his thinking, writing, and speaking is characterized, rather, by a hyperresponsibility, a responsibility to the complexities of the moment, of history, and the history to come, and to the discourses in which we think and judge, all the while committed to resisting some of the suspect and exhausted modes of thinking we have inherited" (207). This is clearly a concern in Derrida's work on animality. Unconditional hospitality is not merely an impossibility but an interpretive and intellectual practice that seeks to question the way the other is related to inside and outside our homes, on the streets, in supermarkets, at our tables and in nature, in texts, traditions, canons and legacies, as well as places such as zoos, laboratories, enclosures, kennels—without pretending there are simple or straightforward solutions to human-animal interactions and obligations. The difficulty in Derrida's ethics of the other lies in its suggestion "that the response cannot be formulated as a 'yes or no.'" What is necessary is a singular response that takes account of a given context and that risks the undecidable (Derrida 2004, 76). As Wolfe (2009, 54, emphasis original) points out, it is in our "confrontation with an ethical situation that is always precisely *not* generic (hence its demand and, in a sense, its trauma); it obeys instead a double articulation in which the difference between law and justice is always confronted in *specific* situations whose details matter a great deal."

Writing on the ethical and political stakes of Derrida's work on animals, Calarco (2007) asks why Derrida does not go on to provide an ethical platform from which moral change and action can take place. However, he rightly points out that Derrida is attempting to think ethics and animality at another level, the conditions for any ethics, and what principles must be in place in order to think ethics at all (Calarco 2007, 12). This attempt at something like a disruptive gesture at the foundations of relations to the other, and the engagement with traditions, canons and philosophical inheritance, is why Derrida is such a valuable thinker for the question of the animal today. As Calarco puts it: "deconstruction is situated precisely at this level, namely, that of trying to articulate another thought of relation (ethics) and practice (politics) that moves beyond the limits of anthropocentric traditions and institutions" (12).

Graham Ward (2001, 285) criticizes what he sees as the "tyrannous demand for infinite responsibility" that can only be endured, implied by the impossible responsibility and regard for life signified in Derrida's God and represented in my reading of Gen 9. He suggests that such an ethics becomes a Sisyphean task, questioning whether there is anything ethical about the "infinite guilt" which, Ward (2001, 285) argues, this thinking of responsibility entails. But as John D. Caputo's (2001, 296) response to Ward testifies, it is rather a matter of "always responding and at the same time always asking what we are responding to, always choosing and at the same time asking what we have chosen or has chosen us, what we are doing in the midst of the concrete decisions we always and invariably make." Deconstruction is "not a philosophy of undecidability *tout court*, but of deciding-in-the-midst-of-undecidability" (296). Condemning Derrida's thought-world as "an ironic and constantly shifting world without borders and without the moral teleology of apocalyptic thought, that is, without final solutions," as Juliet Flower MacCannell (2003, 71) puts it, and thus avoiding such a world, would be to accept a cessation of thought, of critical attention, and of final, or one might say terminal, appropriations of texts as well as others.

There are two movements in deconstruction, Caputo suggests: historical association and messianic dissociation. Deconstruction situates itself *in* the contexts, histories, and traditions given to us *and* dissociates itself from these names, terms, narratives, and dreams for a messianic justice to come. "If the first movement, historical dissociation, has to do with the *fore-given*, the second movement has to do with the *un-fore-seeable*, which is *never* given" (Caputo 2001, 304, emphasis original). Derrida moves between this sense of what is dreamt—an unconditional justice, infinite responsibility, a hospitality without limits—and the awakened, urgent,

contextual, and material that must be lived *with* and lived *in-the-midst-of.*
For the question of the animal, Derrida posits his philosophical reflection in the gaze of the animal other—with his cat as a singular other who
is encountered in a particular context. Human relations to "the animal"
must change, he insists, and there is a hope that justice will come as a
result of this exhortation (Derrida 2004, 64). But at the same time, we
must acknowledge, and sadly live with the reality, that hospitality toward
animal others may continue to be limited, even sometimes impossible.

Animals on the Table

Many of the themes emerging in the biblical texts I present revolve around
the relationship between eating and being eaten. One common theme,
then, has been the table as a locus of power but also a symbol of hospitality. This theme is also important for Derrida, and it is with the question of
eating that Derrida's (2004, 67–68) ambivalence as to the animal question
fully emerges. It is not enough to avoid eating animals, he states: the other
is also consumable in more symbolic and unconscious ways. Predominantly, this highlights that there can be no simple solution that avoids the
suffering of others or that abstains from violence. There can be no hospitality of the table that is immune from appropriation and consumption
of my other. For Derrida, a justice to come is not teleological, but rather,
it remains as a horizon of justice in which his dream of hospitality to the
other as any other can awaken but is never free from the risks of violence.
The "opening to the future or to the coming of the other as the advent of
justice," is what Derrida (2002, 56) calls the messianic. This opening of the
future and coming of the other cannot but be unknown, bringing potentially the worst as well as the best outcome (56). The table can be seen as
the metaphorical place on which subjects are drawn from the margins and
on which they are placed for discussion, *to do (or give) them justice*: putting animals *on the table*. But the table is also that place on which animals
are eaten and appropriated—done justice in the sense of a sentencing to
killability and edibility, what Gross (2014, 145) calls "the most literal form
of sacrifice today." The table is the place for fellowship with my neighbor,
fellow, and friend, but it is also a place of exclusion for those who are not
invited. The table is an ambivalent site for animals. Following Caputo, it
is a matter of ceaselessly thinking and offering hospitality, while always
already questioning what kind of hospitality we are offering, and what or
who is left outside the economy of the table. As Derrida (1969, 57) con-

cluded in "The Ends of Man," the words that must interrupt our thinking are perhaps these three: "But who, we?"

Perhaps the only way to conclude, then, is with Derrida's double imperative. On the one hand, everything must be done to decrease significantly the suffering and systematic exploitation and industrialization of animal bodies. This might involve imperfect short-term solutions, even clumsy practical attempts that risk contradiction and unsustainability. On the other hand, it is crucial to be and remain critical to the practices, institutions, canons, and customs that regulate and inform our lives in relation to the category of the *nonhuman*, the *animal*. Here, a slow and rigorous approach must be endured to ensure that systematic and accepted abuse of animals is critiqued, questioned, and hopefully stopped, or at least limited. "All the archaic, anachronistic forms are there ready to re-emerge, intact and timeless, like the viruses deep in the body," Baudrillard (1994, 27) writes of history. "History has only wrenched itself from cyclical time to fall into the order of the recyclable" (27). But it is perhaps in the recyclable that an engagement of the past that is allied to the future may be found: an engagement that does not naively suppose that the past and its intellectual inheritance can be shrugged off, that does not balk at relocating "the 'new' ground on the older one" (Derrida 1969, 56), and that abides in a world in which our archives may be inhabited in such a way as to rethink today as well as what is to come.

Bibliography

Adams, Carol J. 1990. *The Sexual Politics of Meat: A Feminist-Vegetarian Critical Theory*. New York: Continuum.

———. 2004. *The Pornography of Meat*. London: Continuum.

———. 2018. *Neither Man nor Beast: Feminism and the Defense of Animals*. London: Bloomsbury. [originally 1994]

Adams, Carol J., and Josephine Donovan, eds. 1995. *Animals and Women: Feminist Theoretical Explorations*. Durham, NC: Duke University Press.

———. 2007. *Feminist Care Tradition in Animal Ethics: A Reader*. New York: University of Columbia Press.

Adams, Carol J., and Marie M. Fortune. 1995. *Violence against Women and Children: A Christian Theological Sourcebook*. London: Continuum.

Adorno, Theodor W., and Max Horkheimer. (1944) 1997. *Dialectic of Enlightenment*. VC. London: Verso Books.

Allsen, Thomas T. 2006. *The Royal Hunt in Eurasian History*. EA. Philadelphia: University of Pennsylvania Press.

Alter, Robert. 1997. *Genesis: Translation and Commentary*. New York: Norton.

Arnold, Bill T. 2008. *Genesis*. NCBC. Cambridge: Cambridge University Press.

Assmann, Jan. 2006. *Religion and Cultural Memory: Ten Studies*. Translated by Rodney Livingstone. CMP. Stanford, CA: Stanford University Press.

———. 2012. "Martyrdom, Violence, and Immortality: The Origins of a Religious Complex." Pages 39–60 in *Dying for the Faith, Killing for the Faith: Old-Testament Faith-Warriors (1 and 2 Maccabees) in Historical Perspective*. Edited by Gabriela Signori. BSIH 206. Leiden: Brill.

Auguet, Roland. 1994. *Cruelty and Civilization: The Roman Games*. London: Routledge.

Augustine. 2008. *Confessions*. Translated by Henry Chadwick. OWC. Oxford: Oxford University Press.

Aune, David E. 1998. *Revelation 17–22*. WBC 52C. Edited by Bruce M. Metzger. Nashville: Nelson.

Badmington, Neil, ed. 2007. *Derridanimals*. OLR 29: v–vii.

Bailey, Lloyd R. 1989. *Noah: The Person and the Story in History and Tradition*. SPOT. Columbia: University of South Carolina Press.

Balfour, Ian, ed. 2007. *Late Derrida*. Durham: Duke University Press.

Balsdon, John P. V. D. 1969. *Life and Leisure in Ancient Rome*. London: Bodley Head.

Barton, Stephen C., and David Wilkinson, eds. 2009. *Reading Genesis after Darwin*. Oxford: Oxford University Press.

Bataille, Georges. 1989. *Theory of Religion*. New York: Zone Books.

Bauckham, Richard. 1993. *The Theology of the Book of Revelation*. NTT. Cambridge: Cambridge University Press.

Baudrillard, Jean. 1994. *The Illusion of the End*. Translated by Chris Turner. Cambridge: Polity.

Beale, Gregory K. 1984. *The Use of Daniel in Jewish Apocalyptic Literature and in the Revelation of St. John*. Lanham, MD: University Press of America.

———. 1999. *The Book of Revelation: A Commentary on the Greek Text*. NIGTC. Grand Rapids: Eerdmans.

Beauchamp, Tom L., and R. G. Frey, eds. 2011. *The Oxford Handbook of Animal Ethics*. OH. Oxford: Oxford University Press.

Beauvoir, Simone de. 2010. *The Second Sex*. Translated by Constance Borde and Sheila Malovany-Chevallier. London: Vintage Books.

Bennett, Jane. 2010. *Vibrant Matter: A Political Ecology of Things*. Durham, NC: Duke University Press.

Berger, Anne Emmanuelle, and Marta Segarra, eds. 2011. *Demenageries: Thinking (of) Animals after Derrida*. CriticalSt 35. Amsterdam: Rodopi.

Bergsma, John Sietze, and Scott Walker Hahn. 2005. "Noah's Nakedness and the Curse on Canaan (Genesis 9:20–27)." *JBL* 124:25–40.

Beyerle, Stefan. 2001. "The Book of Daniel and Its Social Setting." Pages 205–28 in vol. 1 of *The Book of Daniel: Composition and Reception*. Edited by John J. Collins and Peter W. Flint. VTSup 83; FIOTL 2. Leiden: Brill.

Bezan, Sarah, and James Tink, eds. 2017. *Seeing Animals after Derrida*. ETP. Lanham, MD: Lexington Books.

Bovon, François. 2003. *Studies in Early Christianity*. WUNT 161. Tübingen: Mohr Siebeck.

Brett, Mark G. 2000. *Genesis: Procreation and the Politics of Identity*. OTR. London: Routledge.

Bruce, F. F. 1963. "Acts of the Apostles." In *The Wycliffe Bible Commentary*. Edited by Charles F. Pfeiffer and Everett F. Harrison. London: Oliphants.

Bruch, Debra. 2004. "The Prejudice against Theatre." *JRT* 3:1–18.

Brueggemann, Walter. 2003. *An Introduction to the Old Testament: The Canon and Christian Imagination*. Louisville: Westminster John Knox.

Buell, Denise Kimber. 2005. *Why This New Race? Ethnic Reasoning in Early Christianity*. New York: Columbia University Press.

Calarco, Matthew. 2007. "Thinking through Animals: Reflections on the Ethical and Political Stakes of the Question of the Animal in Derrida." *OLR* 29:1–15.

———. 2008. *Zoographies: The Question of the Animal from Heidegger to Derrida*. New York: Columbia University Press.

Calarco, Matthew, and Peter Atterton, eds. 2004a. *Animal Philosophy: Essential Readings in Continental Thought*. London: Continuum.

———. 2004b. "Editors' Introduction: The Animal Question in Continental Philosophy." Pages xv–xx in *Animal Philosophy: Essential Readings in Continental Thought*. Edited by Matthew Calarco and Peter Atterton. London: Continuum.

Cantrell, Deborah O'Daniel. 2011. *The Horsemen of Israel: Horses and Chariotry in Monarchic Israel (Ninth–Eighth Centuries B.C.E.)*. HACL 1. Winona Lake, IN: Eisenbrauns.

Caputo, John D. 2001. "What Do I Love When I Love My God? Deconstruction and Radical Orthodoxy." Pages 291–317 in *Questioning God*. Edited by John D. Caputo, Mark Dooley, and Michael J. Scanlon. ISPR. Bloomington: Indiana University Press.

Carr, David M. 1996. *Reading the Fractures of Genesis: Historical and Literary Approaches*. Louisville: Westminster John Knox.

Cavalieri, Paola, ed. 2009. *The Death of the Animal: A Dialogue*. New York: Columbia University Press.

Cavalieri, Paola, and Peter Singer, eds. 1995. *The Great Ape Project: Equality beyond Humanity*. New York: St. Martin's.

Cavell, Stanley, Cora Diamond, John McDowell, Ian Hacking, and Cary Wolfe. 2010. *Philosophy and Animal Life*. New York: Columbia University Press.

Chrulew, Matthew. 2006. "Feline Divinanimality: Derrida and the Discourse of Species in Genesis." *BCT* 2.2:18.1–18.23. https://doi.org/10.2104/bc060018.

Chrystal, Paul. 2013. *Women in Ancient Rome*. Gloucestershire: Amberley.

Cixous, Helene. 1998. "Love of the Wolf." Pages 84-99 in *Stigmata: Escaping Texts*. Translated by Keith Cohen. RC. London: Routledge..

Clark, Stephen R. L. 1999. *The Political Animal: Biology, Ethics, and Politics*. London: Routledge.

———. 2013. "'Ask Now the Beasts and They Shall Teach Thee.'" Pages 15–34 in *Animals as Religious Subjects: Transdisciplinary Perspectives*. Edited by Celia Deane-Drummond, Rebecca Artinian-Kaiser, and David L. Clough. T&TCT. London: T&T Clark.

Clark, Timothy. 2015. *Ecocriticism on the Edge: The Anthropocene as a Threshold Concept*. London: Bloomsbury.

Clough, David L. 2009. "All God's Creatures: Reading Genesis on Human and Nonhuman Animals." Pages 145–62 in *Reading Genesis after Darwin*. Edited by Stephen C. Barton and David Wilkinson. Oxford: Oxford University Press.

———. 2012. *On Animals*. Vol. 1 of *Systematic Theology*. T&TCT. London: T&T Clark.

Cohen, Jeffrey Jerome, ed. 2012. *Animal, Vegetable, Mineral: Ethics and Objects*. Washington, DC: Oliphaunt Books.

Cohn, Norman. 1996. *Noah's Flood: The Genesis Story in Western Thought*. New Haven: Yale University Press.

———. 1999. "Biblical Origins of the Apocalyptic Tradition." Pages 28–42 in *The Apocalypse and the Shape of Things to Come*. Edited by Frances Carey. Toronto: University of Toronto Press.

Coleman, Kathleen M. 1990. "Fatal Charades: Roman Executions Staged as Mythological Enactments." *JRS* 80:44–73.

Collins, Adela Yarbro. 2009. "Feminine Symbolism in the Book of Revelation." Pages 121–30 in *A Feminist Companion to the Apocalypse of John*. Edited by Amy-Jill Levine and Maria Mayo Robbins. FCNTECW 13. London: T&T Clark.

Collins, John J. 1977. *The Apocalyptic Vision of the Book of Daniel*. HSM 16. Missoula, MT: Scholars Press.

———. 1981. *Daniel, First Maccabees, Second Maccabees, with an Excursus on the Apocalyptic Genre*. OTM 15. Wilmington, DE: Glazier.

Cone, James. 2001. "Whose Earth Is It, Anyway?" Pages 23–32 in *Earth*

Habitat: Eco-injustice and the Church's Response. Edited by Dieter Hessel and Larry Rasmussen. Minneapolis: Fortress.

Cunningham, David S. 2009. "The Way of All Flesh: Rethinking the *Imago Dei*." Pages 100–117 in *Creaturely Theology: On God, Humans and Other Animals*. Edited by Celia Deane-Drummond and David L. Clough. London: SCM.

Davies, Phillip R. 1985. *Daniel*. OTG 4. Sheffield: JSOT Press.

Deane-Drummond, Celia, and David L. Clough. 2009. *Creaturely Theology: God, Humans and Other Animals*. London: SCM.

Deane-Drummond, Celia, Rebecca Artinian-Kaiser, and David L. Clough, eds. 2013. *Animals as Religious Subjects: Transdisciplinary Perspectives*. T&TCT. London: T&T Clark.

DeGrazia, David. 1996. *Taking Animals Seriously: Mental Life and Moral Status*. Cambridge: Cambridge University Press.

DeMello, Margo. 2012. *Animals and Society: An Introduction to Human-Animal Studies*. New York: Columbia University Press.

Derrida, Jacques. (1967a) 1998. *Of Grammatology*. Translated by Gayatri Chakravorty Spivak. Baltimore: Johns Hopkins University Press.

———. (1967b) 2001. *Writing and Difference*. Translated by Alan Bass. RC. New York: Routledge.

———. 1969. "The Ends of Man." *PhilPR* 30.1:31–57.

———. (1972) 1983. *Dissemination*. Translated by Barbara Johnson. Chicago: University of Chicago Press.

———. (1974) 1986. *Glas*. Translated by John P. Leavey Jr. and Richard Rand. Lincoln: University of Nebraska Press.

———. (1978) 1987. *The Truth in Painting*. Translated by Geoffrey Bennington and Ian McLeod. Chicago: University of Chicago Press.

———. (1987) 1991. *Of Spirit: Heidegger and the Question*. Translated by Geoffrey Bennington and Rachel Bowlby. Chicago: University of Chicago Press.

———. 1989. "*Geschlecht* II: Heidegger's Hand." Pages 161–96 in *Deconstruction and Philosophy: The Texts of Jacques Derrida*. Edited by John Sallis. Translated by John P. Leavey Jr. Chicago: University of Chicago Press.

———. 1992. "Afterw.rds: Or, at Least, Less than a Letter about a Letter Less." Pages 197–203 in *Afterwords*. Edited by Nicholas Royle. Translated by Geoffrey Bennington. TES 1. Tampere: Outside Books.

———. (1993) 2006. *Specters of Marx: The State of the Debt, the Work of*

Mourning and the New International. Translated by Peggy Kamuf. RC. New York: Routledge.

———. 1995b. With Jean-Luc Nancy. "'Eating Well,' or the Calculation of the Subject." Pages 255–87 in *Points...: Interviews, 1974–1994*. Edited by Elisabeth Weber. Translated by Peter Connor and Avital Ronell. Meridian. Stanford, CA: Stanford University Press.

———. 1995c. *The Gift of Death*. Translated by David Willis. RP. Chicago: University of Chicago Press.

———. 2000. *Of Hospitality*. With Anne Dufourmantelle. Translated by Rachel Bowlby. CMP. Stanford, CA: Stanford University Press.

———. 2001. *On Cosmopolitanism and Forgiveness*. Translated by Mark Dooley. TA. New York: Routledge.

———. 2002. "Faith and Knowledge: The Two Sources of 'Religion' at the Limits of Reason Alone." Pages 42–100 in *Acts of Religion*. Edited by Gil Anidjar. New York: Routledge.

———. 2004. "Violence against Animals." Pages 62–75 in *For What Tomorrow ...: A Dialogue*. With Elisabeth Roudinesco. Translated by Jeff Fort. CMP. Stanford, CA: Stanford University Press.

———. 2005. *Rogues: Two Essays on Reason*. Translated by Pascale-Anne Brault and Michael Naas. Meridian. Stanford, CA: Stanford University Press.

———. 2008. *The Animal That Therefore I Am*. Edited by Marie-Louise Mallet. Translated by David Wills. PCPhil. New York: Fordham University Press.

———. 2009–2011. *The Beast and the Sovereign*. Edited by Michel Lisse, Marie-Louise Mallet, and Ginette Michaud. Translated by Geoffrey Bennington. 2 vols. Chicago: University of Chicago Press.

Descartes, René. 1989. *Discourse on Method and the Meditations*. Translated by John Veitch. GBP. Amherst, NY: Prometheus.

Donaldson, Sue, and Will Kymlicka. 2011. *Zoopolis: A Political Theory of Animal Rights*. Oxford: Oxford University Press.

Donovan, Josephine. 1990. "Animal Rights and Feminist Theory." *Signs* 15:350–75.

Donovan, Josephine, and Carol J. Adams, eds. 2007. *The Feminist Care Tradition in Animal Ethics: A Reader*. New York: Columbia University Press.

Douglas, Mary. 1966. *Purity and Danger: An Analysis of Concepts of Pollution and Taboo*. London: Routledge & Kegan Paul.

Dunn, James D. G. 1996. *The Acts of the Apostles*. EC. Peterborough: Epworth.

———. 2013. "Why and How Did Embryonic Christianity Expand beyond the Jewish People?" Pages 183–204 in *The Rise and Expansion of Christianity in the First Three Centuries of the Common Era*. Edited by Clare K. Rothschild and Jens Schröter. WUNT 301. Tübingen: Mohr Siebeck.

Embry, Brad. 2011. "The 'Naked Narrative' from Noah to Leviticus: Reassessing Voyeurism in the Account of Noah's Nakedness in Genesis 9.22–24." *JSOT* 35:417–33.

Esler, Philip Francis. 1987. *Community and Gospel in Luke-Acts: The Social and Political Motivations of Lucan Theology*. SNTSMS 57. Cambridge: Cambridge University Press.

Evans, William McKee. 1980. "From the Land of Canaan to the Land of Guinea: The Strange Odyssey of the 'Sons of Ham.'" *AHR* 85:15–43.

Fagan, Madeleine, Ludovic Glorieux, Indira Hašimbegović, and Marie Suetsugu, eds. 2007. *Derrida: Negotiating the Legacy*. Edinburgh: Edinburgh University Press.

Fellenz, Marc R. 2007. *The Moral Menagerie: Philosophy and Animal Rights*. Champaign: University of Illinois Press.

Ferry, Luc. 1995. *The New Ecological Order*. Translated by Carol Volk. Chicago: University of Chicago Press.

Fewell, Danna Nolan. 1988. *The Circle of Sovereignty: A Story of Stories in Daniel 1–6*. JSOTSup 72; BLS 20. Sheffield: Almond Press.

Forti, Tova L. 2008. *Animal Imagery in the Book of Proverbs*. VTSup 118. Leiden: Brill.

France, Peter. 1986. *An Encyclopedia of Bible Animals*. London: Croom Helm.

Friesen, Steven J. 2005. "Satan's Throne, Imperial Cults and the Social Settings of Revelation." *JSNT* 27:351–73.

Frilingos, Christopher A. 2004. *Spectacles of Empire: Monsters, Martyrs, and the Book of Revelation*. Divinations. Philadelphia: University of Pennsylvania Press.

Fukuyama, Francis. 1992. *The End of History and the Last Man*. London: Penguin Books.

Garner, Robert, ed. 1997. *Animal Rights: The Changing Debate*. New York: New York University Press.

Gilhus, Ingvild Sælid. 2006. *Animals, Gods and Humans: Changing Atti-*

tudes to Animals in Greek, Roman and Early Christian Ideas. London: Routledge.

Glancy, Jennifer A., and Stephen D. Moore. 2011. "How Typical a Roman Prostitute is Revelation's 'Great Whore'?" *JBL* 130:551–69.

Goldenberg, David M. 2005. *The Curse of Ham: Race and Slavery in Early Judaism, Christianity, and Islam*. Princeton: Princeton University Press.

Gordon, Lewis R. 2013. "Race, Theodicy, and the Normative Emancipatory Challenges of Blackness." *SAQ* 112:725–36.

Grant, Robert M. 1999. *Early Christians and Animals*. London: Routledge.

Gross, Aaron S. 2009. "The Question of the Creature: Animals, Theology and Levinas' Dog." Pages 121–37 in *Creaturely Theology: On God, Humans and Other Animals*. Edited by Celia Deane-Drummond and David L. Clough. London: SCM.

———. 2014. *The Question of the Animal and Religion: Theoretical Stakes, Practical Implications*. New York: Columbia University Press.

Gruen, Lori, and Kari Weil, eds. 2012. *Animal Others. Hypatia* 27.3.

Habel, Norman C., and Shirley Wurst, eds. 2000. *The Earth Story in Genesis*. The Earth Bible 2. Sheffield: Sheffield Academic.

Haraway, Donna J. 1990. *Primate Visions: Gender, Race, and Nature in the World of Modern Science*. New York: Routledge.

———. 1991. "A Cyborg Manifesto: Science, Technology, and Socialist-Feminism in the Late Twentieth Century." Pages 149–81 in *Simians, Cyborgs, and Women: The Reinvention of Nature*. London: Free Association Books.

———. 2003. *The Companion Species Manifesto: Dogs, People, and Significant Otherness*. Chicago: Prickly Paradigm.

———. 2007. *When Species Meet*. Minneapolis: University of Minnesota Press.

Harrington, Wilfrid J. 1969. *The Apocalypse of St. John*. London: Chapman.

Haynes, Stephen R. 2007. *Noah's Curse: The Biblical Justification of America Slavery*. RA. Oxford: Oxford University Press.

Heidegger, Martin. 1993. "Letter on Humanism." Pages 217–65 in *Basic Writings*. Second revised and expanded edition. Edited by David F. Krell. Translated by Frank A. Capuzzi. RC. San Francisco: HarperSanFrancisco.

———. 2001. *The Fundamental Concepts of Metaphysics: World, Finitude, Solitude*. Translated by William McNeill and Nicholas Walker. SCT. Bloomington: Indiana University Press.

Hengel, Martin. 1979. *Acts and the History of Earliest Christianity*. Translated by John Bowden. London: SCM.

Himmelfarb, Martha. 2012. *The Apocalypse: A Brief History*. BBHRS. Chichester: Wiley-Blackwell.

Hird, Myra J. 2009. *The Origins of Sociable Life: Evolution after Science Studies*. New York: Palgrave Macmillan

Hobgood-Oster, Laura. 2008. *Holy Dogs and Asses: Animals in the Christian Tradition*. Champaign, IL: University of Illinois Press.

———. 2014. "And Say the Animal Really Responded: Speaking Animals in the History of Christianity." Pages 210–22 in *Divinanimality: Animal Theory, Creaturely Theology*. Edited by Stephen D. Moore. New York: Fordham University Press.

Hoffmann, Matthias Reinhard. 2005. *The Destroyer and the Lamb: The Relationship between Angelomorphic and Lamb Christology in the Book of Revelation*. WUNT 2/203. Tübingen: Mohr Siebeck.

Houston, Walter. 1993. *Purity and Monotheism: Clean and Unclean Animals in Biblical Law*. JSOTSup 140. Sheffield: Sheffield Academic.

———. 1998. "What Was the Meaning of Classifying Animals as Clean or Unclean?" Pages 18–24 in *Animals on the Agenda: Questions about Animals for Theology and Ethics*. Edited by Andrew Linzey and Dorothy Yamamoto. London: SCM.

Howard-Brook, Wes, and Anthony Gwyther. 1999. *Unveiling Empire: Reading Revelation Then and Now*. Maryknoll, NY: Orbis Books.

Howell, Justin R. 2008. "The Imperial Authority and Benefaction of Centurions and Acts 10.34–43: A Response to C. Kavin Rowe." *JSNT* 31:25–51.

Huggan, Graham. 2001. *The Postcolonial Exotic: Marketing the Margins*. New York: Routledge.

Humphreys, W. Lee. 2001. *The Character of God in the Book of Genesis: A Narrative Appraisal*. Louisville: Westminster John Knox.

Jameson, Michael H. 1988. "Sacrifice and Animal Husbandry in Classical Greece." Pages 87–119 in *Pastoral Economies in Classical Antiquity*. Edited by C. R. Whittaker. CPSSup 14. Cambridge: Cambridge Philological Society.

Kamuf, Peggy. 2010. *To Follow: The Wake of Jacques Derrida*. FT. Edinburgh: Edinburgh University Press.

Kemmerer, Lisa. 2011. *Animals and World Religions*. Oxford: Oxford University Press.

Kim, Jean K. 1999. "'Uncovering Her Wickedness': An Inter(Con)textual Reading of Revelation 17 from a Postcolonial Feminist Perspective." *JSNT* 73:61–81.

Klauck, Hans-Josef. 2000. *The Religious Context of Early Christianity: A Guide to Graeco-Roman Religions*. Translated by Brian McNeil. SNTW. London: T&T Clark.

Klawans, Jonathan. 2009. "Sacrifice in Ancient Israel: Pure Bodies, Domesticated Animals, and the Divine Shepherd." Pages 65–80 in *A Communion of Subjects: Animals in Religion, Science, and Ethics*. Edited by Paul Waldau and Kimberly Patton. New York: Columbia University Press.

Knapp, Robert. 2013. *Invisible Romans: Prostitutes, Outlaws, Slaves, Gladiators, Ordinary Men and Women; The Romans That History Forgot*. London: Profile Books.

Knight, Jonathan. 1999. *Revelation*. Readings. Sheffield: Sheffield Academic.

Koester, Craig R. 2001. *Revelation and the End of All Things*. Grand Rapids: Eerdmans.

Koosed, Jennifer L., ed. 2014a. *The Bible and Posthumanism*. SemeiaSt 74. Atlanta: Society of Biblical Literature.

———. 2014b. "Humanity at Its Limits." Pages 3–12 in *The Bible and Posthumanism*. Edited by Jennifer L. Koosed. SemeiaSt 74. Atlanta: Society of Biblical Literature.

Koosed, Jennifer L., and Robert Paul Seesengood. 2014. "Daniel's Animal Apocalypse." Pages 182–95 in *Divinanimality: Animal Theory, Creaturely Theology*. Edited by Stephen D. Moore. New York: Fordham University Press.

Korsgaard, Christine M. 2009. "Facing the Animal You See in the Mirror." *HRP* 16:2–7.

Kovacs, Judith, and Christopher Rowland. 2004. *Revelation: The Apocalypse of Jesus Christ*. Oxford: Blackwell.

Krell, David F. 2013. *Derrida and Our Animal Others: Derrida's Final Seminar, "The Beast and the Sovereign."* SCT. Bloomington: Indiana University Press.

Kristeva, Julia. 1982. *Powers of Horror: An Essay on Abjection*. Translated by Leon S. Roudiez. EP. New York: Columbia University Press.

Lacocque, André. 1979. *The Book of Daniel*. Translated by David Pellauer. London: SPCK.

Lawlor, Leonard. 2007. *This Is Not Sufficient: An Essay on Animality and Human Nature in Derrida*. New York: Columbia University Press.

Levinas, Emmanuel. 1969. *Totality and Infinity: An Essay on Exteriority*. Translated by Alphonso Lingis. Pittsburgh: Duquesne University Press.

———. 2004. "The Name of the Dog, or Natural Rights." Pages 47–50 in *Animal Philosophy: Essential Readings in Continental Thought*. Edited by Matthew Calarco and Peter Atterton. London: Continuum.

Lewis, Jack P. 1968. *A Study of the Interpretation of Noah and the Flood in Jewish and Christian Literature*. Leiden: Brill.

Lindstrøm, Torill Christine. 2010. "The Animals of the Arena: How and Why Could Their Destruction and Death Be Endured and Enjoyed?" *WA* 42:310–23.

Linzey, Andrew. 1976. *Animal Rights: A Christian Assessment of Man's Treatment of Animals*. London: SCM.

———. 1987. *Christianity and the Rights of Animals*. London: SPCK.

———. 1994. *Animal Theology*. London: SCM.

———. 1998. "Introduction: Is Christianity Irredeemably Speciesist?" Pages xi–xx in *Animals on the Agenda: Questions about Animals for Theology and Ethics*. Edited by Andrew Linzey and Dorothy Yamamoto. London: SCM.

Linzey, Andrew, and Dan Cohn-Sherbok. 1997. *After Noah: Animals and the Liberation of Theology*. London: Mowbrays.

Linzey, Andrew, and Dorothy Yamamoto, eds. 1998. *Animals on the Agenda: Questions about Animals for Theology and Ethics*. London: SCM.

Lipschitz, Ruth. 2012. "Skin/ned Politics: Species Discourse and the Limits of 'The Human' in Nandipha Mntambo's Art." *Hypatia* 27:546–66.

Livingstone, David N. 2008. *Adam's Ancestors: Race, Religion, and the Politics of Human Origins*. MSRHC. Baltimore: Johns Hopkins University Press.

Longman, Tremper, III. 2005. *How to Read Genesis*. HRS. Downers Grove, IL: InterVarsity Press.

MacCannell, Juliet Flower. 2003. "Kristeva's Horror." Pages 69–97 in *The Kristeva Critical Reader*. Edited by John Lechte and Mary Zournazi. Edinburgh: Edinburgh University Press.

Mansfield, Nick. 2000. *Subjectivity: Theories of the Self from Freud to Haraway*. New York: New York University Press.

Marshall, John W. 2009. "Gender and Empire: Sexualized Violence in John's Anti-Imperial Apocalypse." Pages 17–32 in *A Feminist Companion to the Apocalypse of John*. Edited by Amy-Jill Levine and Maria Mayo Robbins. FCNTECW 13. London: T&T Clark.

Martin, Clarice J. 2005. "Polishing the Unclouded Mirror: A Womanist Reading of Revelation 18:13." Pages 82–109 in *From Every People and Nation: The Book of Revelation in Intercultural Perspective*. Edited by David Rhoads. Minneapolis: Fortress.

Matson, David L. 1996. *Household Conversion Narratives in Acts: Pattern and Interpretation*. JSNTSup 123. Sheffield: Sheffield Academic.

McConville, J. G. 2006. *God and Earthly Power: An Old Testament Political Theology; Genesis–Kings*. LHB 454. London: T&T Clark.

Midgley, Mary. 2004. *The Myths We Live By*. New York: Routledge.

Moberly, R. W. L. 2009. *The Theology of the Book of Genesis*. OTT. Cambridge: Cambridge University Press.

Montaigne, Michel de. 1987. *An Apology for Raymond Sebond*. Translated by M. Screech. PC. London: Penguin Books.

Moore, Stephen D. 2006. *Empire and Apocalypse: Postcolonialism and the New Testament*. BMW 12. Sheffield: Sheffield Phoenix.

———. ed. 2014a. *Divinanimality: Animal Theory, Creaturely Theology*. New York: Fordham University Press.

———. 2014b. "Ecotherology." Pages 196–209 in *Divinanimality: Animal Theory, Creaturely Theology*. Edited by Stephen D. Moore. New York: Fordham University Press.

Moore, Stephen D., and Yvonne Sherwood. 2011. *The Invention of the Biblical Scholar: A Critical Manifesto*. Minneapolis: Fortress.

Morton, Timothy. 2007. *Ecology without Nature: Rethinking Environmental Aesthetics*. Cambridge: Harvard University Press.

———. 2008. "Thinking Ecology: The Mesh, the Strange Stranger and the Beautiful Soul." Pages 265–93 in vol. 6 of *Collapse: Philosophical Research and Development*. Edited by Robin Mackay. Falmouth: Urbanomic.

———. 2010. *The Ecological Thought*. Cambridge: Harvard University Press.

Morton, Stephen. 2013. "Troubling Resemblances, Anthropological Machines and the Fear of Wild Animals: Following Derrida after Agamben." Pages 105–23 in *The Animal Question in Deconstruction*. Edited by Lynn Turner. Edinburgh: Edinburgh University Press.

Murphy, James G. 1863. *A Critical and Exegetical Commentary on the Book of Genesis: With a New Translation*. Edinburgh: T&T Clark.

Murray, Robert. 1992. *The Cosmic Covenant: Biblical Themes of Justice, Peace and the Integrity of Creation*. HM 7. London: Sheed & Ward.

Naas, Michael B. 2003. *Taking on the Tradition: Jacques Derrida and the Legacies of Deconstruction*. CMP. Stanford, CA: Stanford University Press.

———. 2008. *Derrida from Now On*. PCPhil. New York: Fordham University Press.

Nasrallah, Laura. 2008. "The Acts of the Apostles, Greek Cities, and Hadrian's Panhellenion." *JBL* 127:533–66.

Norwood, F. Bailey, and Jason L. Lusk. 2011. *Compassion, by the Pound: The Economics of Farm Animal Welfare*. Oxford: Oxford University Press.

O'Hear, Natasha, and Anthony O'Hear. 2015. *Picturing the Apocalypse: The Book of Revelation in the Arts over Two Millennia*. Oxford: Oxford University Press.

Olley, John. 2000. "Mixed Blessings for Animals: The Contrasts of Genesis 9." Pages 130–39 in *The Earth Story in Genesis*. Edited by Norman C. Habel and Shirley Wurst. The Earth Bible 2. Sheffield: Sheffield Academic.

O'Toole, Robert F. 1983. "Luke's Position on Politics and Society in Luke-Acts." Pages 1–17 in *Political Issues in Luke-Acts*. Edited by Richard J. Cassidy and Philip J. Scharper. Maryknoll, NY: Orbis Books.

Pao, David W. 2000. *Acts and the Isaianic New Exodus*. WUNT 2/130. Tübingen: Mohr Siebeck.

Perkins, Judith. 1995. *The Suffering Self: Pain and Narrative Representation in the Early Christian Era*. London: Routledge.

Perry, Peter S. 2007. "Critiquing the Excess of Empire: A *Synkrisis* of John of Patmos and Dio of Prusa." *JSNT* 29:473–96.

Pervo, Richard I. 2009. *Acts: A Commentary*. Herm. Minneapolis: Fortress.

Pippin, Tina. 1999. *Apocalyptic Bodies: The Biblical End of the World in Text and Image*. London: Routledge.

Plumwood, Val. 2002. *Environmental Culture: The Ecological Crisis of Reason*. EPS. London: Routledge.

Pomeroy, Sarah B. 1975. *Goddesses, Whores, Wives, and Slaves: Women in Classical Antiquity*. New York: Schocken Books.

Porter, Paul A. 1983. *Metaphors and Monsters: A Literary-Critical Study of Daniel 7 and 8*. CBOTS 20. Lund: Gleerup.

Potter, David S. 1993. "Martyrdom as Spectacle." Pages 53–88 in *Theater and Society in the Classical World*. Edited by Ruth Scodel. Ann Arbor: University of Michigan Press.

Pyper, Hugh S. 2012. "Looking into the Lions' Den: Otherness, Ideology, and Illustration in Children's Versions of Daniel 6." Pages 51–72 in *Text, Image, and Otherness in Children's Bibles: What Is in the Picture?* Edited by Caroline Vander Stichele and Hugh S. Pyper. SemeiaSt 56. Atlanta: Society of Biblical Literature.

———. 2014. "The Lion King: Yahweh as Sovereign Beast in Israel's Imaginary." Pages 59–74 in *The Bible and Posthumanism*. Edited by Jennifer L. Koosed. SemeiaSt 74. Atlanta: Society of Biblical Literature.

Regan, Tom. 2004. *The Case for Animal Rights*. Berkeley: University of California Press.

Rejali, Darius. 2007. *Torture and Democracy*. Princeton: Princeton University Press.

Ricoeur, Paul. 1979. Foreword to *The Book of Daniel*, by André Lacocque. London: SPCK.

Robinson, John A. T. 1957. *The Body: A Study in Pauline Theology*. SBT 5. London: SCM.

Robinson, O. F. 1994. *Ancient Rome: City Planning and Administration*. London: Routledge.

Roof, Judith. 2003. "From Protista to DNA (and Back Again): Freud's Psychoanalysis of the Single-Celled Organism." Pages 101–20 in *Zoontologies: The Question of the Animal*. Edited by Cary Wolfe. Minneapolis: University of Minnesota Press.

Rosenzweig, Franz. 2005. *The Star of Redemption*. Translated by Barbara E. Galli. MJPR. Madison: University of Wisconsin Press.

Rothschild, Clare K. 2013a. "Etumologia, Dramatis Personae, and the Lukan Invention of an Early Christian Prosopography." Pages 279–98 in *The Rise and Expansion of Christianity in the First Three Centuries of the Common Era*. Edited by Clare K. Rothschild and Jens Schröter. WUNT 301. Tübingen: Mohr Siebeck.

———. 2013b. "Introduction: The Rise and Expansion of Christianity in the First Three Centuries of the Common Era." Pages 1–10 in *The Rise and Expansion of Christianity in the First Three Centuries of the Common Era*. Edited by Clare K. Rothschild and Jens Schröter. WUNT 301. Tübingen: Mohr Siebeck.

Rowland, Christopher. 1993. *Revelation*. EC. London: Epworth.

———. 2001. Foreword to *Studies in the Book of Revelation*. Edited by Stephen Moyise. Edinburgh: T&T Clark.

Royle, Nicholas, ed. 2000. *Deconstructions: A User's Guide*. New York: Macmillan.

———. 2009. *In Memory of Jacques Derrida*. Edinburgh: Edinburgh University Press.

Rudy, Kathy. 2011. *Loving Animals: Toward a New Animal Advocacy*. Minneapolis: University of Minnesota Press.

Schochet, Elijah Judah. 1984. *Animal Life in Jewish Tradition: Attitudes and Relationships*. New York: Ktav.

Schüssler Fiorenza, Elisabeth. 1991. *Revelation: Vision of a Just World*. Edinburgh: T&T Clark.

Sedgwick, Peter. 2001. *Descartes to Derrida: An Introduction to European Philosophy*. Oxford: Blackwell.

Seesengood, Robert Paul. 2006. *Competing Identities: The Athlete and the Gladiator in Early Christian Literature*. LNTS 346; Playing the Texts 12. London: T&T Clark.

Shaw, Brent D. 1996. "Body/Power/Identity: Passions of the Martyrs." *JECS* 4:269–312.

Sheehan, James J., and Morton Sosna, eds. 1991. *The Boundaries of Humanity: Humans, Animals, Machines*. Berkeley: University of California Press.

Sherwood, Yvonne. 2004. "Introduction: Derrida's Bible." Pages 1–20 in *Derrida's Bible: Reading a Page of Scripture with a Little Help from Derrida*. Edited by Yvonne Sherwood. RCC. New York: Macmillan.

———. 2014. "Cutting Up Life: Sacrifice as a Device for Clarifying—and Tormenting—Fundamental Distinctions between Human, Animal, and Divine." Pages 247–300 in *The Bible and Posthumanism*. Edited by Jennifer L. Koosed. SemeiaSt 74. Atlanta: Society of Biblical Literature.

Sherwood, Yvonne, and Kevin Hart, eds. 2004. *Derrida and Religion: Other Testaments*. London: Routledge.

Signori, Gabriela. 2012. Introduction to *Dying for the Faith, Killing for the Faith: Old-Testament Faith-Warriors (1 and 2 Maccabees) in Historical Perspective*. Edited by Gabriela Signori. BSIH 206. Leiden: Brill.

Singer, Peter. 2004. Preface. Pages xi–xiv in *Animal Philosophy: Essential Readings in Continental Thought*. Edited by Matthew Calarco and Peter Atterton. London: Continuum.

Skinner, John. 1910. *A Critical and Exegetical Commentary on Genesis*. ICC. Edinburgh: T&T Clark.

Smith, Shanell T. 2014. *The Woman Babylon and the Marks of Empire: Reading Revelation with a Postcolonial Womanist Hermeneutics of Ambivalence*. Minneapolis: Fortress.

Smith-Christopher, Daniel L. 1989. *The Religion of the Landless: The Social Context of the Babylonian Exile*. Bloomington: Meyer-Stone Books.

———. 2001. "Prayers and Dreams: Power and Diaspora Identities in the Social Setting of the Daniel Tales." Pages 266–90 in vol. 1 of *The Book of Daniel: Composition and Reception*. Edited by John J. Collins and Peter W. Flint. VTSup 83; FIOTL 2. Leiden: Brill.

Soards, Marion L. 1994. *The Speeches in Acts: Their Content, Context, and Concerns*. Louisville: Westminster John Knox.

Spittler, Janet E. 2008. *Animals in the Apocryphal Acts of the Apostles: The Wild Kingdom of Early Christian Literature*. WUNT 2/247. Tübingen: Mohr Siebeck.

———. 2013. "Christianity at the Edges: Representations of the Ends of the Earth in the Apocryphal Acts of the Apostles." Pages 353–78 in *The Rise and Expansion of Christianity in the First Three Centuries of the Common Era*. Edited by Clare K. Rothschild and Jens Schröter. WUNT 301. Tübingen: Mohr Siebeck.

Spivak, Gayatri Chakravorty. 1987. "Subaltern Studies: Deconstructing Historiography." Pages 197–221 in *In Other Worlds: Essays in Cultural Politics*. New York: Methuen.

Stichele, Caroline Vander. 2009. "Re-membering the Whore: The Fate of Babylon according to Revelation 17.16." Pages 106–20 in *A Feminist Companion to The Apocalypse of John*. Edited by Amy-Jill Levine and Maria Mayo Robbins. FCNTECW 13. London: T&T Clark.

Still, Judith. 2015. *Derrida and Other Animals: The Boundaries of the Human*. Edinburgh: Edinburgh University Press.

Stone, Ken. 2014. "The Dogs of Exodus and the Question of the Animal." Pages 36–50 in *Divinanimality: Animal Theory, Creaturely Theology*. Edited by Stephen D. Moore. New York: Fordham University Press.

Strawn, Brent A. 2005. *What Is Stronger than a Lion? Leonine Image and Metaphor in the Hebrew Bible and the Ancient Near East*. OBO 212. Göttingen: Vandenhoeck & Ruprecht.

Strohm, Paul. 2000. *Theory and the Premodern Text*. MC 26. Minneapolis: University of Minnesota Press.

Strømmen, Hannah, 2018. "The Politics of the Beast." *Relegere: Studies in Religion and Reception*.

Strong, James. 2001. *The New Strong's Expanded Dictionary of Bible Words.* Nashville: Nelson.

Thompson, Leonard L. 1990. *The Book of Revelation: Apocalypse and Empire.* New York: Oxford University Press.

Toynbee, J. M. C. 1996. *Animals in Roman Life and Art.* Baltimore: Johns Hopkins University Press.

Trever, John C. 1985. "The Book of Daniel and the Origin of the Qumran Community." *BArch* 48.2:89–102.

Turner, Laurence A. 2009. *Genesis.* Readings. Sheffield: Sheffield Phoenix.

Turner, Lynn, ed. 2013. *The Animal Question in Deconstruction.* Edinburgh: Edinburgh University Press.

Tyler, Tom. 2012. *Ciferae: A Bestiary in Five Fingers.* Post 19. Minneapolis: University of Minnesota Press.

Tyson, Joseph B. 1992. *Images of Judaism in Luke-Acts.* Columbia: University of South Carolina Press.

Valeta, David M. 2008. "The Book of Daniel in Recent Research (Part 1)." *CBR* 6:330–54.

Van Der Toorn, Karel. 2001. "Scholars at the Oriental Court: The Figure of Daniel against Its Mesopotamian Background." Pages 37–54 in vol. 1 of *The Book of Daniel: Composition and Reception.* Edited by John J. Collins and Peter W. Flint. VTSup 83; FIOTL 2. Leiden: Brill.

Van Henten, Jan Willem. 2001. "Daniel 3 and 6 in Early Christian Literature." Pages 149–70 in vol. 1 of *The Book of Daniel: Composition and Reception.* Edited by John J. Collins and Peter W. Flint. VTSup 83; FIOTL 2. Leiden: Brill.

Van Kooten, George H. 2007. "The Year of the Four Emperors and the Revelation of John: The 'Pro-Neronian' Emperors Otho and Vitellius, and the Images and Colossus of Nero in Rome." *JSNT* 30:205–48.

Vries, Hent de. 1999. *Philosophy and the Turn to Religion.* Baltimore: Johns Hopkins University Press.

Waldau, Paul. 2011. *Animal Rights: What Everyone Needs to Know.* Oxford: Oxford University Press.

———. 2013. *Animal Studies: An Introduction.* Oxford: Oxford University Press.

Waldau, Paul, and Kimberly Patton, eds. 2009. *A Communion of Subjects: Animals in Religion, Science, and Ethics.* New York: Columbia University Press.

Walton, John. 2001. "The Anzu Myth as Relevant Background for Daniel 7?" Pages 69–90 in vol. 1 of *The Book of Daniel: Composition and*

Reception. Edited by John J. Collins and Peter W. Flint. VTSup 83; FIOTL 2. Leiden: Brill.

Ward, Graham. 2001. "Questioning God." Pages 274–90 in *Questioning God.* Edited by John D. Caputo, Mark Dooley, and Michael J. Scanlon. ISPR. Bloomington: Indiana University Press.

Way, Kenneth C. 2011. *Donkeys in the Biblical World: Ceremony and Symbol.* HACL 2. Winona Lake, IN: Eisenbrauns.

Weber, Elizabeth. 2007. "Suspended from the Other's Heartbeat." *SAQ* 106:325–44.

Weiner, Allison, and Simon Morgan Wortham, eds. 2007. *Encountering Derrida: Legacies and Futures of Deconstruction.* CSCP. London: Continuum.

Wesselius, Jan-Wim. 2005. "The Literary Nature of the Book of Daniel and the Linguistic Character of its Aramaic." *AS* 3:241–83.

Westermann, Claus. 1994. *Genesis 1–11: A Continental Commentary.* Translated by John J. Scullion. Minneapolis: Fortress.

Wills, Lawrence M. 1990. *The Jew in the Court of the Foreign King: Ancient Jewish Court Legends.* HDR 26. Minneapolis: Fortress.

White, Lynn, Jr. 1967. "The Historical Roots of Our Ecological Crisis." *Sci* 155:1203–7.

Whitford, David M. 2009. *The Curse of Ham in the Early Modern Era: The Bible and the Justifications for Slavery.* StASRH. London: Routledge.

Wolfe, Cary, ed. 2003. *Zoontologies: The Question of the Animal.* Minneapolis: University of Minnesota Press.

———. 2009. "Humanist and Posthumanist Antispeciesism." Pages 45–58 in *The Death of the Animal: A Dialogue.* Edited by Paola Cavalieri. New York: Columbia University Press.

Wortham, Simon Morgan. 2011. " 'By Force of Love … Something Should Happen to God, and *Someone* Happen to Him': The Other's Other(s) in Derrida." *TP* 25:1051–73.

Wynter, Sylvia. 2003. "Unsettling the Coloniality of Being/Power/Truth/ Freedom: Towards the Human, After Man, Its Overrepresentation— An Argument." *CR* 3:257–337.

Young, Edward J. 1949. *The Prophecy of Daniel: A Commentary.* Grand Rapids: Eerdmans.

ANCIENT SOURCES INDEX

Modern Authors Index

Subject Index

abject, the/abjection, 123, 126, 126 n. 21, 127, 128, 129
accountability, 32, 39, 40, 46, 47, 51, 56, 57, 65, 129, 136
Adam, 37, 104, 124
   and Eve, fruit-eating, 51, 57,
   naming the animals, 49, 50, 58
   new Adam, 37, 102 n. 14
accountability, 11, 32, 39, 40, 46, 46 n. 13, 47, 51, 56, 57, 129, 136
   to God, 46, 59, 65
Adorno, Theodor, 6, 7, 21
Althusser, Louis, 6
ambiguity
   of abjection, 123, 126 n. 21, 127,
   of covenant with God, 43, 48
   of the Bible, 143
   of human sovereignty, 135
angel, 110
   of god, 68
animal liberation, 2
animal rights, 2, 39, 81 n. 12, 144, 146,
animal studies, 1, 2, 3, 5, 10, 11, 15, 16, 19, 22, 24, 25 n. 17, 28, 28 n. 20, 37, 51, 124, 125 n. 20, 140, 141, 142
anthropocene, 8, 26
anthropocentrism/anthropocentric, 1, 4, 10, 11, 12, 15, 18, 25, 38, 81, 82, 88, 143, 144, 147
anthropology, 23, 142
Aristotle, 3 n. 2, 6, 11, 12, 21, 22, 23, 30 n. 23, 124
apocalyptic, 93 n. 5, 97, 115, 139, 140, 144, 147
   genre of, 93

apocalyptic (*cont.*)
   imagination, 91
   literature, 92
Aquinas, Thomas, 11, 38 n. 4
Augustine, 11, 38 n. 4, 85
   Confessions, 57
autonomy, 6, 7, 31, 61
awakening, to ethics
   Derrida on, 26, 29, 30, 31, 32, 33, 58, 77, 81, 147, 148. *See also* wakeful-ness.
Babylon/Babylonian, 93, 94, 95, 96, 98, 98 n. 8, 99, 100 n. 10, 103, 105, 122, 123. *See also* Whore of Babylon and empire.
baptism, 72, 83
Bataille, Georges, 14
beast, 21, 34, 43 nn. 11–12, 47, 49, 52, 55, 56, 60, 61, 65, 69, 86, 91, 92, 94, 95, 98, 100, 104, 106, 109, 110, 111, 112, 113, 114, 115, 116, 117, 135
   and the Roman arena, 121, 130
   animal as, 95, 112, 121, 131
   as evil, 131, 132, 133, 137, 138
   god as beast. *See* god as carnivorous.
   imagery of the, 119, 122, 131 n. 25, 133, 137
   political order as beastlike, 91, 94, 95, 97, 98, 103, 110, 116, 117, 118, 121, 132
   Rome as beast, 109, 111, 112, 113, 119, 121, 127, 133, 137
   Whore and/Whore as, 122, 123, 124, 125, 126 n. 21, 127, 128, 132, 133, 137

-177-